H. Clay Gorton

First Printing, August 1993

International Standard Book Number
0-88290-475-2

Horizon Publishers' Catalog and Order Number
1033

Printed and distributed
in the United States of America by

& Distributors, Incorporated
P.O. Box 490 Bountiful, Utah 84011-0490

ACKNOWLEDGMENTS

First, I would like to express appreciation to Peggy McFarland who willingly and kindly poured over several versions of the manuscript in a valiant attempt to drag it from the stolid realms of a technical treatise into a more readable format.

Appreciation is also due to my dear wife whose painstaking editorial efforts have found many nearly imperceptible yet grammatically significant errors in spelling, grammar and construction.

We are also deeply indebted to Duane Crowther who has made many helpful suggestions both for style and content, and proofread several drafts of the manuscript.

Finally, we make no claim of completeness. Since we are dealing with artistic expression, we may be blind to chiastic expressions that are apparent to others more versed in the art. What prospector can say that he has discovered all the diamonds in a diamond mine? Likewise, there are undoubtedly undiscovered chiastic gems in the linguistic mines of the Language of the Lord.

TABLE OF CONTENTS

SEQUENTIAL INDEX OF CHIASMA IN THE DOCTRINE AND COVENANTS

INTRODUCTION

Extensive effort has been spent identifying specific literary forms used in the Bible. E.W. Bullinger, who has written the definitive work on the subject,[1] has identified, named and given examples of 217 distinct figures of speech used in the Bible. He affirms that such figures of speech are of inspired origin, and are employed by Deity as sign posts to draw the reader's attention to the particular force of specific passages. Of the chiasmus he states, "This is by far the most stately and dignified presentation of a subject; and is always used in the most solemn and important portions of the Scriptures.[2] He cites Bengel as stating that "its employment is never without some use; *vis.*, in perceiving the ornament and in observing the force of the language; in understanding the true and full sense; in making clear the sound interpretation; in demonstrating the tone and neat analysis of the sacred text."[3]

Chiastic Form Unknown to Joseph Smith

Although the chiastic form had been identified and used by the ancients in various cultures as a literary artifact, it was virtually unknown at the time of Joseph Smith. Of over 500 literature references to the chiasmus which have been identified, only three were published prior to 1828, when the first revelations published in the Doctrine and Covenants were received; and only four more references appeared prior to the prophet's martyrdom in 1844. The three papers published prior to 1828 were all London publications, although the four published between 1833 and 1836 were published in New York and Philadelphia. None of these publications were primers on the chiasmus, but were studies of the Holy Scriptures that made mention of the chiasmus as a literary structure in the scriptures. It is impossible that Joseph Smith could have gained from these publications sophistication in the employment of the chiasmus in the revelations he recorded even if the

---

1. Bullinger, E.W., *Figures of Speech Used in the Bible*. Grand Rapids, Michigan: Baker Book House, 1968, originally published by Mesrs. Eyre and Spottiswoode, London, 1898.
2. Ibid., p. 374.
3. Ibid., p. 374.

publications were at his disposal, which undoubtedly they were not. There were only 22 more publications on the subject in the next 100 years.

Chiasmus—A Compelling Evidence of the Divine Origin of the Doctrine and Covenants

Since Joseph Smith was without doubt unaware of the chiastic structure as a literary form, discovery of its use in the revelations that he recorded represents yet another compelling evidence of the authenticity and divine origin of the Doctrine and Covenants. Two hundred twenty-five chiastic structures have been identified in the Doctrine and Covenants, representing over one third of the total volume of the text, and perhaps set it apart, with the exception of the Bible, as the scriptural volume containing the very highest density of chiastic structures.

This writing makes a case for the divine origin of the chiastic form in the Doctrine and Covenants and in the Book of Mormon, and concurs with Bullinger's thesis in reference to the Bible that such literary forms are inspired by the Holy Spirit, "and the Spirit that inspired the words in the Book must inspire its truth in our hearts, for they can and must be 'spiritually discerned'"(1 Cor. 2:1-14).

3 Lord, Be With Me
2 I Need You Near
1 To Comfort and Love
1 My Weakened Spirit
I shan't not cry
2 While You're Near By
And So, I sigh
3 Lord, Be With Me.

1

WHAT IS A CHIASMUS?

Basic Chiastic Structures

The chiasmus is a literary form found extensively in the scriptures and occasionally in some of the secular literature. The structure of the chiasmus comprises two sets of identical or related words, phrases or concepts, the second set of which is a repetition of the first; however, the second set is repeated in inverse order, as A,B,C,D,...D,C,B,A. Thus, the first element of the first series is related to the last element of the second series; the second element of the first series is related to the penultimate element of the second series, and so forth. Finally, the first and second sets of elements converge on a central theme in the middle of the chiasmus.

Chiasma in the scriptures are essentially subliminal. They are not generally apparent as one reads the scriptures; i.e., the repeated elements are not generally perceived as such. Yet they are there, and undoubtedly serve to impress on the mind by the process of repetition the concepts that the Lord is conveying to those who *feast upon the words of Christ* (2 Ne. 32:3).

The simplest form of chiastic structure comprises two sets of two elements each (AB-BA), and thus lacks a central theme. An example of a two-element chiasmus is found in Matt. 19:30, *the first shall be last and the last shall be first.* The two-element chiasmus may be diagrammed in the following manner—

the *first* shall be *last*

and the *last* shall be *first.*

Lines connecting the parallel elements form an X; hence, from the Greek, the word CHI-asmus.

In the above example, the words "first" and "last" are repeated in inverse order. However, the chiasmus may also repeat a phrase word for word, or repeat a concept with different phraseology in the parallel elements. In addition, the chiastic elements in conceptual chiasma, i.e., those containing elements composed of phrases or sentences, rather than single words, may be juxtaposed in many different forms. For example, the relationship of the parallel elements may be positive to negative, past to future, spiritual to temporal, general to specific, cause to effect, etc. The most common relationship of chiastic elements is that of parallel concepts, i.e., to repeat a given concept in different words. We have found in the Doctrine and Covenants fifty-seven chiasma comprised entirely of parallel concepts, with the number of elements in the chiasma ranging from two to seven. We have also found nineteen chiasma in which each of the elements repeats identical words, and five chiasma in which each of the elements bears a positive to negative relation with its mirror element. In all of the other 144 chiasma in the Doctrine and Covenants more than one type of relationship between parallel elements exists in the same chiasmus.

Chiasma may be classified according to the relationship of their parallel elements as follows:

Type One: Identical Phrases. The parallel or mirror elements contain identical phrases or strings of words. The following chiasmus is comprised of a repeated series of identical phrases, except for a minor variation in the fourth or outer elements, wherein 'one soul' in the initial fourth element is changed to 'many souls' in the final fourth element.

D&C 18:15,16

4] And *if* it so be that *you should* labor all your days in crying repentance unto this people, and *bring, save it be one soul unto me*,
3] *how great shall be your joy* with him
2] *in the kingdom of my Father!*
1] 16 And now, if your joy will be great with one soul that you have brought unto me
2] *into the kingdom of my Father,*
3] *how great will be your joy*
4] *if you should bring many souls unto me!*

Type Two: Identical Words. The mirror elements contain the same words. In a pure structure there would be no intervening words that would not be chiastically related. The following chiasmus is comprised of a repeated series of identical words.

D&C 27:6,7

4] 6 And also with *Elias*, to whom I have committed the keys of bringing to pass the restoration of all things spoken by the mouth of all the holy prophets since the world began, concerning the last days;
3] 7 And also *John*
2] *the son*
1] of *Zacharias,*
1] which *Zacharias*
2] he (Elias) visited and gave promise that he should have *a son,*
3] and his name should be *John,*
4] and he should be filled with the spirit of *Elias;*

Type Three: Parallel Concepts. The mirror elements repeat the same concepts or concepts related to those contained in the initial elements, but expressed in different words, as shown in the following chiasmus.

D&C 18:21-24

5] 21 *Take upon you the name of Christ*, and speak the truth in soberness.
4] 22 *And as many as repent and are baptized*
3] *in my name,*
2] *which is Jesus Christ,*
1] and endure to the end, the same shall be saved.
2] 23 *Behold, Jesus Christ is the name which is given of the Father,*
3] and *there is none other name* given
4] *whereby man can be saved;*
5] 24 Wherefore, *all men must take upon them the name which is given of the Father*, for in that name shall they be called at the last day;

Type Four: Positive to Negative. The initial concepts may be either positive or negative, but the mirror concepts are the opposite. The elements in the following chiasmus bear a positive-to-negative relationship one with another.

D&C 42:13,14

3] and *these shall be their teachings,*
2] as *they shall be directed by the Spirit.*
1] 14 And the Spirit shall be given unto you by the prayer of faith;
2] and *if ye receive not the Spirit*
3] *ye shall not teach.*

Type Five: Mixed or Hybrid. The relationships between parallel elements are different for different pairs of parallel elements in the same chiasmus. In the following two chiasma, each pair of elements bears a different relationship than the others. The nature of the relationships between chiastic elements is printed following the chiasmus.

D&C 22:1-4

4] 1 Behold, I say unto you that all old covenants have I caused to be done away in this thing; and *this is a new and an everlasting covenant,*
3] *even that which was from the beginning.*
2] 2 Wherefore, although a man should be baptized an hundred times it availeth him nothing, *for you cannot enter in at the strait gate by the law of Moses,*
1] neither by *your dead works.*
1] 3 For it is because of *your dead works*
2] that *I have caused this last covenant and this church to be built up unto me,*
3] *even as in days of old.*
4] 4 *Wherefore, enter ye in at the gate,* as I have commanded, and seek not to counsel your God. Amen.

4] **general/specific**—(The new and everlasting covenant—*general*— is defined as the gate through which the Kingdom is entered, i.e., baptism—*specific*.)
3] **parallel concepts**—(*even as in days of old* expresses the same general concept as *even that which was from the beginning*)
2] **negative/positive**—(i.e. salvation cannot come by obedience to *the law of Moses*, but can only come by obedience to the new and everlasting covenant, *this last covenant*, administered by *this church to be built up unto me,*)
1] **identical words**—(*your dead works*)

D&C 24:1-8

4] and *I have lifted thee up out of thine afflictions,* and have counseled thee, that *thou hast been delivered from all thine enemies, and thou hast been delivered from the powers of Satan and from darkness!*
3] 2 Nevertheless, thou art not excusable in thy transgressions; nevertheless, go thy way and sin no more.
3 *Magnify thine office; and after thou hast sowed thy fields and secured them, go speedily unto the church which is in Colesville, Fayette, and*

Manchester, and they shall support thee; and I will bless them both spiritually and temporally;

2] 4 But if they receive thee not, *I will send upon them a cursing instead of a blessing.*

1] 5 And thou shalt continue in calling upon God in my name, and writing the things which shall be given thee by the Comforter, and expounding all scriptures unto the church.

2] 6 And it shall be given thee in the very moment what thou shalt speak and write, and they shall hear it, or *I will send unto them a cursing instead of a blessing.*

3] 7 *For thou shalt devote all thy service in Zion; and in this thou shalt have strength.*

4] 8 *Be patient in afflictions, for thou shalt have many; but endure them, for, lo, I am with thee, even unto the end of thy days.*

4] **past/future**—(Both elements refer to afflictions of Joseph and Oliver. The first element reveals that the Lord has delivered them from prior afflictions and *from the powers of Satan and from darkness*. The mirror element speaks of afflictions to come, and promises the sustaining companionship of the Lord, *for, lo, I am with thee, even unto the end of thy days*.)

3] **specific/general**—(The first element gives specific instructions for particular activities, '*and after thou hast sowed thy fields and secured them, go speedily unto the church which is in Colesville, Fayette, and Manchester*'; whereas in the mirror element they are given the general counsel to '*devote all thy service in Zion*'.)

2] **identical words**—(*I will send upon/unto them a cursing instead of a blessing*.)

1] **central theme**—(Each of the elements of this chiasmus is related to, and leads to the Lord's encouragement to Joseph and Oliver to continue in the sacred work to which they were called, '*Behold, thou wast called and chosen to write the Book of Mormon, and to my ministry*').

In addition to the types of relationships between parallel elements specified in the first four types of chiasma, a number of additional relationships are used in different parallel elements of the type five chiasmus. Following is a list of the different types of chiastic relationships that have been identified in the Doctrine and Covenants. After each item will be an alpha numeric specifying the Section in the Doctrine and Covenants containing the chiasmus (number) and the number of the chiasmus in that Section (alpha).

1. **Worldly to spiritual**—1B (Section 1, second chiasmus in Section 1).
2. **Satan's commands versus the Lord's commands**—10C.
3. **Temporal to eternal**—11A.
4. **Concept and it's clarification**—18C.
5. **Action and it completion**—18I.
6. **Instruction and it's consequence**—19B.
7. **Permissive to restrictive**—20B.
8. **Old versus new**—22A.
9. **First to last**—29D.
10. **Public to private**—38A,
11. **Cause to effect**—39B, 101A,
12. **Promise to fulfillment**—45A, 66A.
13. **Temporal to spiritual**—93G.
14. **Mortal conflict versus Divine displeasure**—87A.
15. **Question to answer**—88F.
16. **Singular to plural**—107J.
17. **Persecutors versus persecuted**—109D.

Type Six: Chiasma Containing Parallelisms as Chiastic Elements. More complex forms of the chiasmus include both parallel structures and chiastic structures as elements of a larger chiasmus. In chiasma containing a series of concepts repeated in parallel elements of the chiasmus, the series is repeated in the mirror element without being inverted. This repeated series thus represents a single element of the chiasmus of which it is a part. In this work, the elements of a series that are repeated in the same order are identified by alpha characters, while the elements of the chiastic series that are repeated in inverse order are identified by numeric characters. Thus 3A, 3B, 2, 1,—1, 2, 3A, 3B, represents a three-element chiasmus, (3, 2, 1,), the third, or outer, element of which is comprised of a series of two items (A,B). The fact that the series is repeated in its mirror element in the same order as in the first element (rather than in reverse order) sets the series apart as a single chiastic element.

Examples of parallel structures as chiastic elements are shown in the following two chiasma, the first with a two-element series as the outer chiastic element, and the second with a four-element series as the central chiastic element.

D&C 76:31-38

3A] 32 *They are they who are the sons of perdition,*
3B] *of whom I say that it had been better for them never to have been born;*
2] 33 *For they are vessels of wrath, doomed to suffer the wrath of God, with the devil and his angels in eternity;*
1] 34 *Concerning whom I have said there is no forgiveness in this world nor in the world to come--*
1] 35 *Having denied the Holy Spirit after having received it, and having denied the Only Begotten Son of the Father, having crucified him unto themselves and put him to an open shame.*
2] 36 *These are they who shall go away into the lake of fire and brimstone, with the devil and his angels--*
3A] 37 *And the only ones on whom the second death shall have any power;*
3B] 38 *Yea, verily, the only ones who shall not be redeemed in the due time of the Lord, after the sufferings of his wrath.*

Incidentally, in this chiasmus, the mirror element is a more detailed or specific explanation of the first element. Thus, as is the case with many, but not all chiasma, this chiasmus may be read element-for-element rather than sequentially as it is written, which helps to clarify and establish the meaning and emphasize the thought. Thus, if the mirror elements are placed together, the meaning is retained, and the concepts reinforced, as is shown below:

3A] 32 *They are they who are the sons of perdition,*
3A]' 37 *And the only ones on whom the second death shall have any power;*
3B] 32 *of whom I say that it had been better for them never to have been born;*
3B]' 38 *Yea, verily, the only ones who shall not be redeemed in the due time of the Lord, after the sufferings of his wrath.*
2] 33 *For they are vessels of wrath, doomed to suffer the wrath of God, with the devil and his angels in eternity;*
2]' 36 *These are they who shall go away into the lake of fire and brimstone, with the devil and his angels—*
1] 34 *Concerning whom I have said there is no forgiveness in this world nor in the world to come—*
1]' 35 *Having denied the Holy Spirit after having received it, and having denied the Only Begotten Son of the Father, having crucified him unto themselves and put him to an open shame.*

Note that the following chiasmus has a repeated pair of central elements, each element comprised of a series of four units.

D&C 87:1-8

6] 1 *Verily, thus saith the Lord concerning the wars that will shortly come to pass, beginning at the rebellion of South Carolina,*

5] *which will eventually terminate in the death and misery of many souls;*

4] 2 *And the time will come that war will be poured out upon all nations, beginning at this place.*

3] 3 *For behold, the Southern States shall be divided against the Northern States, and the Southern States will call on other nations, even the nation of Great Britain, as it is called, and they shall also call upon other nations, in order to defend themselves against other nations;*

2] *and then war shall be poured out upon all nations.*

1A] 4 *And it shall come to pass*, after many days,

1B] *slaves shall rise up against their masters,*

1C] *who shall be marshaled*

1D] *and disciplined for war.*

1A] 5 *And it shall come to pass* also

1B] *that the remnants who are left of the land*

1C] *will marshal themselves,*

1D] *and shall become exceedingly angry, and shall vex the Gentiles with a sore vexation.*

2] 6 *And thus, with the sword and by bloodshed the inhabitants of the earth shall mourn;*

3] *and with famine, and plague, and earthquake, and the thunder of heaven, and the fierce and vivid lightning also, shall the inhabitants of the earth be made to feel the wrath, and indignation, and chastening hand of an Almighty God,*

4] *until the consumption decreed hath made a full end of all nations;*

5] 7 *That the cry of the saints, and of the blood of the saints, shall cease to come up into the ears of the Lord of Sabaoth, from the earth, to be avenged of their enemies.*

6] 8 *Wherefore, stand ye in holy places, and be not moved, until the day of the Lord come*; for behold, it cometh quickly, saith the Lord. Amen.

Type Seven: Interdigitated Chiasmus and Parallelism. An interdigitated chiasmus and parallelism exists in D&C 29:32. Only three such structures have been found in the Doctrine and Covenants. The interdigitated chaismus and parallelism in D&C 29:32, is shown below, and the other two, found in D&C 74:1 and D&C 77:2, are identified and outlined in Chapter four. In the following example, the parallel elements are underlined, and the chiastic structure is in italics. As may be observed, the parallel or series elements are not part of a chiastic element, as is the case with chiasma D&C

76:31-38 and D&C 87:1-8 on pages 17 and 18, but are an independent repeated series artfully interleaved as an integral part of the chiasmus to express a complete thought. Neither the chiasmus nor the repeated series makes sense by itself. The verse, *First spiritual, secondly temporal, which is the beginning of my work; and again, first temporal, and secondly spiritual, which is the last of my work*—is diagrammed as follows:

D&C 29:32

A]		First	2] *spiritual,*
B]		secondly	1] *temporal,*
C]		which is the beginning of my work;	
A']	and again,	first	1] *temporal,*
B']	and	secondly	2] *spiritual,*
C']		which is the last of my work—	

Type Eight: Interleaved or Included Chiasma. There are cases where a chiasmus may exist between elements of a larger chiasmus, or where one or more of the elements of a larger chiasmus may be chiastic in form. There are also overlapping or chained chiasma where one or more elements of one chiasmus are common to an adjacent chiasmus. These complex chiastic forms will be treated in detail in chapter four. An example of a chiasmus within a chiasmus is shown in D&C 63:5-13. Verses 9 and 10, which comprise elements 4] through 2], and the two central elements 1] form another chiasmus, as shown below.

D&C 63:5-13

6] 5 *Behold, I, the Lord, utter my voice, and it shall be obeyed.*

5A] 6 *Wherefore, verily I say, let the wicked take heed, and let the rebellious fear and tremble; and let the unbelieving hold their lips, for the day of wrath shall come upon them as a whirlwind, and all flesh shall know that I am God.*

5B] 7 *And he that seeketh signs shall see signs, but not unto salvation.*

5C] 8 *Verily, I say unto you, there are those among you who seek signs, and there have been such even from the beginning;*

4] 9 But, behold, *faith*

3] *cometh*

2] not by *signs,*

1] but *signs follow those that believe.*

1] 10 Yea, *signs come by faith*, not by the will of men, nor as they please, but by the will of God.

2] 11 Yea, *signs*

3] *come* by

4] *faith*, unto mighty works, for without faith no man pleaseth God;
5A] *and with whom God is angry he is not well pleased;*
5B] *wherefore, unto such he showeth no signs, only in wrath unto their condemnation.*
5C] 12 *Wherefore, I, the Lord, am not pleased with those among you who have sought after signs and wonders for faith, and not for the good of men unto my glory.*
6] 13 *Nevertheless, I give commandments, and many have turned away from my commandments and have not kept them.*

The included independent chiasmus, comprising verses 9 and 10 follows:

D&C 63:9-10
4a] 9 But, behold, *faith*
3a] *cometh*
2a] not by *signs*
1a] but signs follow those that believe.
2a] 10 Yea, *signs*
3a] *come*
4a] by *faith*,

Literary Comparisons: Non-scriptural Chiasma

The chiastic structure has apparently been used as a literary formalism since ancient times. It is pervasive in both the Old and the New Testaments. Although we have been unable to obtain estimates of that fraction of the Bible which is written in chiastic form, Ronald Man[4] has identified from the published literature 605 chiasma in the New Testament alone. One would assume that the chiastic density in the Old Testament would be at least as great, as Man reflects the commonly held position that chiasmus is part of the thought and speech pattern of Semitic culture, and that New Testament writers in using chiasma were calling upon their Hebrew backgrounds, specifically Paul, or their familiarity with Old Testament literary style. Bullinger[5] states that it is by far the most stately and dignified presentation of a subject; and is always used in the most solemn and important portions of the Scriptures.

---

4. Man, Ronald E., *Chiasm in the New Testament*. Dallas: Master of Theology Thesis, Dallas Theological Seminary, 1982.
5. Bullinger, E.W., *Figures of Speech Used in the Bible*. Baker Book House Co., p. 374, 1968.

The chiasmus has also been identified from early times outside of religious literature. The literary form was known among both the Greeks and Latins—called by the Greeks *Chiasmos*, *Chiaston* or *Allelouchia*, and by the Latins *Chiasmus* or *Decussata oratio*. Nonscriptural applications of the chiasmus include the following: Beregovskaya[6] cites the Latin chiasmus, *edimus, ut vivamus, non vivimus, ut edamus*, 'we eat to live, not live to eat'. Ronald Man[7] suggests that chiasm was a common form in ancient Greek and Latin literature. Fukuchi[8] has identified the chiastic structure as an integral part of old English riddles. Karl Marx used the chiastic form in his satire of Louis Napoleon.[9]

The author and others have identified extensive chiasma in the *Popol Vuh*; which, interestingly enough, was handed down as oral tradition by the Quiché Indians until it was written with Roman characters in the Quiché idiom by one of the princes of the conquered Quiché nation following the Spanish inquisition.

Shakespeare also appears to have used the form in many of his word plays. For instance, in Hamlet, Act III, scene iv, we find—

2] *eyes*
1]   without *feeling*
1]   *feeling*
2] without *sight.*

3] When *you* are
2]   *desirest*
1]   to be *blest*
1]   I'll *blessings*
2]   *beg*
3] of *you*.

---

6. Beregovskaya, E. M., "To the Theory of Figures [Semantic and Functional Characteristics of Chiasmus]." *Seriya literatury i yazyka, Isvestiya Akademii nauk SSSR*, 3,43, pp. 227-37, May-June 1984.
7. Man, Ronald E., "The Value of Chiasm for the New Testament Interpretation." *Bibliotheca Sacra*, 141, pp. 146-57, April-June, 1984.
8. Fukuchi, Michael Seiji, "A Study of Old English Riddles." *Dissertation Abstracts International*, 41/04-A, p. 1609, 1980.
9. Riquelme, John Paul, "The Eighteenth Brumaire of Karl Marx as Symbolic Action." *History and Theory*, 19(1), pp. 58-72, 1980.

3] *If words be made of breath*
2] and *breath*
1] of *life*
1] I have no *life*
2] to *breathe*
3] *what thou hath said to me.*

In addition, Hamlet, in Act V, scene ii, quotes a most interesting interdigitated chiasmus and parallelism, which includes two chained chiasma in which the final two elements of the first chiasmus represent the first two elements of the final chiasmus, as

A] If it be — 2] *now*
B] 'tis not — 1] *to come*
A] If it be not — 1] 2) *to come*
B] it will be — *2] 1) now*
A] If it be not — *1) now*
B] yet it will — 2) *come.*

Purposes of Chiasma in Ancient Literature

Much has been written on the purpose of the chiastic form in ancient literature. The writings for the most part attempt to rationalize its use as a literary artifact developed by the authors for particular grammatical or literary purposes. Bullinger[1] cites Bengel as recording with regard to the chiastic form that "its employment is never without some use: *vis.*, in perceiving the ornament and in observing the force of the language; in understanding the true and full sense; in making clear the sound interpretation; in demonstrating the true and neat analysis of sacred text." Clark,[10] however, suggests that the use of the form may be subconscious, and results as a natural consequence of the structure of the language, since "each speaking human being unconsciously uses structures on all language levels."

---

10. Clark, David J., "Criteria for Identifying Chiasm." *Linguistica Biblica*, 35, pp. 63-72, September 1975.

A number of authors, including Gow[11] and Parunak,[12] cite the chiasm and other Hebrew literary forms as a literary convention to indicate divisions in a text, since ancient Hebrew manuscripts lacked punctuation. It has also been suggested that the form was imposed in Hebrew religious texts as a memory aid because of the appreciable oral liturgy in the Hebrew religion. These conclusions beg the question of the use of the chiastic form in languages that do contain punctuation and in areas where memorization is not formally imposed.

The chiastic form has also been cited as an artifact to protect the integrity of the text,[13] since alterations would be obvious (unless the perpetrators were also chiastically literate and both members of parallel chiastic elements were similarly altered). Such a reason would imply the unlikely suspicion on the part of the author that future generations would attack his text. It would seem, however, that the artistic and poetic value of the chiastic form would be sufficient to justify its existence in any literature.

In some communities the chiastic structure was evidently a part of the culture. Stock[14] refers to certain aspects of classical Hellenistic education in which the children learned the alphabet by repeating the names of the letters from alpha to omega, backwards from omega to alpha, and then from each end towards the middle—alpha-omega, beta-psi, . . . mu-nu, which is the chiastic form. Radday,[15] investigating chiasm in the Book of Kings, concludes that chiastic techniques constituted a widespread principle of narrative writing of the time.

Nevertheless, the application of the chiasm as an objective literary artifact may still be examined on the basis of Clark's thesis.[10] Undoubtedly, two- or three-element chiasma could easily be inadvertent. In *The Tragedy of Hamlet* was Shakespeare merely playing with words or invoking chiasma? If it were assumed that Shakespeare intentionally invoked chiastic structures,

---

11. Gow, Murray D. "The Significance of Literary Structure for the Translation of the Book of Ruth." *The Bible Translator*, 35, 3, pp. 309-320, July 1984.
12. Parunak, Henry Van Dyke, "Oral Typesetting: Some uses of Biblical Structure." *Biblica*, 62 No. 2, pp. 153-68, 1981.
13. Garrett, Duane A., "The Structure of Amos as a Testimony to its Integrity." *Journal of the Evangelical Theological Seminary*, 27, pp. 275-76, September 1984.
14. Stock, Augustine, "Chiastic Awareness and Education in Antiquity." *Biblical Theology Bulletin*, 14, pp. 23-27, January 1984.
15. Radday, Yehuda T., "Chiasm in Kings." *Linguistica Biblica*, 31, pp. 52-67, May 1974.

one would certainly not expect that he would be miserly and elemental in the use of such a sophisticated literary form—specifically, one that could be turned to such intricate plays on words and grammar for which Shakespeare is so noted.

The phrase "Smart is dumb and dumb is smart" is chiastic in structure, but it is extremely doubtful that the originator of the phrase was chiastically literate. One of the cited norms for oral discourse in our own society is, "Tell them what you are going to tell them, then tell them, then tell them what you told them." The formalism of repetition of concepts in a dissertation could well lead to a chiastic arrangement of concepts. However, it is obvious that the probability of the chance arrangement of text in chiastic order would decrease with the increasing number of elements in the chiasmus. In chiasma with as many as ten elements, for instance, the probability of the chance arrangement of the second set of ten elements in the proper chiastic order would be one in over three million. And chiasma with as many as thirty-three single elements have been found in the Doctrine and Covenants!

Much of the literature on chiasmus promotes the form as a characteristic of ancient Hebrew religious literature that represented a literary style of the authors. Since the chiastic form is found so extensively in the Doctrine and Covenants, and since Joseph Smith undoubtedly was not acquainted with chiasmus as a literary form, it is concluded that the chiastic structure, at least in the Doctrine and Covenants and possibly in all of sacred literature, is of Divine origin.

2

USE OF THE CHIASTIC FORM IN THE DOCTRINE AND COVENANTS

Comparison of Book of Mormon and Doctrine and Covenants Chiasma

The chiasm as a literary form in the Book of Mormon was first identified by Dr. John Welsh in 1969.[1] While considerable study has been devoted to Book of Mormon chiasma, very little has been done to study chiastic forms in the Doctrine and Covenants. The lack of attention to this rich treasure of chiasm was undoubtedly influenced by the pervasive concept that chiasm is a literary element of ancient Hebrew religious writing, and since the writings of the Prophet Joseph Smith had no connection with ancient Hebrew, the form would not be expected in the works that he authored. Nevertheless, this author has identified 225 chiasma in the Doctrine and Covenants, which reveals a density comparable to that in the Book of Mormon.

Finding the chiastic form as such an integral part of the Doctrine and Covenants has profound implications with respect to both the Doctrine and Covenants and the chiasmus itself. Of particular significance is the fact that of the 225 chiasma in the Doctrine and Covenants, 194 of them are in the words of Jesus Christ. On the other hand, in the Book of Mormon, among over 500 chiasma, only 48 may be attributed to the direct words of the Lord. However, in 3 Nephi, for example, of 387 verses in which the Savior is speaking, 29% are chiastic. Thus, the chiastic density of the Savior's words in the Book of Mormon is comparable to that in the Doctrine and Covenants, but a much smaller fraction of the Book of Mormon contains direct quotations of the Savior than does the Doctrine and Covenants.

In Doctrine and Covenants, Section 11, for example, which is entirely comprised of a single 33-element chiasmus, we find the words, *"Behold, I am God," "For behold, it is I that speak," "by my power I give these words unto*

1. Welsh, John W., "Chiasmus in the Book of Mormon." *BYU Studies*, 10, 1, pp. 9-84, Autumn 1969.

thee," "Behold, I speak unto all who have good desires," "Behold, I am Jesus Christ, the son of God." In fact, first-person personal pronouns referring to the Lord are used in this chiasmus 55 times. So it is with the other 193 chiasma in which the Lord is speaking. It is inconceivable that Joseph Smith would have taken the Lord's words, which were given to him by the Spirit or which he heard with his own ears, and would have rearranged them in some peculiar literary form. The conclusion is obvious—the Lord speaks chiastically! Certainly not exclusively so, but frequently. And nowhere is this more evident than in the Doctrine and Covenants.

Since Joseph Smith could not have written the chiastic structure as an objective literary form, it would necessarily follow that the chiastic form itself in the Doctrine and Covenants was of inspired origin. It is significant in this regard to note that the Section containing the chiasmus with the most elements, Section 11, with sixteen sets of parallel elements plus a central theme, is one of at least eight sections that were received by means of the Urim and Thummim. Again, it is not expected that the Prophet would use his own terminology, let alone compose a literary form, when receiving revelation via the Urim and Thummim. Recognizing the divine source of the chiastic form in the Doctrine and Covenants establishes the divinity of the subject matter of which the chiasma are a part.

Guidelines for Evaluating Chiasma

It is essential in this context to examine the validity of the structures as true chiasma. Dr. Welsh has developed a list of 15 criteria by which he would judge the "degree of chiasticity" of a proposed structure.[2] To approach the question of "chiasticity" of the inverse parallelisms found in the Doctrine and Covenants, we may subject the lengthiest chiasmus, that found in Section 11, to the Welsh criteria. The 15 items by which Dr. Welsh judges the degree of chiasticity are itemized below:

1. **Objectivity**—To what degree is the proposed pattern clearly evident in the text? How complete is the chiasticity?

2. **Purpose**—Is there an identifiable literary reason why the author might have employed chiasmus in the text?

---

2. Welsh, John W., "Criteria for Identifying the Presence of Chiasmus. Provo, Utah." *Foundation for Ancient Research and Mormon Studies*, WEL-89b. 1987.

3. **Boundaries**—A chiasm is stronger if it operates across a literary unit as a whole and not only upon fragments or sections which overlap or cut across significant organizational lines intrinsic to the text.

4. **Competition with other forms**—Chiasmus is more dominant in a passage when it is the only structuring device employed there.

5. **Length**—The longer the proposed chiasm the higher its degree of chiasticity. Having a large number of proposed elements, however, is not alone very significant, for all the elements must bear their own weight. An extended chiasm is probably not much stronger than its weakest links.

6. **Density**—How many words are there between the dominant elements?

7. **Dominance**—A convincing analysis must account for and embrace the dominant nouns, verbs and distinctive phrases in the text.

8. **Mavericks**—A chiasm loses potency when key elements in the system appear extraneously outside the proposed structure.

9. **Reduplication**—If the same word or element appears over and over within the system, the greater the likelihood that some other kind of repetition is predominant in the passage instead of chiasmus.

10. **Centrality**—The crux of a chiasm is generally its central turning point. Without a well-defined centerpiece or distinct crossing effect, there is little reason for seeing chiasmus.

11. **Balance**—How balanced is the proposed chiasm? Ideally, the elements on both sides of the proposed focal point should be nearly equal in terms of number of words, lines or elements.

12. **Climax**—A strong chiasm will emphasize the central element of the passage as its focal climax.

13. **Return**—A chiasm is more complete where its beginning and end combine to create a strong sense of return and completion.

14. **Compatibility**—The chiasticity of a passage is greater when it works comfortably and consistently together with the overall style of the author.

15. **Aesthetics**—Relevant factors include fluency with the form, consistency in sustaining the structure, balance and harmony, pliability at the turning point, and meaningful application of the form.

A Chiastic Analysis of Doctrine and Covenants 11

Section 11, comprising 30 verses, is identified as a single chiasmus containing 16 pairs of elements, and it contains the greatest number of elements of any chiasmus identified in the Doctrine and Covenants. The section is reproduced below in chiastic form, with the parallel elements printed in italics.

16] 1 *A great and marvelous work is about to come forth among the children of men.*

15] 2 *Behold, I am God*; give heed to my word, which is quick and powerful, sharper than a two-edged sword, to the dividing asunder of both joints and marrow; therefore give heed unto my word.

14A] 3 Behold, the field is white already to harvest; *therefore, whoso desireth to reap*

14B] *let him thrust in his sickle* with his might, *and reap* while the day lasts,

13] *that he may treasure up for his soul everlasting salvation in the kingdom of God.*

12] 4 *Yea, whosoever will thrust in his sickle and reap, the same is called of God.*
5 Therefore, if you will ask of me you shall receive; if you will knock it shall be opened unto you.

11] 6 Now, as you have asked, behold, I say unto you, keep my commandments, and *seek to bring forth and establish the cause of Zion.*

10A] 7 *Seek not for riches but for wisdom;*

10B] and, *behold, the mysteries of God shall be unfolded unto you*, and then shall you be made rich. Behold, he that hath eternal life is rich.

9] 8 Verily, verily, I say unto you, even as you desire of me so it shall be done unto you; and, *if you desire, you shall be the means of doing much good in this generation.*

8] 9 *Say nothing but repentance unto this generation.*

7] *Keep my commandments*, and assist to bring forth my work,

6A] *according to my commandments,*

6B] *and you shall be blessed.*

5A] 10 Behold, thou hast a gift, or thou shalt have a gift *if thou wilt desire of me*

5B] *in faith*, with an honest heart, believing in the power of Jesus Christ, or in my power which speaketh unto thee;

4] 11 For, behold, it is I that speak; *behold*, I am the light which shineth in darkness, and *by my power I give these words unto thee.*

3] 12 And now, verily, verily, I say unto thee, *put your trust in that Spirit which leadeth to do good*—yea, to do justly, to walk humbly,

2] *to judge righteously*; and this is my Spirit.

1] 13 Verily, verily, I say unto you, I will impart unto you of my Spirit, which shall enlighten your mind, which shall fill your soul with joy;

2] 14 And then shall ye know, or by this shall you know, all things whatsoever you desire of me, which are *pertaining unto things of righteousness,*

3] *in faith believing in me that you shall receive.*

4] 15 *Behold, I command you* that you need not suppose that you are called to preach until you are called.

16 Wait a little longer, until you shall have my word, my rock, my church, and my gospel, that you may know of a surety my doctrine.

5A] 17 And then, behold, *according to your desires,*

5B] yea, *even according to your faith* shall it be done unto you.

6A] 18 *Keep my commandments*; hold your peace; appeal unto my Spirit;

6B] 19 Yea, cleave unto me with all your heart, *that you may assist in bringing to light those things of which has been spoken—yea, the translation of my work*; be patient until you shall accomplish it.

7] 20 Behold, this is your work, to *keep my commandments*, yea, with all your might, mind and strength.

8] 21 Seek not to declare my word, but *first seek to obtain my word, and then shall your tongue be loosed;*

9] then, *if you desire, you shall have my Spirit and my word, yea, the power of God unto the convincing of men.*

10A] 22 But now hold your peace; *study my word which*
hath gone forth among the children of men, and
also study my word which shall come forth among
the children of men, or that which is now translat-
ing, yea, until you have obtained all which I shall
grant unto the children of men in this generation,
10B] *and then shall all things be added thereto.*
11] 23 Behold thou art Hyrum, my son; *seek the kingdom*
of God, and all things shall be added according to
that which is just.
12] 24 Build upon my rock, which is my gospel;
25 *Deny not the spirit of revelation, nor the spirit of*
prophecy, for wo unto him that denieth these things;
13] 26 Therefore, *treasure up in your heart until the time which*
is in my wisdom that you shall go forth.
14A] 27 Behold, *I speak unto all who have good desires,*
14B] *and have thrust in their sickle to reap.*
15] 28 *Behold, I am Jesus Christ, the Son of God.* I am the life and the
light of the world.
29 I am the same who came unto mine own and mine own
received me not;
16] 30 *But verily, verily, I say unto you, that as many as receive me, to them*
will I give power to become the sons of God, even to them that believe
on my name. Amen.

The Evaluation of D&C 11 According to the Welsh Criteria

1. Objectivity

The chiastic pattern is clearly evident in the text. Over 50% of the words in the Section comprise strictly parallel elements of the chiasmus. The clarity of the chiastic pattern may be observed by a comparison of the relationship in the meanings of each of the parallel elements. (See Analysis 11A, page 318.)

2. Purpose

A. The entire revelation is a single chiasmus, identifying it as a single literary entity.

B. It is mirrored around a strong central theme, which defines the means for accomplishing the work, and the effect of that means on the person.

C. The contrasts between parallel elements are with one exception conceptual, indicating a purposeful, intellectual arrangement rather than one which is merely mechanical. This is striking in a chiasmus with as many as 16 elements.

D. This chiasmus invokes a strong sense of closure in both the ultimate and penultimate elements. First, the great and marvelous work in 16a is defined in 16b, and the authorship of Jesus Christ is defined in the proximate elements 15a and 15b.

E. Intentionality— Although a simple, two-element chiasmus may indeed be accidental, it is difficult to imagine that the chiastic arrangement of as many as sixteen elements could be anything but intentional. The greater the number of parallel elements, the less the probability that an inverse parallelism would result from the chance arrangement of the elements. The probability of purposeful arrangement is further enhanced by the density of chiasticity of the section. Density is treated in criterion No. 6.

3. **Boundaries**

This section is perfectly bounded chiastically since the entire section, which treats a single subject, comprises a single chiasmus.

4. **Competition with other forms**

This criteria would be applicable if the different literary forms were independent and competitive. In this section of the Doctrine and Covenants four of the sixteen elements are comprised of two-element series. These series, however, are intrinsic to the chiastic structure, and hence, give it more intricacy and sophistication, thus enhancing, rather than detracting from, the chiasticity of the section.

5. **Length**

Each of the elements of the subject chiasmus appear to be of similar weight, i.e., the connecting elements are all obvious, and there appears to be no need for contrivance or explanation to demonstrate the connections between parallel passages.

6. **Density**

In the analysis of Section 11, identified as "ANALYSIS 11A D&C 11:1-30," only the strictest parallel phrases have been cited. In some cases, additional wording amplifies the concept of the element and could logically have been included. For instance, element 11b: "Behold thou are Hyrum, my son" identifies the subject "you" in element 11a, and those phrases could well have been included in the rather terse comparisons in the Analysis.

Similarly, the entire segment cited in the first element 10B could easily have been incorporated, completing the thought. Nevertheless, comparing the strictly parallel phrases cited in the analysis with the totality of the section, omitting from the totality only the non-essential words such as articles and exclamations, we find by word count that the section is over 73% chiastic.

7. Dominance

The chiastic elements in this section do contain dominant phrases and essential grammatical elements, but not exclusively so. Twenty-seven percent of the section is non-chiastic, but the non-chiastic fraction also contains essential and meaningful phrases. However, they are not more meaningful than those in the chiastic elements, so the dominance factor could be rated on a par with the density factor.

8. Mavericks

One does not find in Section 11 key elements of the section that are extraneous to the chiastic text. The chiastic structure is pervasive, and the extraneous elements are fragmentary.

9. Reduplication

The only significant word that bridges more than one pair of elements is the word *commandments*, which is common to and predominant in elements 7 and 6. Thus, it appears that the chiasmus in this section does not violate the concept of reduplication.

10. Centrality

Section 11 comprises a series of instructions and commandments from the Lord to Hyrum Smith. Verse 13, set off in the center of the section as the hub of the chiasmus, contains the Lord's commitment to Hyrum—the promise of His Spirit, to enlighten Hyrum's mind and fill his soul with joy. This centralized change-over from that which is required by the Lord to that which may be expected from the Lord provides a well-defined central theme comprised of a specific significant blessing promised to Hyrum Smith.

11. Balance

There is little disparity in the length of parallel elements in Section 11. However, the idea of mechanical balance perhaps should not be weighted too heavily. In some cases the purpose of chiasmus is served by a parallel element providing a detailed explanation of a given concept stated in both brief and general terms (see 1. Objectivity), which would serve the intent of objectivity and purpose. Mild disparities in length that fulfil the concept of detailed explanation are found in the general-to-specific elements 16, 10A, and 6B of this chiasmus.

12. **Climax**

The central element of this chiasmus is significant, but does not show a high degree of predominance. The theme of the Section is a call to preach the gospel. The power by which that is to be accomplished comprises the focal point. However, the concepts of which the chiasmus is comprised build in strength and specificity toward the center. Elements 16a through 12a are written in the third person, and specific instructions in the second person begin with element 11a, "Now, as *you* have asked" and continue to the center. The second person is again used from the center through 11b, which element identifies the antecedent of the pronoun, you, in element 11a. Elements 14Ab and 14Bb again identify the third-person intent of the outer segments.

13. **Return**

The end elements in this chiasmus are perhaps more powerful than the center. The implied definition of the *great and marvelous work* as the *power to become the sons of God*, followed and correspondingly preceded by the statement of divine authorship, gives this chiasmus a powerful sense of return and completion.

14. **Compatibility**

This statement of style implies that the chiasmus is a conscious literary artifact of the author. This could well apply to non-scriptural writing, and would be a strong argument in favor of intent. However, in scriptural writing, where *holy men of God spake as they were moved by the Holy Ghost*, we are concerned with divine authorship, and the question of style may take on another dimension. The concept of style and authorship of chiastic structure in the Doctrine and Covenants will be treated in detail later.

15. **Aesthetics**

Although aesthetics to a degree is in the eye of the beholder, yet consensus establishes the validity of opinion. Thus this subjective criterion may best be evaluated by each reader.

Joseph Smith Could Not Have Originated the Chiastic Style in the Doctrine and Covenants

Joseph Smith cannot be considered, in a strict sense, as the author of the Doctrine and Covenants. In the same sense that he was the translator of the Book of Mormon, he was the revelator of the Doctrine and Covenants. It is of critical importance to consider whether the Prophet received the revelations in the form of mental concepts and used his own wording in recording them and either accidentally or intentionally invoked the chiastic structure, or whether he transcribed the revelations in the phraseology in which they were received, which would imply that the form itself in the Doctrine and Covenants would be of Divine origin.

Consider the possibility that the Prophet received the revelations as mental concepts and recorded them in his own phraseology. With the exception of Section 2, which contains only three verses and was received in September, 1823 when the Prophet was 17 years old, and Sections 135, 136 and 138, received by John Taylor, Brigham Young and Joseph F. Smith, respectively, in 1844, 1847 and 1918, the revelations recorded in the Doctrine and Covenants span the period from 1828 to 1843, corresponding to the Prophet's age from 22 to 37 years old. The Prophet studied Hebrew in 1836 in the School of the Prophets, under the tutelage of professor Joshua Seixas, a Hebrew scholar, and it might be suggested that he acquired a knowledge of the form from his acquaintance with Hebrew, although the likelihood is minimal since the chiastic form had hardly been recognized by other Bible scholars of the time. Had he nevertheless learned the chiastic form from his Hebrew studies, one would expect that the use of the form would not begin before 1836, when he began to study Hebrew, and would increase in frequency as sophistication in its application increased with learning. If we were to assume that the Prophet had learned the chiastic form from his own studies and objectively incorporated the form in the revelations that he recorded, it would be necessary to conclude that revelation was received in the form of concepts or ideas and expressed in the Prophet's own phraseology. As earlier mentioned, Section 11, containing the longest chiasmus in the Doctrine and Covenants and which was received via the Urim and Thummim, argues against the concept of free-form transcription.

The Frequency of Occurrences of D&C Chiasma

To examine the frequency of occurrence of chiasma in the Doctrine and Covenants, we need a measure of chiastic density in the revelations. The frequency of occurrence of the chiastic form in the Doctrine and Covenants as a function of time could be expressed by the percent of the revelations received in a given year that contained the chiastic form. This measure may give a distorted view however, since for example, only three revelations were recorded in 1839, one of which, or 33%, contains a chiastic structure. However, the chiasmus consists of only five verses of the revelation that contains 46 verses. So in 1843, 33% of the revelations contained chiasma, but chiastic elements were found in only 7% of the verses. It would seem that the more appropriate measure of chiastic frequency would be the fractional chiastic content of the revelations, i.e., the percent of the verses in any given revelation encompassed within chiastic structures.

Figure 1 is a graph of chiastic frequency based on the percent of the verses in a given year with chiastic structures. The three revelations received by others than the Prophet Joseph and the early 1823 revelation are not included. Also excluded are Section 102, Minutes of the organization of the first high council of the Church, written by Oliver Cowdery and Orson Hyde, and Section 113, answers to certain questions on the writings of Isaiah, which contains one-verse questions and generally one-verse answers—improbable for chiastic structures. The revelations included in the figure have an average chiastic content of 43%. It is noted that the revelations received in 1828 and 1829 have a higher chiastic content than those of any other year except 1835. This immediately rules out the postulate that Joseph Smith became acquainted with chiasmus through his Hebrew studies, since chiastic structures occurred in the Doctrine and Covenants more frequently before the Prophet could have learned anything about them from his study of Hebrew than they did afterwards.

Since it cannot be conceived that the prophet contrived the chiastic structure as a conscious literary form in the revelations prior to 1836, and that the chiastic structures are far too complex to have been originated by chance, it must be concluded that the chiastic structure in the Doctrine and Covenants is of divine origin. The Prophet was undoubtedly unaware of its existence as a literary form. This conclusion is further supported by the fact that a number of revelations containing chiastic structures were dictated as they were received, precluding the possibility of organizing the writing in a complicated literary form in which each element is some sort of a reflection of its mirror image in the second part.

Figure 1.

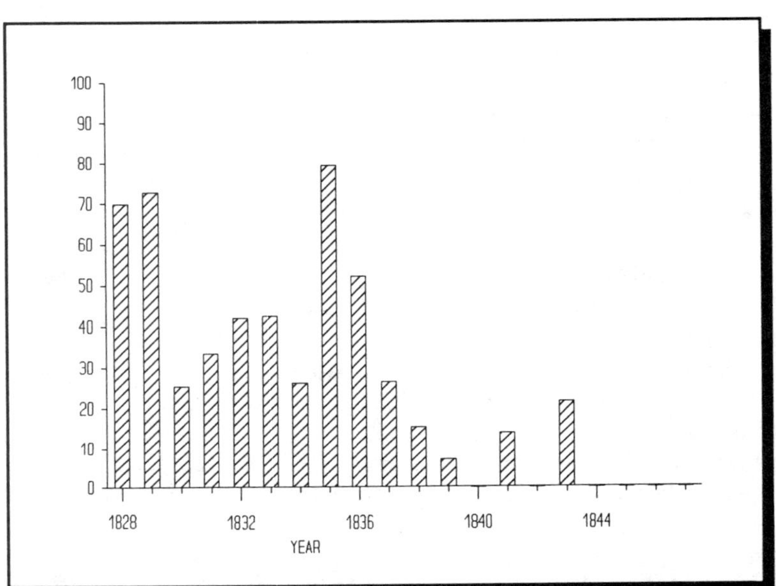

CHIASTIC FREQUENCY IN THE DOCTRINE AND COVENANTS

A Chiastic Analysis of D&C 76

An additional evidence of the chiasticity of the Doctrine and Covenants may be appreciated by examining the complex structure of Section 76, which contains the greatest number of chiasma of any Section in the Doctrine and Covenants. As mentioned before, Section 76 contains 11 chiasma. Different subjects within the section are chiastically bounded; there exist chiasma within chiasma; and the four series of parallel "these are they" elements outlining the conditions of the three degrees of glory are chiastically related!

The chiastic nature of the section is particularly striking in view of the fact that it is the record of a vision received by Joseph Smith and Sidney Rigdon, and that the entire text was recorded shortly after the vision was received. Apart from a non-chiastic introduction, vs 1-4, and a non-chiastic conclusion, vs 108-119, the section is comprised of 11 chiasma, each bounding a given topic, as outlined below:

vs 1-4 Non-chiastic Introduction, declaring the attributes of the Savior.

vs 5-10 Three-element chiasmus with two-element parallelism in the first (internal) chiastic elements, declaring the Lord's mercy and grace toward those who fear and serve him.

vs 11-25 Four-element chiasmus with a three-element chiastic structure comprising part of the initial fourth element, and a two-element chiastic structure comprising part of the final fourth element, testifying of the vision of the Father and the Son, and of Lucifer, as seen by Joseph Smith and Sidney Rigdon.

v 13 Three-element chiasmus which forms a part of the initial fourth element of Chiasmus 76B, declaring that the things of God given to the understanding of Joseph and Sidney were from the beginning.

v 27 Two-element chiasmus which forms a part of the final fourth element of chiasm 76B describing the fall of Lucifer.

vs 28-30 Three-element chiasmus, including the commandment to write the vision and declaring that they had beheld Satan.

vs 32-38 Three-element chiasmus with two-element parallelisms in the third chiastic elements, describing the sons of perdition.

vs 36-44 Five-element chiasmus, the initial elements 5] and 4] being the same as the final elements 2], 3A] and 3B] of the preceding chiasmus, describing the fate of the sons of perdition, and the power of the Lamb to redeem all else.

vs 45-48 Three-element chiasmus declaring that the fate of the sons of perdition is not revealed to those not ordained to this condemnation.

vs 50-65 Four-element chiasmus with triple parallelisms in the first (internal) chiastic elements, describing the characteristics of those who come forth in the resurrection of the just.

vs 63-107 Complex four-element chiasmus in which the initial and final fourth elements are composed of 8- and 7-element parallelisms, respectively; and the initial and final second elements are comprised of 6- and 5-element parallelisms, respectively. The initial fourth element lists eight "these are they" describing the characteristics of those who inherit the celestial glory, and the final fourth element lists seven "these are they" describing the characteristics of those who inherit the telestial glory. The initial third element introduces the subject of the terrestrial world, and the final third element, comprising verses 89-98, is a three-element chiasmus summarizing the vision of the three degrees of glory.

The initial second element lists six "these are they" describing the characteristics of those who inherit the terrestrial kingdom, and the final second element lists five "these are they" describing the characteristics of those who inherit the telestial kingdom. The two internal first elements summarize the visions of the terrestrial and telestial glories, respectively.

vs108-112 Non-chiastic segment.

vs113-119 Conclusion.

The chiasma in Section 76, and the section itself as a complex chiastic literary structure, emphatically fulfill all of the 15 Welsh criteria for a high degree of chiasticity.

To demonstrate how precisely and neatly each topic in Section 76 is bounded by chiastic structures, the chiastic content of Section 76 is displayed below. (Incidentally, verse 13, which forms a part of the initial fourth element of the chiasmus in verses 11-27, is itself a three-element chiasmus, as are verses 26 and 27, which form a two-element chiasmus as part of the final fourth element of the same chiasmus! These two chiasma are identified by brackets [ ].)

D&C 76:5-10, THE LORD'S PREFACE

3] 5 *For thus saith the Lord—I, the Lord, am merciful and gracious unto those who fear me, and delight to honor those who serve me in righteousness and in truth unto the end.*

2] 6 *Great shall be their reward and eternal shall be their glory.*

1A] 7 *And to them will I reveal all mysteries,*

1B] *yea, all the hidden mysteries of my kingdom from days of old, and for ages to come, will I make known unto them the good pleasure of my will concerning all things pertaining to my kingdom.*

1A] 8 *Yea, even the wonders of eternity shall they know,*

1B] 9 *And things to come will I show them, even the things of many generations.*

2] *And their wisdom shall be great, and their understanding reach to heaven; and before them the wisdom of the wise shall perish, and the understanding of the prudent shall come to naught.*

3] 10 *For by my Spirit will I enlighten them, and by my power will I make known unto them the secrets of my will—yea, even those things which eye has not seen, nor ear heard, nor yet entered into the heart of man.*

D&C 76:11-27, THE VISION OF THE FATHER AND THE SON

4] 11 We, Joseph Smith, Jun., and Sidney Rigdon, being in the Spirit on the sixteenth day of February, in the year of our Lord one thousand eight hundred and thirty-two—

12 By the power of the Spirit *our eyes were opened and our understandings were enlightened, so as to see and understand the things of God—*

[D&C 76:13]

13 Even those things

a3] *which were from the beginning* before the world was,

a2] which were ordained *of the Father,*

a1] through his Only Begotten Son,

a2] who was in the bosom *of the Father,*

a3] *even from the beginning;*

3] 14 *Of whom we bear record; and the record which we bear is the fullness of the gospel of Jesus Christ, who is the Son,*

2] *whom we saw and with whom we conversed in the heavenly vision.*

1] 15 For while we were doing the work of translation, which the Lord had appointed unto us, we came to the twenty-ninth verse of the fifth chapter of John, which was given unto us as follows:

16 Speaking of the resurrection of the dead, concerning those who shall hear the voice of the Son of Man, and shall come forth—

17 They who have done good in the resurrection of the just, and they who have done evil in the resurrection of the unjust—

18 Now this caused us to marvel, for it was given unto us of the Spirit.

19 And while we meditated upon these things, the Lord touched the eyes of our understandings and they were opened, and the glory of the Lord shone round about.

20 And we beheld the glory of the Son, on the right hand of the Father, and received of his fullness;

21 And saw the holy angels, and them who are sanctified before his throne, worshiping God, and the Lamb, who worship him forever and ever.

22 And now, after the many testimonies which have been given of him, this is the testimony, last of all, which we give of him: That he lives!

2] *For we saw him, even on the right hand of God;*
3] 23 *and we heard the voice bearing record that he is the Only Begotten of the Father—*
24 *That by him, and through him, and of him, the worlds are and were created, and the inhabitants thereof are begotten sons and daughters unto God.*
4] 25 *And this we saw also*, and bear record, that an angel of God who was in authority in the presence of God, who rebelled against the Only Begotten Son whom the Father loved and who was in the bosom of the Father, was thrust down from the presence of God and the Son,
26 And was called Perdition, for the heavens wept over him—he was Lucifer,

[D&C 76:26,27], THE FALL OF SATAN

a2] *a son of the morning.*
27 And we beheld, and lo,
a1] *he is fallen!*
a1] *is fallen,*
a2] even *a son of the morning!*

D&C 76:28-30, THE VISION OF SATAN

3] 28 And while we were yet in the Spirit, *the Lord commanded us that we should write the vision;*
2] *for we beheld Satan, that old serpent, even the devil, who rebelled against God,*
1] *and sought to take the kingdom of our God and his Christ—*
1] *29 Wherefore, he maketh war with the saints of God, and encompasseth them round about.*
2] 30 *And we saw a vision of the sufferings of those with whom he made war and overcame,*
3] *for thus came the voice of the Lord unto us:*

D&C 76:31-38, THE SONS OF PERDITION

31 Thus saith the Lord concerning all those who know my power, and have been made partakers thereof, and suffered themselves through the power of the devil to be overcome, and to deny the truth and defy my power—
3A] 32 *They are they who are the sons of perdition,*
3B] *of whom I say that it had been better for them never to have been born;*
2] 33 *For they are vessels of wrath, doomed to suffer the wrath of God, with the devil and his angels in eternity;*

1] 34 *Concerning whom I have said there is no forgiveness in this world nor in the world to come—*
1] 35 *Having denied the Holy Spirit after having received it, and having denied the Only Begotten Son of the Father, having crucified him unto themselves and put him to an open shame.*
2] 36 *These are they who shall go away into the lake of fire and brimstone, with the devil and his angels—*
3A] 37 *And the only ones on whom the second death shall have any power;*
3B] 38 *Yea, verily, the only ones who shall not be redeemed in the due time of the Lord, after the sufferings of his wrath.*

D&C 76:36-44, THE SAVIOR REDEEMS ALL BUT THE SONS OF PERDITION

6] 36 *These are they who shall go away into the lake of fire and brimstone, with the devil and his angels—*
5] 37 *And the only ones on whom the second death shall have any power;* 38 *Yea, verily, the only ones who shall not be redeemed in the due time of the Lord, after the sufferings of his wrath.*
4] 39 *For all the rest shall be brought forth by the resurrection of the dead,*
3] *through the triumph and the glory of the Lamb,*
2] *who was slain,* who was in the bosom of the Father before the worlds were made.
1] 40 And this is the gospel, the glad tidings, which the voice out of the heavens bore record unto us—
2] 41 *That he came into the world, even Jesus, to be crucified for the world,*
3] *and to bear the sins of the world, and to sanctify the world, and to cleanse it from all unrighteousness;*
4] 42 *That through him all might be saved whom the Father had put into his power and made by him;*
5] 43 Who glorifies the Father, and saves all the works of his hands, *except those sons of perdition who deny the Son after the Father has revealed him.*
6] 44 *Wherefore, he saves all except them—they shall go away into everlasting punishment, which is endless punishment, which is eternal punishment, to reign with the devil and his angels in eternity,* where their worm dieth not, and the fire is not quenched, which is their torment—

D&C 76:45-48, THE FATE OF THE SONS OF PERDITION

3] 45 *And the end thereof, neither the place thereof, nor their torment, no man knows;*

2] 46 *Neither was it revealed, neither is, neither will be revealed unto man,*

1] *except to them who are made partakers thereof;*

1] 47 *Nevertheless, I, the Lord, show it by vision unto many,*

2] *but straightway shut it up again;*

3] 48 *Wherefore, the end, the width, the height, the depth, and the misery thereof, they understand not, neither any man except those who are ordained unto this condemnation.*

49 And we heard the voice, saying: Write the vision, for lo, this is the end of the vision of the sufferings of the ungodly.

D&C 76:50-65, THE RESURRECTION OF THE JUST

4] 50 And again we bear record—for we saw and heard, and this is the testimony of the gospel of Christ *concerning them who shall come forth in the resurrection of the just—*

3] 51 *They are they who received the testimony of Jesus, and believed on his name and were baptized after the manner of his burial,* being buried in the water in his name, and this according to the commandment which he has given—

52 That by keeping the commandments they might be washed and cleansed from all their sins, and receive the Holy Spirit by the laying on of the hands of him who is ordained and sealed unto this power;

2] 53 *And who overcome by faith, and are sealed by the Holy Spirit of promise,* which the Father sheds forth upon all those who are just and true.

1A] 54 *They are they who are the church of the Firstborn.*

1B] 55 *They are they into whose hands the Father has given all things—*

1C] 56 *They are they who are priests and kings, who have received of his fullness, and of his glory;*

57 *And are priests of the Most High, after the order of Melchizedek, which was after the order of Enoch, which was after the order of the Only Begotten Son.*

1A] 58 *Wherefore, as it is written, they are gods, even the sons of God—*

1B] 59 *Wherefore, all things are theirs, whether life or death, or things present, or things to come, all are theirs*
1C] *and they are Christ's, and Christ is God's.*
2] 60 *And they shall overcome all things.*
3] 61 Wherefore, let no man glory in man, but rather let him glory in God, who shall subdue all enemies under his feet.
62 *These shall dwell in the presence of God and his Christ forever and ever.*
63 These are they whom he shall bring with him, when he shall come in the clouds of heaven to reign on the earth over his people.
64 These are they who shall have part in the first resurrection.
4] 65 *These are they who shall come forth in the resurrection of the just.*

D&C 76:63-106, THE THREE DEGREES OF GLORY

4] **PARALLELISM D&C 76:63-70**

1) 63 These are they whom he shall bring with him, when he shall come in the clouds of heaven to reign on the earth over his people.
2) 64 These are they who shall have part in the first resurrection.
3) 65 These are they who shall come forth in the resurrection of the just.
4) 66 These are they who are come unto Mount Zion, and unto the city of the living God, the heavenly place, the holiest of all.
5) 67 These are they who have come to an innumerable company of angels, to the general assembly and church of Enoch, and of the Firstborn.
6) 68 These are they whose names are written in heaven, where God and Christ are the judge of all.
7) 69 These are they who are just men made perfect through Jesus the mediator of the new covenant, who wrought out this perfect atonement through the shedding of his own blood.
8) 70 These are they whose bodies are celestial, whose glory is that of the sun, even the glory of God, the highest of all, whose glory the sun of the firmament is written of as being typical.

3] 71 And again, we saw the terrestrial world, and behold and lo, these are they who are of the terrestrial, whose glory differs from that of the church of the Firstborn who have received the fullness of the Father, even as that of the moon differs from the sun in the firmament.

2] **PARALLELISM D&C 76:72-79**

1) 72 Behold, these are they who died without law;
2) 73 And also they who are the spirits of men kept in prison, whom the Son visited, and preached the gospel unto them, that they might be judged according to men in the flesh;
74 Who received not the testimony of Jesus in the flesh, but afterwards received it.
3) 75 These are they who are honorable men of the earth, who were blinded by the craftiness of men.
4) 76 These are they who receive of his glory, but not of his fullness.
5) 77 These are they who receive of the presence of the Son, but not of the fullness of the Father.
78 Wherefore, they are bodies terrestrial, and not bodies celestial, and differ in glory as the moon differs from the sun.
6) 79 These are they who are not valiant in the testimony of Jesus; wherefore, they obtain not the crown over the kingdom of our God.

1] 80 And now this is the end of the vision which we saw of the terrestrial, that the Lord commanded us to write while we were yet in the Spirit.

1] 81 And again, we saw the glory of the telestial, which glory is that of the lesser, even as the glory of the stars differs from that of the glory of the moon in the firmament.

2] **PARALLELISM D&C 76:82-88**

1) 82 These are they who received not the gospel of Christ, neither the testimony of Jesus.
2) 83 These are they who deny not the Holy Spirit.
3) 84 These are they who are thrust down to hell.
4) 85 These are they who shall not be redeemed from the devil until the last resurrection, until the Lord, even Christ the Lamb, shall have finished his work.
5) 86 These are they who receive not of his fullness in the eternal world, but of the Holy Spirit through the ministration of the terrestrial;

87 And the terrestrial through the ministration of the celestial.
88 And also the telestial receive it of the administering of angels who are appointed to minister for them, or who are appointed to be ministering spirits for them; for they shall be heirs of salvation.

3] **[D&C 76:89-98]**

3) 89 And thus we saw, in the heavenly vision, *the glory of the telestial*, which surpasses all understanding;
90 And no man knows it except him to whom God has revealed it.

2) 91 And thus we saw *the glory of the terrestrial* which excels in all things the glory of the telestial, even in glory, and in power, and in might, and in dominion.

1) 92 And thus we saw *the glory of the celestial*, which excels in all things--where God, even the Father, reigns upon his throne forever and ever;
93 Before whose throne all things bow in humble reverence, and give him glory forever and ever.
94 They who dwell in his presence are the church of the Firstborn; and they see as they are seen, and know as they are known, having received of his fullness and of his grace;
95 And he makes them equal in power, and in might, and in dominion.

1) 96 And *the glory of the celestial* is one, even as the glory of the sun is one.

2) 97 And *the glory of the terrestrial* is one, even as the glory of the moon is one.

3) 98 And *the glory of the telestial* is one, even as the glory of the stars is one; for as one star differs from another star in glory, even so differs one from another in glory in the telestial world;

4] **PARALLELISM D&C 76:99-107**

1) 99 For these are they who are of Paul, and of Apollos, and of Cephas.

2) 100 These are they who say they are some of one and some of another—some of Christ and some of John, and some of Moses, and some of Elias, and some of Esaias, and some of Isaiah, and some of Enoch;
101 But received not the gospel, neither the testimony of Jesus, neither the prophets, neither the everlasting covenant.

3) 102 Last of all, these all are they who will not be gathered with the saints, to be caught up unto the church of the Firstborn, and received into the cloud.

4) 103 These are they who are liars, and sorcerers, and adulterers, and whoremongers, and whosoever loves and makes a lie.

5) 104 These are they who suffer the wrath of God on earth.

6) 105 These are they who suffer the vengeance of eternal fire.

7) 106 These are they who are cast down to hell and suffer the wrath of Almighty God, until the fullness of times, when Christ shall have subdued all enemies under his feet, and shall have perfected his work;
107 When he shall deliver up the kingdom, and present it unto the Father, spotless, saying: I have overcome and have trodden the wine-press alone, even the wine-press of the fierceness of the wrath of Almighty God.

How D&C 76 Was Received and Recorded

The complicated literary format of Section 76 is all the more striking considering the manner in which the revelation was received and recorded. The revelation was received as a vision by the Prophet and Sidney Rigdon in the house of Father Johnson, in Hyrum, Ohio, in the presence of about a dozen persons. Philo Dibble was among those present, and recorded the following eye-witness account:[3]

> Joseph would, at intervals, say: "What do I see?" as one might say while looking out the window and beholding what all in the room could not see. Then he would relate what he had seen or what he was looking at.

3. *The Juvenile Instructor*. May 15, 1892, pp. 303, 304.

> Then Sidney replied, "I see the same." Presently Sidney would say "what do I see?" and would repeat what he had seen or was seeing, and Joseph would reply, "I see the same."
>
> This manner of conversation was repeated at short intervals to the end of the vision, and during the whole time not a word was spoken by any other person. Not a sound nor motion made by anyone but Joseph and Sidney, and it seemed to me that they never moved a joint or limb during the time I was there, which I think was over an hour, and to the end of the vision.

Of major significance is the fact that Joseph Smith apparently did not write Section 76. The commandment was given in verse 28, *And while we were yet in the Spirit, the Lord commanded us that we should write the vision.* Ivan J. Barrett reports in his book entitled *Joseph Smith and the Restoration*, that Joseph requested Sidney Rigdon to write the vision, and that he stayed up the entire night following the vision to put it in written form.[4] In an attempt to find the original reference to the Prophet's instructions to Sidney to write the revelation, we contacted Brother Barrett, who unfortunately had not retained that information. The staff of the library in the Church Historical Department also were unable to identify the original reference. However, such action was characteristic of the Prophet, who commonly used scribes to record the revelations. In those revelations that were dictated by the Prophet, the dictation stood as first pronounced. There was never any reading back to alter the wording in order to improve the form or impose a style. Parley P. Pratt records,

> All his written revelations were dictated and written. There was never any hesitation, reviewing, or reading back, in order to keep the run of the subject; neither did any of these communications undergo revisions, interlinings, or corrections. As he dictated them, so they stood, so far as I have witnessed; and I was present to witness the dictation of several communications of several pages each.[5]

---

4. Barrett, Ivan J., *Joseph Smith and the Restoration*. Provo, Utah, Brigham Young University Press, p. 204, 1967 (Rev. Ed. 1973).
5. *The Autobiography of Parley P. Pratt, One of the Twelve Apostles of The Church of Jesus Christ of Latter-Day Saints*. Chicago: Pratt Brothers, by Law, King and Law, pp. 65-66, 1880.

Although Section 76 was probably written by Sidney Rigdon rather than being dictated by the Prophet, this Section nevertheless contains the most complex and sophisticated chiastic structures in the Doctrine and Covenants! To assume that both Joseph and Sidney were secretly masters of the chiasmus as a literary form is beyond belief.

It is interesting to note that in 1843 the Prophet wrote a poetic version of Section 76.[6] This has been examined for chiastic content and has been found to be non-chiastic except for one elementary couplet found in verse 69— "from the least unto the greatest, and greatest to least." Such an elementary structure, as an isolated case in a much larger presentation, would be assumed to be accidental. The fact that chiasmus is virtually non-existent in the Prophet's own rendition of a highly chiastic revelation further supports the contention that Joseph Smith was not aware of the chiastic form. Furthermore, the magnitude of the chiastic content and the complexity of the chiastic structures in Section 76 and in the Doctrine and Covenants as a whole preclude the possibility that the literary structure could have been contrived and composed by the ingenuity of the Prophet while dictating to a scribe, and in addition provide strong evidence that the contents, structure and wording of the Doctrine and Covenants are of Divine origin.

---

6. *Times and Seasons*, 4, 1 Feb. 1843, pp. 82-85.

3

EXTENSION OF THE CONCEPT OF THE DIVINE ORIGIN OF THE CHIASTIC FORM TO THE BOOK OF MORMON

Accepting the divine origin of the chiastic structure in the Doctrine and Covenants leads to the question of the origin of the chiastic structure in other scriptures, and in the Book of Mormon in particular. The Book of Mormon is a particularly useful vehicle to investigate the premise of the inspirational source of chiasma in religious literature. The Jaredite record was written in the Adamic language, undoubtedly before the Hebrew tongue was developed. The abridgement of that Jaredite record by Moroni, the Book of Ether, contains at least 46 chiasma. Were those chiasma in the original text, or were they imposed by Moroni, or by Joseph Smith?

What of the chiastic content of the Small Plates, that were a direct translation by the Prophet Joseph Smith of the original authors? How does the chiastic content of the Small Plates compare with that of Mormon's abridgement of the Large Plates? What about the first-person writings of Mormon and Moroni?

The question of inspiration versus writer-imposed literary artifact as the origin of the chiastic form in the Book of Mormon may be considered in light of the distribution of chiasma in the various literary segments of the book. We have identified over 500 chiasma in the Book of Mormon. While undoubtedly there are more, nevertheless the 500+ chiasma identified, comprising fully 30% of the Book of Mormon, represent a sample of major statistical significance.

Literary Divisions of the Book of Mormon

For purposes of examining the question, the Book of Mormon may be divided into four literary segments: (1) the direct translation by Joseph Smith of the early prophets' writings from the Small Plates of Nephi, comprising the six books from First Nephi to the Words of Mormon;

(2) Mormon's abridgement of the Large Plates of Nephi, comprising the books from Mosiah to Mormon; (3) Moroni's abridgement of the record of the Jaredites; and (4) the commentaries and writings of Mormon and Moroni.

The abridgement of the Large Plates can further be divided into three categories:

1. **The abridged record.** The abridgement is written in the third person, and is frequently introduced by the phrase "and it came to pass."

2. **Direct quotations from the early prophets and others.** Direct quotations are written in the first person. The first-person accounts include complete discourses or writings, such as Alma's counsel to his sons, comprising Alma, chapters 36 through 42, in addition to shorter excerpts, and accounts of numerous conversations in the first person, such as between Alma and Zeezrom in Alma 15:6-10, and between Ammon and King Limhi in Alma 18:14-35, in each of which Mormon appears to be copying directly from the original record.

3. **Mormon's commentaries.** Mormon's commentaries on the scene, such as in Mosiah 23:21-23, are of course in the first person, and are the words of Mormon interposed in the text of the abridgement. Of 125 verses of commentary in Mormon's abridgement, most are in segments of one to three verses. However, the last two chapters of Third Nephi, comprising incidentally only 11 verses, are the words of Mormon.

Moroni's abridgement of the record of the Jaredites can also be subdivided as above. However, Moroni's commentaries in the Book of Ether are much more prolific than those of Mormon in his abridgement. We have found that nineteen percent of the verses in Ether are Moroni's commentary, whereas only three percent of the verses in Mormon's abridgement are commentary.

Considering the popular explanation of the origin of the chiastic form as a literary artifact of ancient religious Hebrew literature, two possibilities of chiastic distribution may be considered:

1. **Nephi and Lehi as possible originators of the chiastic form.** Nephi and Lehi could have been conversant with the form from their Hebrew heritage, and employed it in their writings. Indeed, such a conclusion could be read into Nephi's statement as he opens the account in First Nephi, *Yea, I make a record in the language of my father, which consists of the learning of the Jews and the language of the Egyptians.* "The learning of the Jews" could imply their acquisition of the chiastic form from learned Jews.

Were this the case, one would expect that the use of the form in the Book of Mormon would be most prolific at the beginning and gradually diminish as ties to the Hebrew culture were attenuated by time. Thus, one would expect to find the highest chiastic content in the Small Plates and a diminishing frequency with time in quotations of the prophets in the abridgement of the Large Plates.

The abridged account by Mormon and Moroni might also contain chiasma, as the form could have been passed down to them by the succession of earlier authors. Regarding the Book of Ether, however, if Moroni had learned the form from his father or from his own study of the records, it would be expected that the chiastic frequency in the Book of Ether would be highest in Moroni's commentary, lower in his abridgement and absent in direct quotations, since the Jaredites were separated from their eastern origins at the time of the tower of Babel, which predated the Hebrew language.

2. **Mormon as the possible originator of the chiastic form.** The other possible scenario would be that the earlier Book of Mormon writers were chiastically illiterate, and that Mormon, as a historian, had identified the form from his study of the Brass Plates of Laban, and used it in his writings in the Book of Mormon. We would then expect that the higher chiastic density would be in Mormon's own account and in his commentaries in the abridged record, and a lower chiastic density would be found in the abridged part of the record, since it would seem more natural to impose a given literary style in original writings than in an abridgement of the writings of others; and that direct quotations from the early writers would be non-chiastic.

Ground Rules for Evaluating Chiasma Authorship in the Book of Mormon

In examining the chiastic content of the various literary segments of the Book of Mormon, the following considerations were made:

(1) *The chapters of Isaiah quoted in First and Second Nephi were not considered*, since they do not represent original input by the Book of Mormon writers.

(2) *A verse is considered a quotation verse if it contains a quote, regardless of the fraction of the verse employed in the quotation.* For instance,

Alma 18:13

> And one of the king's servants said unto him, "Rabbanah," which is, being interpreted, powerful or great king, considering their kings to be powerful; and thus he said unto him: "Rabbanah, the king desireth thee to stay."

would be considered a quotation verse. However, the chiasmus contained in this verse

2] *powerful*
1]   or great *king*,
1]   considering their *kings*
2] to be *powerful*

would not be counted as a quotation chiasmus since it is not part of the quote.

(3) *A quotation verse is considered chiastic only if the chiasmus is within the quote, but not if the quote is within the chiasmus.* For instance, the quotation of Ammon in Alma 26:11-37 contains two chiasma, the verses of which would be considered chiastic, since the chiasma are within the quotes.

Alma 26:11,12

But Ammon said unto him:
4] *I do not boast*
3]   *in my own strength*, nor in my own wisdom;
2]   but behold, *my joy*
1]   *is full*
1]   my heart *is brim*
2]   *with joy*, and I will rejoice in my God.
3]   Yea, I know that I am nothing; *as to my strength* I am weak;
4] therefore *I will not boast* of myself,
but I will boast of my God, for in his strength I can do all things;

Alma 26:13,14

Behold, how many thousands of
2A]   *our brethren*
2B]   *has* he *loosed*
2C]   *from the pains of hell*; and they are brought to sing redeeming love, and this because of the power of his word which is in us,
1]   *therefore have we not great reason to rejoice*?
1]   *Yea, we have reason to praise him forever*, for he is the Most

High God,
2B] and *has loosed*
2A] *our brethren*
2C] *from the chains of hell.*

However, the chiasmus in Alma 27:6-8 consists of a conversation between King Anti-Nephi-Lehi and Ammon. One would not consider that they spoke to one another chiastically, but that the account was put together in chiastic form. Therefore, these verses are not listed as chiastic, since the quote is within a larger chiasmas.

Alma 27:6-8

But the king said unto them: "Behold, the Nephites will destroy us, because of
4] *the many murders and sins we have committed against them.*"
3] And Ammon said: "I will go and inquire of the Lord, and if he say unto us, go *down unto our brethren,*
2] *will ye go:*"
1] *And the king said unto him:*
1] "Yea, *if the Lord saith unto us* go,
2] *we will go*
3] *down unto our brethren,*
4] and we will be their slaves until we repair unto them *the many murders and sins which we have committed against them.*"

(Quotation marks added.)

Evidence that Nephi and Lehi Did Not Originate the Chiastic Form in the Book of Mormon

Examining the postulate that Nephi and Lehi were the originators of the chiastic form in the Book of Mormon, we would anticipate, as mentioned above, a decrease in chiastic content with time from the earlier to the later writers. Table 1 lists the chronological sequence of the Nephite writers and their chiastic content. Shown in the table are the number of verses of direct quotation attributed to each author and the percent of those verses that were defined as chiastic. Omitted are single-verse direct quotations, such as are found in Alma 11:26-35, which records a conversation between Amulek and Zeezrom; as well as isolated single-verse references such as the questions posed by Giddonah in Alma 30:22—the reason being that forming

Table 1.

NAME	DATE	N° of VERSES	PERCENT CHIASTIC
Nephi	BC- 600-545	924	42
Jacob	544-420	312	70
Enos	544-421	27	63
Jarom	399	15	60
Amaleki	279	19	11
Zeniff	200	41	61
Abinadi	150-148	107	16
Alma	142-92	14	29
Benjamin	130-124	115	70
Alma, son of Alma	91-73	461	58
Amulek	82	89	26
Ammon	90-73	461	58
Gen. Moroni	74-62	53	58
Helaman	65-62	134	3
Helaman, son of H.	30	7	57
Nephi, son of H.	23-16	64	0
Samuel	6	82	32
THE LORD	AD- 34-35	372	34
Mormon	345-385	394	16
Moroni	401-421	232	50

CHIASTIC FREQUENCY OF NEPHITE WRITERS

chiastic structures from such short statements is highly improbable. Chiastic structures in isolated quotation verses in the abridgement of the Large Plates have been found in only three out of 168 such verses (Alma 18:13; 22:16 and Third Nephi 11:7). The years listed in the table represent the interval during which the quoted writings occurred.

A visual representation of the chiastic content with time is shown in Figure 2, which plots the percent chiastic content of each Nephite author against the first year of the author's writing, as listed in Table 1. It is apparent that there is not a general decrease in chiastic frequency with time. The relative consistency of the chiastic frequency over time is striking considering that the data covers a 1000-year period. The wide disparity in chiastic content between contemporaries, such as between Helaman and General Moroni (3% vs 58%) or between Mormon and Moroni (16% vs 50%), suggests that the form was not invoked because of social mores, as being characteristic of the manner of writing of the society at a given time. It is apparent from the observed distribution of chiastic frequency that Nephi was not the originator of the chiastic style in the Book of Mormon.

Figure 2.

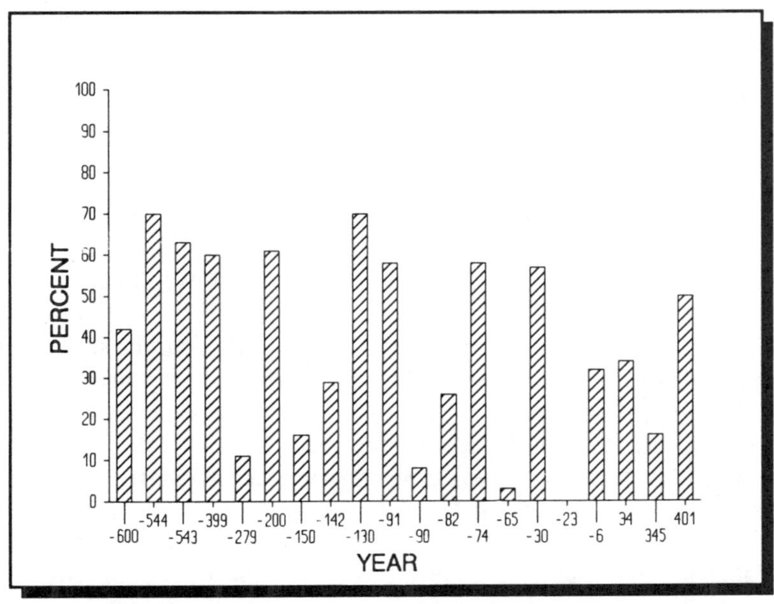

CHIASTIC CONTENT OF NEPHITE WRITERS

The relative uniformity of distribution over the 1000-year period supports the concept that the form was of inspired origin.

Evidence that Mormon and Moroni Did Not Originate the Chiastic Form in the Book of Mormon

We next examine the postulate that Mormon and Moroni originated the chiastic form and imposed it in their compilation of the Nephite and Jaredite records. A comparison of the chiastic content of the various pertinent literary elements in Mormon's writings is shown in Table 2.

Table 2.

ITEM	N° OF VERSES	% CHIASTIC
Mormon's Record— Books of Mormon and Moroni	253	21
Abridgement— Mormon's Commentaries	141	8
Abridgement Verses	1827	18
Quotation Verses	2075	33
Total, Large Plates	4043	19

CHIASTIC FREQUENCY IN MORMON'S WRITINGS

Although the difference may be too small to be significant, the slightly lower frequency of the chiastic form in Mormon's third-person account in the Abridgement, 18% compared to his own record in the Books of Mormon and Moroni of 21%, would be consistent with his authorship of the form, since, were that the case, it would be expected that a chiastic construction would be used less in copying and reducing a document than in writing in original form. The lower chiastic frequency of his commentaries in the Abridgement, 8% vs 21% in his own record, is logical since they are for the most part brief statements contained in segments of one to three verses.

However, if the early writers were non-chiastic, as postulated above, one would expect the quotation verses from the abridgement to contain no chiasma. On the contrary, they contain the highest chiastic content of Mormon's writings. This observation strongly supports the postulate that chiasmus in the Book of Mormon is an inspired structure, consistent with its appearance in the Doctrine and Covenants.

Examination of Moroni's writings in the same light leads to conclusions that are yet less ambiguous. Table 3 shows the relative chiastic content of the various elements of the Book of Ether compared with Moroni's personal account. Examining Table 3, we find a slight increase in chiastic frequency in Moroni's commentaries in the Book of Ether over his writings in the Books of Mormon and Moroni—56 to 51 percent, which is in the wrong direction if he were the author of the form. However, there is a marked decrease in the chiastic content of his abridgement over his own record, which would be consistent with Moroni's authorship of the form. The striking observation is that 79% of the quotation verses in the Book of Ether are chiastic! It is highly unlikely that an abridger would change the language of

Table 3.

ITEM	N° OF VERSES	% CHIASTIC
Moroni's Record	137	51
Moroni's Commentaries	79	56
Abridgement Verses	321	15
Quotation Verses	33	79
Total	433	27

CHIASTIC FREQUENCY IN MORONI'S WRITINGS

first-person quotations from the original record to impose a literary style. And even if he were to do so, it is yet more unlikely that the imposed literary form would occur at a significantly higher frequency than in the authors' original writings. Thus, the quotation verses in the Book of Ether must be attributed to the original authors, principally the brother of Jared.

The original language of the Jaredite account was that spoken before the confounding of tongues at the tower of Babel. Thus, the chiastic structures in the quotation verses in the Book of Ether predate the beginning of the Hebrew tongue and therefore cannot be considered as an artifact of Hebrew literature.

The Scriptures Testify of Their Own Chiasticity

Such a complicated, sophisticated literary form, one that is common to both Joseph Smith and the brother of Jared, separated by four millennia of time and vastly different cultures, would have to come from a single inspired source! Indeed, Peter tells us in 2 Pet.1:21, "*For prophecy came not in old time by the will of man: but holy men of God spake as they were moved by the Holy Ghost.*" If this scripture were to be taken literally, we may assume that the literary form, as well as the message, was inspired. Further, the Lord says in D&C 18:34,

These words are not of men
3] nor of man,
2] but of me;
1] wherefore, you shall testify
2] they are of me
3] and not of man;

Since the Lord's statement that the words of the scripture are not of men but of him is stated in chiastic form, could there be an esoteric meaning in the construction itself?

A chiastic implication could also be read into the declaration of the Lord in Moses 6:63:

And behold, all things have their likeness,
4] and all things are created and made to bear record of me,
3] both things which are temporal, and things which are spiritual
2] things which are in the heavens above,
1] and things which are on the earth,
1] and things which are in the earth,
2] and things which are under the earth,
3] both above and beneath;
4] all things bear record of me.

Since the statement that *all things bear record of me* is part of a chiastic structure, we may well conclude that the chiastic form itself is intended to bear record of Him.

4

COMPLEX CHIASMA IN THE DOCTRINE AND COVENANTS

Chiasma in the Doctrine and Covenants are not constrained to simple elemental inverse parallelisms. They may be extremely sophisticated in content and complex in form. The chiastic elements themselves may be complex. for instance, a given pair of chiastic elements may be comprised of a parallel series of words or concepts; a chiastic element may itself be a chiasmus; in addition, chiasma may be interlinked with one another, i.e., two or more contiguous chiasma may have common elements. We have identified fifty-six Doctrine and Covenants chiasma that contain parallel elements; six that are found as elements within larger chiasma; three interdigitated parallel and chiastic structures; and five combinations of chiasma with overlapping elements.

To aid in the appreciation of the complexity of the various chiastic structures, this chapter will attempt to categorize, diagram and explain the various degrees of complexity of the chiasma found in the Doctrine and Covenants.

Simple Parallelisms

The parallelism has also been identified as a characteristic of ancient Hebrew religious literature, and it is a prominent component of Doctrine and Covenants chiasma. In the structures represented in this volume, chiastic elements are given numeric designators and parallel elements are given alpha designators, as in the example of chiasmus D&C 104:29-35, below:

3A
3B
3C
  2
    1
  2
3A
3B
3C

Of the 56 chiasma with parallel elements, 45 contain simple parallel series in one or more of the chiastic elements, as in the example above. Two chiasma, D&C 14:2-11 and D&C 45:19-33, each contain a series of five parallel elements as their outermost chiastic elements. Of the remainder, two contain 4-element parallelisms, eight contain 3-element parallelisms and 38 contain 2-element parallelisms. Five chiasma contain two parallelisms each, accounting for 50 parallel elements in 45 chiasma.

Parallel-Chiasma Combinations

In eleven cases the parallelisms as chiastic elements are convoluted to form parallel-chiasma combinations. The following combinations have been observed:

(1) **Two-element parallelism, the second element of which is a two-element chiasmus**, as diagrammed below. Examples are found in element 7 of Chiasmus D&C 84:1-12, element 1 of Chiasmus D&C 18:9-14, element 3 of Chiasmus D&C 61:6-11, element 4 of Chiasmus D&C 84:49-53 and element 4 of Chiasmus D&C 88:34-39.

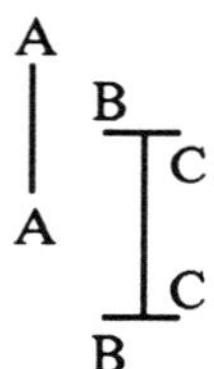

(2) **Two-element parallelism, the first element of which is a two-element chiasmus**, as diagrammed below. Examples are found in element 2 of Chiasmus D&C 27:15-17 and element 1 of Chiasmus D&C 50:4-9.

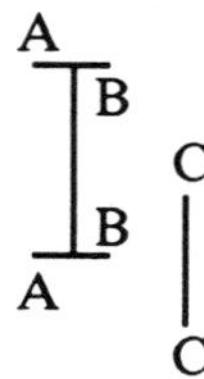

(3) **Three-element parallelism, the first element of which is a two-element chiasmus**, as diagrammed below. Examples are found in element 9 of Chiasmus D&C 63:17-49 and element 1 of Chiasmus D&C 94:3-12.

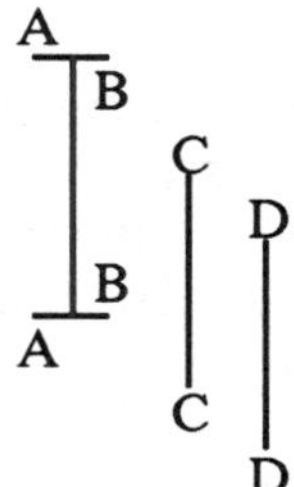

4) **Four-element parallelism, the second and third elements of which are two-element chiasma**, as diagrammed below. This structure is found in element 2 of Chiasmus D&C 132:15-18.

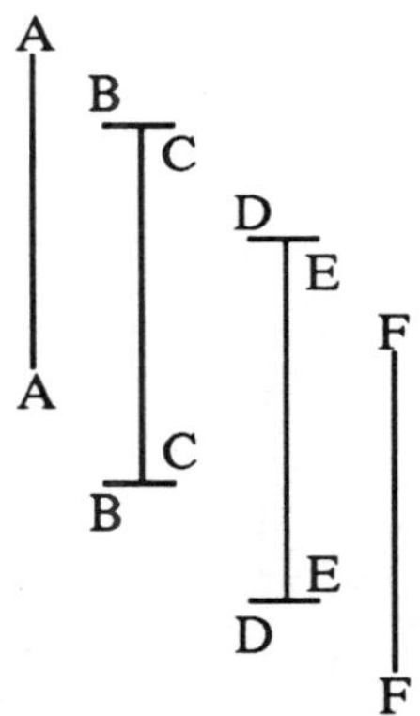

5) **Three-element parallelism, the middle element of which is a four-element chiasmus**, as diagrammed below. This structure is found in element 1 of Chiasmus D&C 10:58-61.

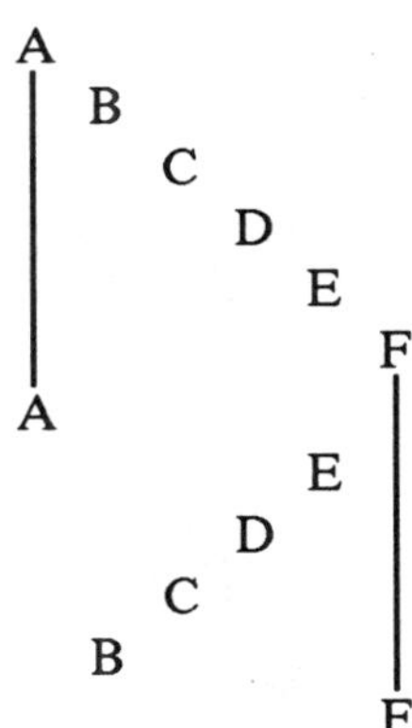

Chiasma Within Chiasma

Six locations have been identified in which chiastic structures are entirely enclosed within larger chiasma. They occur as interpositions, apart from the larger chiasma; also as structures within a given element of a larger chiasmus; and as comprising several elements of the larger chiasmus. These different complex structures are diagrammed below.

Two chiasma have been identified that contain other chiasma within their limits that form independent structures. In other words, they do not form part of the parallel elements of the host chiasmus. They are identified and diagrammed as follows:

D&C 76:11-27

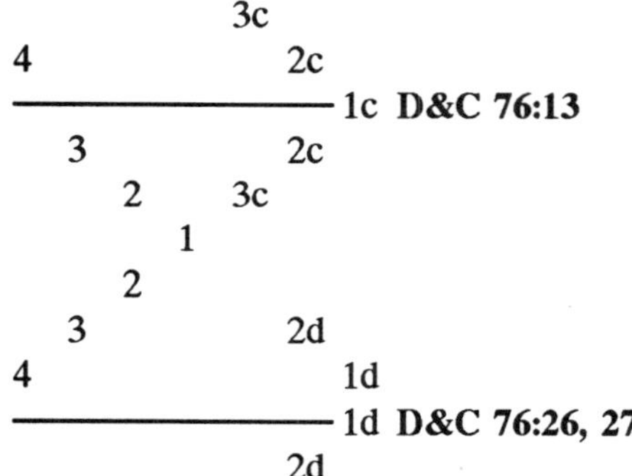

In the above example, the verses 13 and 26, 27 do not form part of the parallel elements of the main chiasmus, but are interpositions without chiastic parallels.

D&C 98:23-44

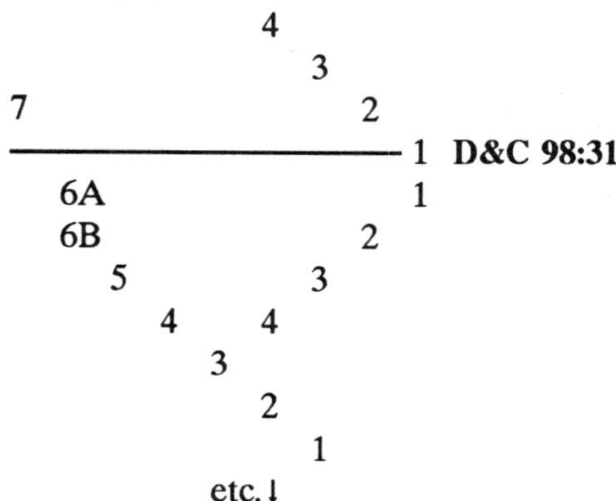

In the above example, a 4-element chiasmus is found between elements 7 and 6A in the first leg of the host chiasmus that forms no part of either elements 7 or 6A.

In the following example, one of the elements of the host chiasmus is itself a chiasmus. It has a parallel element in the mirror leg, but the parallel element is not chiastically arranged.

D&C 76:63-106

```
4 (8-element parallelism)
  3
    2 (6-element parallelism)
      1                     3k
      1                        2k
    2 (5-element parallelism)     1k
  3 ------------------------------1k    D&C 76:89-98
4 ( 7-element parallelism)     2k
                            3k
```

In the following example, two of the elements in the first leg of the chiasmus are themselves chiasma; again, with mirror elements that are not chiastically formed.

D&C 93:7-23

```
            3c
4              2c
  3--------------1c D&C 93:8
    2A         2c    3d
    2B      3c          2d
      1A---------------- 1d D&C 93:12, 13
      1B                2d
      1A             3d
      1B
    2A
    2B
  3
4
```

In the following two examples, several elements of the host chiasmus form a separate internal chiasmus.

D&C 63:5-13

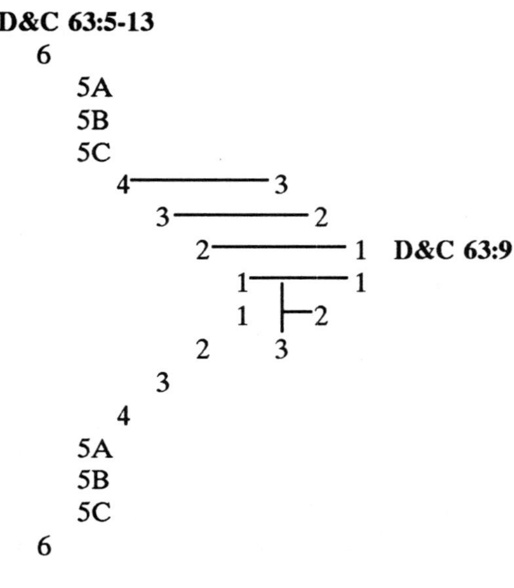

D&C 107:72-76

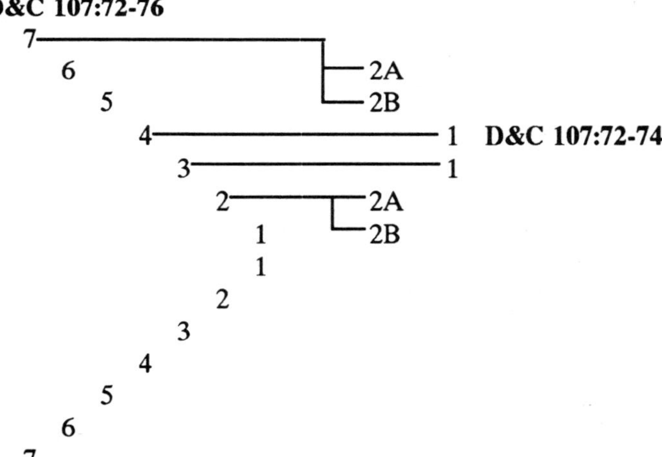

Interdigitated Parallelism and Chiasmus

In addition to the interdigitated parallelism and chiasmus shown in chapter 1 (D&C 29:32), three other similar structures have been identified, similarly containing two chiastic elements, two of which are listed below, with the parallel elements underlined and the chiastic elements in italics:

D&C 74:1

2]	For	the unbelieving	*husband*
1]		is sanctified by the	*wife*
1]	and	the unbelieving	*wife*
2]		is sanctified by the	*husband*

D&C 77:2

2]		that which is	*spiritual*
1]	being	in the likeness of that which is	*temporal*
1]	and	that which is	*temporal*
2]		in the likeness of that which is	*spiritual*

Overlapping Chiasma

Overlapping chiasma consist of pairs or strings in which the final elements of the prior chiasmus are common to the initial elements of the following chiasmus. Varying degrees of overlapping have been observed, as shown below in examples 1 through 4:

Example 1.

```
2A
2B
2C
      1     D&C 107:23-34
      1
2A
2B
2C---------3
              2
                 1     D&C 107:34-38
              2
           3
```

Example 2.

```
3A
3B
   2
      1       D&C 76:31-38
      1
   2————————6
3A————————————5
3B               4
                    3
                       2
                          1  D&C 76:36-44
                       2
                    3
                 4
              5
           6
```

Example 3.

```
4
   3
      2
         1A
         1B
         1C          D&C 76:50-65
         1A
         1B
         1C
      2                 4
   3————————————┬———————1)  D&C 76:63-106
                └———————2)
4———————————————————————3)
                        4)
                        5)
                        6)
                        7)
                        8)
                           3
                              2
                              etc.↓
```

Example 4.

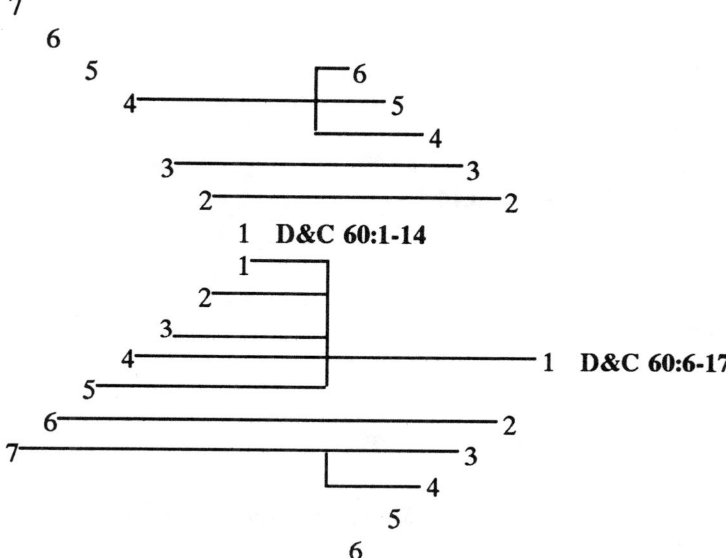

Doctrine and Covenants Section 10 contains a string of three chiasma, each overlapping the next. The middle 4-element chiasmus has the first two elements in common with the prior chiasmus and three of the final four elements in common with the following chiasmus, as shown below:

Example 5.

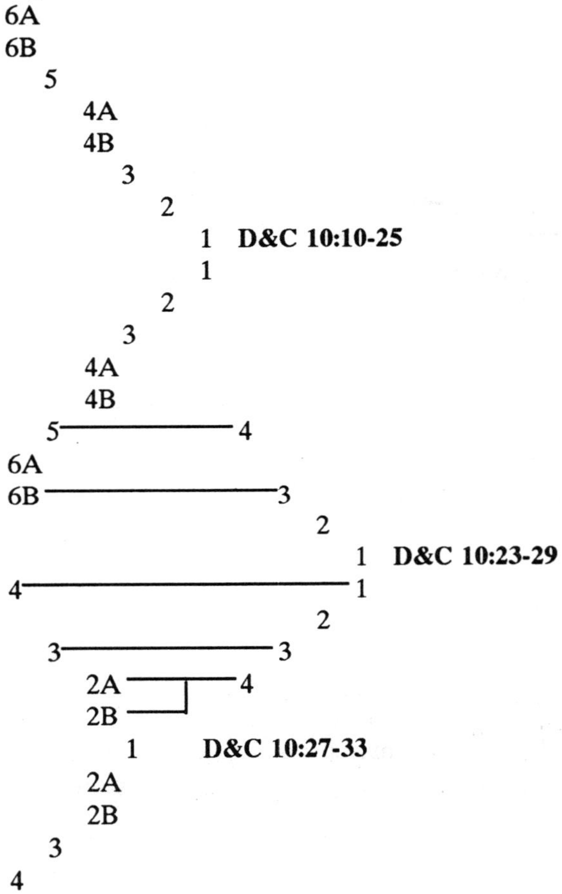

```
6A
6B
  5
    4A
    4B
      3
        2
          1   D&C 10:10-25
          1
        2
      3
    4A
    4B
  5 ———————— 4
6A
6B ——————————— 3
                 2
                   1   D&C 10:23-29
4 ————————————————— 1
                 2
  3 —————————— 3
    2A ——┬—— 4
    2B ——┘
      1      D&C 10:27-33
    2A
    2B
  3
4
```

Additional Considerations

Twelve of the 138 Sections in the Doctrine and Covenants are comprised of single chiasma; and an additional section is fully chiastic, but contains two chiasma. The fully chiastic sections are 7, 8, 9, 11, 22, 34, 40, 47, 57, 60 (two chiasma) and 66. By comparison, only six of the 239 chapters in the Book of Mormon are comprised of single chiasma—Second Nephi 3 (Lehi's exhortation to his son, Joseph), Alma 36 and 38 (comprising Alma's commandments to his sons, Helaman and Shiblon) and the first three short chapters of the Book of Moroni. In addition, First Nephi 17 and Second Nephi 1 are fully chiastic—First Nephi 17 containing five chiasma and Second Nephi 1 containing nine chiasma.

The chiasma in the Doctrine and Covenants are pervasive, and are both complicated and elegant. If relatively few simple structures were found within a significantly larger volume, they could be conceived as accidental. However, the complexity of the chiastic structures found in the Doctrine and Covenants, the beauty and artfulness of expression they contain, the manner in which they form integral parts of the messages they convey, and the essential subliminal nature of their existence preclude any possibility that they are accidental inclusions or that they were merely artfully conceived in the mind of Joseph Smith. Their existence demands the recognition of a Divine source, and with it the acceptance of both the Doctrine and Covenants and the Book of Mormon as literal transcriptions of the dictation of Deity.

5

THE SIMPLE CHIASTIC FORM IN THE DOCTRINE AND COVENANTS— TWO-ELEMENT CHIASMA

As has been demonstrated in the preceding Chapters, chiasma in the Doctrine and Covenants range from simple two-element structures to extremely complex forms including chiasma within chiasma, chiasma with varying degrees of complex parallelisms as chiastic elements, interdigitated parallel and chiastic elements, and overlapping and chained chiasma.

To help the student in his study of the chiastic form, all of the chiasma identified in the Doctrine and Covenants will be reproduced in order of increasing complexity. Each chiasmus will be followed by an analytical structure in which corresponding mirror elements are placed next to each other to facilitate comparison, and the general nature of the relationship of mirror elements will be defined.

Code for Identifying Chiasma in the Doctrine and Covenants

In the succeeding chapters the sequential order of the chiasma within the Doctrine and Covenants will be identified by a number following the word, "Chiasmus," in the heading at the right margin. The sequential order of the chiasma within each Section will be designated by a number identifying the Section and a letter identifying the order within the Section. Thus, Chiasmus 6, 5B would indicate the 6th chiasmus in the Doctrine and Covenants and the second chiasmus in Section 5; and Chiasmus 141, 88L would indicate the 141st chiasmus in the Doctrine and Covenants and the twelfth chiasmus in Section 88.

In Chapter five we will list all the simple two-element chiasma—i.e., those that contain no complex structures and that are composed of only two sets of parallel elements.

D&C 10:46-48 — Chiasmus 16, 10F

2] 46 And, behold, all the remainder of this work does contain all those parts of *my gospel which my holy prophets, yea, and also my disciples, desired in their prayers should come forth unto this people.*

1] 47 And I said unto them, that it should be granted unto them *according to their faith* in their prayers;
1] 48 Yea, *and this was their faith—*
2] *that my gospel, which I gave unto them that they might preach in their days, might come unto their brethren the Lamanites*, and also all that had become Lamanites because of their dissensions.

D&C 10:46-48 Analysis 10F

2a/2b	Parallel concepts:	**2a-** my gospel which my holy prophets, yea, and also my disciples, desired in their prayers should come forth unto this people.
		2b- my gospel, which I gave unto them that they might preach in their days, might come unto their brethren the Lamanites,
1a/1b	Parallel concepts:	**1a-** according to their faith
		1b- and this was their faith—

D&C 10:49-50 Chiasmus 17, 10G

2] 49 Now, this is not all--their faith *in their prayers*
1] was that this gospel should be made known also, if it were possible *that other nations should possess this land;*
1] 50 And thus *they did leave a blessing upon this land*
2] *in their prayers,*

D&C 10:49-50 Analysis 10G

2a/2b	Identical words:	**2-** in their prayers
1a/1b	Parallel concepts:	**1a-** that other nations should possess this land;
		1b- they did leave a blessing upon this land

D&C 10:62-63 Chiasmus 20, 10J

2] 62 Yea, and I will also bring to light my gospel which was ministered unto them, and, behold, they shall not deny that which you have received, but they shall build it up, and shall bring to light *the true points of my doctrine*, yea, and the only doctrine which is in me.
1] 63 And this I do that I may establish my gospel, *that there may not be so much contention;*

1] yea, *Satan doth stir up the hearts of the people to contention*
2] *concerning the points of my doctrine*; and in these things they do err, for they do wrest the scriptures and do not understand them.

D&C 10:62-63 **Analysis 10J**

2a/2b	Identical words:	**2a-** the . . . points of my doctrine **2b-** the points of my doctrine
1a/1b	Parallel concepts:	**1a-** that there may not be so much contention; **1b-** Satan doth stir up the hearts of the people to contention

D&C 18:37-39 **Chiasmus 34, 18I**

2] 37 And now, behold, I give unto you, Oliver Cowdery, and also unto David Whitmer, that *you shall search out the Twelve,*
1] *who shall have the desires of which I have spoken;*
1] 38 *And by their desires and their works you shall know them.*
2] 39 *And when you have found them* you shall show these things unto them.

D&C 18:37-39 **Analysis 18I**

2a/2b	Completed action:	**2a-** you shall search out the Twelve, **2b-** And when you have found them
1a/1b	Parallel concepts:	**1a-** who shall have the desires of which I have spoken; **1b-** And by their desires and their works you shall know them.

D&C 19:21,22 **Chiasmus 36, 19B**

21 And I command you that you preach naught but repentance,
2] and *show not these things unto the world until it is wisdom in me.*
1] 22 *For they cannot bear meat now,*
1] *but milk they must receive;*
2] wherefore, *they must not know these things, lest they perish.*

D&C 19:21,22 **Analysis 19B**

2a/2b	Parallel concepts:	**2a-** show not these things unto the world until it is wisdom in me. **2b-** they must not know these things, lest they perish.
1a/1b	Negative to positive:	**1a-** For they cannot bear meat now, **1b-** but milk they must receive;

D&C 29:30 **Chiasmus 46, 29B**

2] that the *first*
1] shall be *last*,
1] and that the *last*
2] shall be *first*

D&C 29:30 **Analysis 29B**

2a/2b	Identical word:	**2-** first
1a/1b	Identical word:	**1-** last

D&C 29:36 **Chiasmus 49, 29E**

2] 36 And it came to pass that *Adam*,
1] being tempted of *the devil*—
1] for, behold, *the devil*
2] was before *Adam*, for he rebelled against me, saying, Give me thine honor, which is my power; and also a third part of the hosts of heaven turned he away from me because of their agency;

D&C 29:36 **Analysis 29E**

2a/2b	Identical word:	**2-** Adam
1a/1b	Identical words:	**1-** the devil

D&C 43:2-3 **Chiasmus 63, 43A**

2 For behold, verily, verily, I say unto you,
2] that *ye have received a commandment* for a law unto my church,
1] through him *whom I have appointed unto you* to receive commandments and revelations from my hand.
1] 3 And this ye shall know assuredly—that *there is none other appointed unto you*
2] *to receive commandments* and revelations until he be taken, if he abide in me.

D&C 43:2-3 **Analysis 43A**

2a/2b	Parallel concepts:	**2a-** ye have received a commandment **2b-** to receive commandments
1a/1b	Parallel concepts:	**1a-** whom I have appointed unto you **1b-** there is none other appointed unto you

D&C 43:2-4 **Chiasmus 64, 43B**

2 For behold, verily, verily, I say unto you, that ye have received a commandment for a law unto my church,

2] *through him whom I have appointed unto you* to receive commandments and revelations from my hand.

1] 3 And this ye shall know assuredly—that *there is none other appointed unto you* to receive commandments and revelations until he be taken, if he abide in me.

1] 4 But verily, verily, I say unto you, *that none else shall be appointed unto* this gift except it be through him;

2] for if it be taken from him he shall not have power except *to appoint another in his stead.*

D&C 43:2-4 **Analysis 43B**

2a/2b	Past to future:	**2a-** through him whom I have appointed unto you **2b-** to appoint another in his stead.
1a/1b	Parallel concepts:	**1a-** there is none other appointed unto you **1b-** that none else shall be appointed unto this gift

D&C 44:1,2 **Chiasmus 66, 44A**

2] 1 Behold, thus saith the Lord unto you my servants, *it is expedient in me that the elders of my church should be called together*, from the east and from the west, and from the north and from the youth, by letter or some other way.

1] 2 And it shall come to pass, *that inasmuch as they are faithful,*

1] *and exercise faith in me,*

2] I will pour out my Spirit upon them *in the day that they assemble themselves together.*

D&C 44:1,2 **Analysis 44A**

2a/2b	Parallel concepts:	**2a-** it is expedient in me that the elders of my church should be called together, **2b-** in the day that they assemble themselves together.
1]	Parallel concepts:	**1a-** that inasmuch as they are faithful, **1b-** and exercise faith in me,

D&C 50:43 **Chiasmus 77, 50D**

2] *I* am
1] in *the Father*
1] and *the Father*
2] in *me*;

D&C 50:43 **Analysis 50D**

2a/2b	Parallel concepts:	**2a-** I **2b-** me
1a/1b	Identical words:	**1-** the Father

D&C 50:43 **Chiasmus 78, 50E**

2] *ye*
1] are in *me*
1] and *I*
2] in *you*.

D&C 50:43 **Analysis 50E**

2a/2b	Parallel concepts:	**2a-** ye **2b-** you
	Parallel concepts:	**1a-** me **1b-** I

D&C 61:32-35 **Chiasmus 90, 61D**

2] 32 *And from thence let them journey* for the congregations of their brethren,
1] for their labors even now are wanted more abundantly among them than *among the congregations of the wicked*.
1] And now, concerning the residue, let them journey and declare the word *among the congregations of the wicked*, inasmuch as it is given;
34 And inasmuch as they do this they shall rid their garments, and they shall be spotless before me.
2] *And let them journey together*, or two by two, as seemeth them good, only let my servant Reynolds Cahoon, and my servant Samuel H. Smith, with whom I am well pleased, be not separated until they return to their homes, and this for a wise purpose in me.

D&C 61:32-35 **Analysis 61D**

2a/2b	Parallel concepts:	**2a-** And from thence let them journey **2b-** And let them journey together,
1a/1b	Identical words:	**1-** among the congregations of the wicked
1a/1b	Parallel concepts:	**1a-** me **1b-** I

D&C 64:1-4 **Chiasmus 94, 64A**

2] 1 Behold, *thus saith the Lord your God unto you*, O ye elders of my church,
1] *hearken* ye
1] and *hear*,
2] and *receive my will concerning you*.

D&C 64:1-4 **Analysis 64A**

2a/2b	Parallel concepts:	**2a-** thus saith the Lord your God unto you, **2b-** receive my will concerning you.
1a/1b	Parallel concepts:	**1a-** hearken **1b-** hear

D&C 74:3,4 **Chiasmus 105, 74B**

2] 3 And it came to pass that there arose a great contention among the people concerning the law of circumcision, *for the unbelieving husband was desirous that his children should be circumcised*
1] and *become subject to the law of Moses,* which law was fulfilled.
1] 4 And it came to pass that the children, *being brought up in subjection to the law of Moses,*
2] *gave heed to the traditions of their fathers* and believed not the gospel of Christ, wherein they became unholy.

D&C 74:2,3 **Analysis 74B**

2a/2b	Parallel concepts:	**2a-** for the unbelieving husband was desirous that his children should be circumcised **2b-** gave heed to the traditions of their fathers
1a/1b	Parallel concepts:	**1a-** become subject to the law of Moses, **1b-** being brought up in subjection to the law of Moses,

D&C 76:26,27 **Chiasmus 111 76D**

a2] *a son of the morning.*
27 And we beheld, and lo,
a1] *he is fallen*!
a1] *is fallen*,
a2] even *a son of the morning*!

D&C 76:26,27 **Analysis 76D**

2a/2b	Identical words:	**2-** a son of the morning!
1a/1b	Identical words:	**1-** is fallen!

D&C 82:10 **Chiasmus 123, 82B**

2] 10 *I, the Lord, am bound*
1] *when ye do what I say;*
1] but *when ye do not what I say,*
2] *ye have no promise.*

D&C 82:10 **Analysis 82B**

2a/2b	Positive to negative:	**2a-** I, the Lord, am bound **2b-** ye have no promise.
1a/1b	Positive to negative:	**1a-** when ye do what I say; **1b-** when ye do not what I say,

D&C 82:12,13 **Chiasmus 124, 82C**

2] 12 To manage the affairs of the poor, and all things pertaining to the bishopric both *in the land of Zion*
1] and in *the land of Kirtland;*
1] 13 For I have consecrated *the land of Kirtland* in mine own due time for the benefit of the saints of the Most High,
2] and *for a stake to Zion.*

D&C 82:12,13 **Analysis 82C**

2a/2b	Parallel concepts:	**2a-** in the land of Zion **2b-** for a stake to Zion.
1a/1b	Identical words:	**1-** the land of Kirtland

D&C 82:14 — Chiasmus 125, 82D

2] 14 For *Zion must increase in beauty, and in holiness;*
1] *her borders must be enlarged;*
1] *her stakes must be strengthened;*
2] yea, verily I say unto you, *Zion must arise and put on her beautiful garments.*

D&C 82:14 — Analysis 82D

2a/2b	Parallel concepts:	**2a-** Zion must increase in beauty, and in holiness; **2b-** Zion must arise and put on her beautiful garments.
1a/1b	Parallel concepts:	**1a-** her borders must be enlarged; **1b-** her stakes must be strengthened;

D&C 88:6,7 — Chiasmus 133, 88A

2] the light
1] of *truth*
1] which *truth* shineth
2] This is *the light* of Christ.

D&C 88:6,7 — Analysis 88A

2a/2b	Identical words:	**2-** the light
1a/1b	Identical word:	**1-** truth

D&C 88:66 — Chiasmus 141, 88I

2] 66 Behold, that which you hear is the *voice*
1] of one crying in the *wilderness*—
1] in the *wilderness,*
2] because you cannot see him—my *voice,* because my voice is Spirit; my Spirit is truth; truth abideth and hath no end; and if it be in you it shall abound.

D&C 88:66 — Analysis 88I

2a/2b	Identical word:	**2-** voice
1a/1b	Identical word:	**1-** wilderness

D&C 93:3 **Chiasmus 149, 93A**

2] And that *I* am
1] in *the Father,*
1] and *the Father*
2] in *me,*

D&C 93:3 **Analysis 93A**

2a/2b	Same person:	**2-** I/me
1a/1b	Identical words:	**1-** the Father

D&C 93:26-28 **Chiasmus 153, 93E**

2] *He received a fulness of truth, yea, even of all truth;*
27 And no man receiveth a fulness
1] *unless he keepeth his commandments.*
1] 28 *He that keepeth his commandments*
2] *receiveth truth and light, until he is glorified in truth and knoweth all things.*

D&C 93:26-28 **Analysis 93E**

2a/2b	Parallel concepts:	**2a-** He received a fulness of truth, yea, even of all truth; **2b-** receiveth truth and light, until he is glorified in truth and knoweth all things.
1a/1b	Parallel concepts:	**1a-** unless he keepeth his commandments. **1b-** He that keepeth his commandments

D&C 93:31,32 **Chiasmus 154, 93F**

2] 31 Behold, here is the agency of man, and *here is the condemnation* of man; because that which was from the beginning is plainly manifest unto them,
1] *and they receive not the light.*
1] 32 *And every man whose spirit receiveth not the light*
2] *is under condemnation.*

D&C 93:31,32 **Analysis 93F**

2a/2b	Parallel concepts:	**2a-** here is the condemnation **2b-** is under condemnation
1a/1b	Parallel concepts:	**1a-** and they receive not the light. **1b-** And every man whose spirit receiveth not the light

D&C 98:17 **Chiasmus 166, 98C**

17 And again, the hearts
2] of *the Jews*
1] unto *the prophets,*
1] and *the* prophets
2] unto *the Jews*;

D&C 98:17 **Analysis 98C**

2a/2b	Identical words:	**2-** the Jews
1a/1b	Identical words:	**1-** the prophets

D&C 101:7 **Chiasmus 170 101B**

2] 7 *They were slow to hearken unto the voice*
1] *of the Lord their God;*
1] therefore, *the Lord their God*
2] *is slow to hearken unto their prayers,* to answer them in the day of their trouble.

D&C 101:7 **Analysis 101B**

2a/2b	Parallel concepts:	**2a-** they were slow to hearken unto the voice **2a-** (the Lord their God) is slow to hearken unto their prayers,
1a/1b	Identical words:	**1-** the Lord their God

D&C 101:39,40 **Chiasmus 171, 101C**

39 When men are called unto mine everlasting gospel, and covenant with an everlasting covenant, they are accounted
2] as the *salt of the earth*
1] and *the savor of men*;
1] 40 They are called to be *the savor of men*;
2] therefore, if that *salt of the earth*
lose its savor, behold, it is thenceforth good for nothing only to be cast out and trodden under the feet of men.

D&C 101:39,40 **Analysis 101C**

2a/2b	Identical words:	**2-** salt of the earth
1a/1b	Identical words:	**1-** the savor of men

D&C 101:42 — Chiasmus 172, 101D

2] 42 *He that exalteth himself*
1] *shall be abased,*
1] *and he that abaseth himself*
2] *shall be exalted.*

D&C 101:42 — Analysis 101D

2a/2b	Parallel concepts:	**2a-** He that exalteth himself **2b-** shall be exalted
1a/1b	Parallel concepts:	**1a-** shall be abased **1b-** he that abaseth himself

D&C 110:6-9 — Chiasmus 201, 110A

2] 6 *Let the hearts of your brethren rejoice, and let the hearts of all my people rejoice, who have, with their might, built this house to my name.*
1] 7 For behold, I have accepted this house, and my name shall be here; *and I will manifest myself to my people in mercy in this house.*
1] 8 *Yea, I will appear unto my servants, and speak unto them with mine own voice*, if my people will keep my commandments, and do not pollute this holy house.
2] 9 *Yea the hearts of thousands and tens of thousands shall greatly rejoice in consequence of the blessings which shall be poured out, and the endowment with which my servants have been endowed in this house.*

D&C 110:6-9 — Analysis 110A

2a/2b	Parallel concepts:	**2a-** Let the hearts of your brethren rejoice, and let the hearts of all my people rejoice, who have, with their might, built this house to my name. **2b-** Yea the hearts of thousands and tens of thousands shall greatly rejoice in consequence of the blessings which shall be poured out, and the endowment with which my servants have been endowed in this house.
1a/1b	Parallel concepts:	**1a-** and I will manifest myself to my people in mercy in this house. **1b-** Yea, I will appear unto my servants, and speak unto them with mine own voice,

D&C 112:9 — Chiasmus 206, 112C

2] 9 *Thy voice*
1] *shall be a rebuke* unto the transgressor;
1] and *at thy rebuke*
2] let *the tongue of the slanderer* cease its perverseness.

D&C 112:9 — Analysis 112C

2a/2b	Positive to negative:	**2a-** Thy voice **2b-** the tongue of the slanderer
1a/1b	Parallel concepts:	**1a-** shall be a rebuke **1b-** at thy rebuke

D&C 115:1-5 — Chiasmus 208, 115A

2] 1 *Verily thus saith the Lord unto you, my servant Joseph Smith, Jun., and also my servant Sidney Rigdon, and also my servant Hyrum Smith, and your counselors who are and shall be appointed hereafter;*
2 *And also unto you, my servant Edward Partridge, and his counselors;*
3 *And also unto my faithful servants who are of the high council of my church in Zion,*
1] *for thus it shall be called*, and unto all the elders and people of *my Church of Jesus Christ of Latter-day Saints*, scattered abroad in all the world;
1] 4 *For thus shall my church be called* in the last days, *even The Church of Jesus Christ of Latter-day Saints.*
2] 5 *Verily I say unto you all*: Arise and shine forth, that thy light may be a standard for the nations;

D&C 115:1-5 — Analysis 115A

2a/2b	Parallel concepts:	**2a-** Verily thus saith the Lord unto you, my servant Joseph Smith, Jun., and also my servant Sidney Rigdon, and also my servant Hyrum Smith, and your counselors who are and shall be appointed hereafter; And also unto you, my servant Edward Partridge, and his counselors; And also unto my faithful servants who are of the high council of my church in Zion, **2b-** Verily I say unto you all:
1a/1b	Identical words:	**1a-** for thus it/(my church) shall be called . . . my Church of Jesus Christ of Latter-day Saints,

D&C 115:8-10 **Chiasmus 209, 115B**

2] 8 *Therefore, I command you to build a house unto me*, for the gathering together of my saints, that they may worship me.

1] 9 *And let there be a beginning of this work, and a foundation, and a preparatory work, this following summer*;

1] 10 *And let the beginning be made on the fourth day of July next*;

2] and from that time forth *let my people labor diligently to build a house unto my name*;

D&C 115:8-10 **Analysis 115B**

2a/2b	Parallel concepts:	**2a-** Therefore, I command you to build a house unto me, **2b-** let my people labor diligently to build a house unto my name;
1a/1b	Parallel concepts:	**1a-** And let there be a beginning of this work, and a foundation, and a preparatory work, this following summer; **1b-** And let the beginning be made on the fourth day of July next;

D&C 124:39-41 **Chiasmus 214, 124C**

2] 39 *Therefore, verily I say unto you, that your anointings, and your washings, and your baptisms for the dead, and your solemn assemblies, and your memorials for your sacrifices by the sons of Levi, and for your oracles in your most holy places wherein you receive conversations, and your statutes and judgments, for the beginning of the revelations and foundation of Zion, and for the glory, honor, and endowment of all her municipals,*

1] are ordained by the ordinance of *my holy house, which my people are always commanded to build unto my holy name.*

1] 40 And verily I say unto you, *let this house be built unto my name,* that I may reveal mine ordinances therein unto my people;

2] 41 *For I deign to reveal unto my church things which have been kept hid from before the foundation of the world, things that pertain to the dispensation of the fulness of times.*

D&C 124:39-41 **Analysis 124C**

2a/2b	Specific to general:	**2a-** Therefore, verily I say unto you, that your anointings, and your washings, and your baptisms for the dead, and your

		solemn assemblies, and your memorials for your sacrifices by the sons of Levi, and for your oracles in your most holy places wherein you receive conversations, and your statutes and judgments, for the beginning of the revelations and foundation of Zion, and for the glory, honor, and endowment of all her municipals,
		2b- For I deign to reveal unto my church things which have been kept hid from before the foundation of the world, things that pertain to the dispensation of the fulness of times.
1a/1b	Parallel concepts:	**1a-** my holy house, which my people are always commanded to build unto my holy name.
		1b- let this house be built unto my name,

D&C 124:64-66 — Chiasmus 217, 124F

2] 64 *And they shall not receive less than fifty dollars for a share of stock in that house,*

1] *and they shall be permitted to receive fifteen thousand dollars from any one man for stock in that house.*

1] 65 *But they shall not be permitted to receive over fifteen thousand dollars stock from any one man.*

2] 66 *And they shall not be permitted to receive under fifty dollars for a share of stock from any one man in that house.*

D&C 124:64-66 — Analysis 124F

2a/2b	Parallel concepts:	**2a-** and they shall not receive less than fifty dollars for a share of stock in that house,
		2b- And they shall not be permitted to receive under fifty dollars for a share of stock from any one man in that house.
1a/1b	Positive to negative:	**1a-** and they shall be permitted to receive fifteen thousand dollars from any one man for stock in that house.
		1b- But they shall not be permitted to receive over fifteen thousand dollars stock from any one man.

6

THE SIMPLE CHIASTIC FORM IN THE DOCTRINE AND COVENANTS—THREE-ELEMENT CHIASMA

Chapter six contains all the simple three-element chiasma found in the Doctrine and Covenants—i.e., those that contain no complex structures and that are composed of three sets of parallel elements.

D&C 18:34 **Chiasmus 32, 18G**

3] 34 These words are not of men nor *of man,*
2] but *of me;*
1] wherefore, you shall testify they are
2] *of me*
3] and not *of man;*

D&C 18:34 **Analysis 18G**

3a/3b	Identical words:	**3-** of man,
2a/2b	Identical words:	**2-** of me
1	Central theme:	**1-** wherefore, you shall testify

D&C 18:35,36 **Chiasmus 33, 18H**

3] 35 *For it is my voice which speaketh them unto you;*
2] *for they are given by my Spirit unto you,*
1] and by my power you can read them one to another;
2] *and save it were by my power you could not have them;*
3] 36 *Wherefore, you can testify that you have heard my voice, and know my words.*

D&C 18:35,36 **Analysis 18H**

3a/3b	Parallel concepts:	**3a-** For it is my voice which speaketh them unto you; **3b-** Wherefore, you can testify that you have heard my voice, and know my words.

2a/2b	Parallel concepts:	**2a-** for they are given by my Spirit unto you, **2b-** and save it were by my power you could not have them;
1	Central theme:	**1-** and by my power you can read them one to another;

D&C 20:30-35 **Chiasmus 38, 20A**

3] 30 *And we know that justification through the grace of our Lord and Savior Jesus Christ is just and true;*
31 *And we know also, that sanctification through the grace of our Lord and Savior Jesus Christ is just and true, to all those who love and serve God with all their mights, minds, and strength.*
But there is a possibility that man may fall from grace and depart from the living God;
2] *Therefore let the church take heed and pray always,*
1] lest they fall into temptation;
2] 34 *Yea, and even let those who are sanctified take heed also.*
3] *And we know that these things are true* and according to the revelations of John, neither adding to, nor diminishing from the prophecy of his book, the holy scriptures, or the revelations of God which shall come hereafter by the gift and power of the Holy Ghost, the voice of God, or the ministering of angels.

D&C 20:30-35 **Analysis 20A**

3a/3b	Specific to general:	**3a-** And we know that justification through the grace of our Lord and Savior Jesus Christ is just and true; And we know also, that sanctification through the grace of our Lord and Savior Jesus Christ is just and true, to all those who love and serve God with all their mights, minds, and strength. **3b-** And we know that these things are true
2a/2b	Parallel concepts:	**2a-** Therefore let the church take heed and pray always, **2b-** Yea, and even let those who are sanctified take heed also.
1	Central theme:	**1-** lest they fall into temptation;

D&C 40:1-3 **Chiasmus 57, 40A**

3] 1 Behold, verily I say unto you, that the heart of my servant James Covill was right before me, *for he covenanted with me that he would obey my word.*

2] 2 *And he received the word with gladness,*

1] but straightway Satan tempted him;

2] and the fear of persecution *and the cares of the world caused him to reject the word.*

3] 3 Wherefore *he broke my covenant,* and it remaineth with me to do with him as seemeth me good. Amen.

D&C 40:1-3 **Analysis 40A**

3a/3b	Positive to negative:	**3a-** for he covenanted with me that he would obey my word. **3b-** he broke my covenant,
2a/2b	Positive to negative:	**2a-** And he received the word with gladness, **2b-** and the cares of the world caused him to reject the word.
1	Central theme:	**1-** but straightway Satan tempted him;

D&C 41:1,2 **Chiasmus 58, 41A**

3] 1 *Hearken* and hear, *O ye my people*, saith the Lord and your God,

2] ye *whom I delight to bless with the greatest of all blessings*,

1] *ye that hear me*;

1] and *ye that hear me not*

2] *will I curse*, that have professed my name, *with the heaviest of all cursings.*

3] 2 *Hearken, O ye elders of my church* whom I have called,

D&C 41:1,2 **Analysis 41A**

3a/3b	Parallel concepts:	**3a-** Hearken...O ye my people, **3b-** Hearken, O ye elders of my church
2a/2b	Positive to negative:	**2a-** whom I delight to bless with the greatest of all blessings, **2b-** will I curse...with the heaviest of all cursings.
1a/1b	Positive to negative:	**1a-** Ye that hear me; **1b-** ye that hear me not

D&C 42:13,14 **Chiasmus 60, 42B**

13 And they shall observe the covenants and church articles to do them,
3] and *these shall be their teachings,*
2] as *they shall be directed by the Spirit.*
1] 14 And the Spirit shall be given unto you by the prayer of faith;
2] and *if ye receive not the Spirit*
3] *ye shall not teach.*

D&C 42:13,14 **Analysis 42B**

3a/3b	Positive to negative:	**3a-** these shall be their teachings, **3b-** ye shall not teach.
2a/2b	Positive to negative:	**2a-** they shall be directed by the Spirit. **2b-** if ye receive not the Spirit
1	Central theme:	**1-** And the Spirit shall be given unto you by the prayer of faith;

D&C 46:2-7 **Chiasmus 72, 46A**

1 Hearken, O ye people of my church; for verily I say unto you that these things were spoken unto you for your profit and learning.
3] 2 But notwithstanding those things which are written, *it always has been given to the elders of my church from the beginning, and ever shall be, to conduct all meetings as they are directed and guided by the Holy Spirit.*
2] 3 *Nevertheless ye are commanded never to cast any one out from your public meetings, which are held before the world.*
1] 4 *Ye are also commanded not to cast any one who belongeth to the church out of your sacrament meetings*; nevertheless, if any have trespassed, let him not partake until he makes reconciliation.
1] 5 And again I say unto you, *ye shall not cast any out of your sacrament meetings who are earnestly seeking the kingdom—I speak this concerning those who are not of the church.*
2] 6 And again I say unto you, concerning your confirmation meetings, *that if there be any that are not of the church, that are earnestly seeking after the kingdom, ye shall not cast them out.*
3] 7 But ye are commanded in all things to ask of God, who giveth liberally; *and that which the Spirit testifies unto you even so I would that ye should do in all holiness of heart*, walking uprightly before me, considering the end of your salvation, doing all things with prayer and thanksgiving, that ye may not be seduced by evil spirits, or doctrines of devils, or the commandments of men; for some are of men, and others of devils.

D&C 46:2-7 — Analysis 46A

3a/3b	Parallel concepts:	**3a-** it always has been given to the elders of my church from the beginning, and ever shall be, to conduct all meetings as they are directed and guided by the Holy Spirit. **3b-** and that which the Spirit testifies unto you even so I would that ye should do in all holiness of heart,
2a/2b	Parallel concepts:	**2a-** Nevertheless ye are commanded never to cast any one out from your public meetings, which are held before the world. **2b-** that if there be any that are not of the church, that are earnestly seeking after the kingdom, ye shall not cast them out.
1a/1b	Parallel concepts:	**1a-** Ye are also commanded not to cast any one who belongeth to the church out of your sacrament meetings; **1b-** ye shall not cast any out of your sacrament meetings who are earnestly seeking the kingdom—I speak this concerning those who are not of the church.

D&C 52:3-7 — Chiasmus 80, 52A

3] 3 Wherefore, verily I say unto you, *let my servants Joseph Smith, Jun., and Sidney Rigdon take their journey* as soon as preparations can be made to leave their homes, and journey to the land of Missouri.
2] 4 *And inasmuch as they are faithful* unto me,
1] *it shall be made known unto them what they shall do;*
1] 5 And *it shall* also, inasmuch as they are faithful, *be made known unto them the land of your inheritance.*
2] 6 *And inasmuch as they are not faithful,* they shall be cut off, even as I will, as seemeth me good.
3] 7 And again, verily I say unto you, *let my servant Lyman Wight and my servant John Corrill take their journey* speedily;

D&C 52:3-7 **Analysis 52A**

3a/3b	Parallel concepts:	**3a-** let my servants Joseph Smith, Jun., and Sidney Rigdon take their journey **3b-** let my servant Lyman Wight and my servant John Corrill take their journey
2a/2b	Positive to negative:	**2a-** And inasmuch as they are faithful **2b-** And inasmuch as they are not faithful,
1a/1b	Parallel concepts:	**1a-** it shall be made known unto them what they shall do; **1b-** it shall be made known unto them the land of your inheritance.

D&C 55:1-3 **Chiasmus 82, 55A**

1 Behold, thus saith the Lord unto you, my servant William, yea, even the Lord of the whole earth, thou art called and chosen; and after thou hast been baptized by water, which if you do with an eye single to my glory,

3] *you shall have* a remission of your sins and *a reception of the Holy Spirit*

2] *by the laying on of hands*;

1] 2 And then thou shalt be ordained by the hand of my servant Joseph Smith, Jun., to be an elder unto this church, to preach repentance and remission of sins by way of baptism in the name of Jesus Christ, the Son of the living God.

2] 3 *And on whomsoever you shall lay your hands*, if they are contrite before me,

3] *you shall have power to give the Holy Spirit.*

D&C 55:1-3 **Analysis 55A**

3a/3b	Parallel concepts:	**3a-** you shall have a remission of your sins and a reception of the Holy Spirit **3b-** you shall have power to give the Holy Spirit.
2a/2b	Parallel concepts:	**2a-** by the laying on of hands; **2b-** And on whomsoever you shall lay your hands,
1	Central theme:	**1-** And then thou shalt be ordained by the hand of my servant Joseph Smith, Jun., to be an elder unto this church, to preach repentance and remission of sins by way of baptism in the name of Jesus Christ, the Son of the living God.

D&C 56:12,13 **Chiasmus 83, 56A**

12 And if my servant Joseph Smith, Jun., must needs pay the money, behold, I, the Lord, will pay it unto him again

3] *in the land of Missouri,*
2] that those of whom *he shall receive* may be rewarded again
1] *according to that which they do;*
1] 13 For *according to that which they do*
2] *they shall receive,*
3] even *in lands for their inheritance.*

D&C 56:12,13 **Analysis 56A**

3a/3b	Parallel concepts:	**3a-** in the land of Missouri, **3b-** in lands for their inheritance.
2a/2b	Parallel concepts:	**2a-** he shall receive **2b-** they shall receive,
1a/1b	Identical words:	**1-** according to that which they do;

D&C 63:9 **Chiasmus 92, 63B**

3] 9 But, behold, *faith*
2] *cometh*
1] not by *signs*,
1] but *signs*
2] *follow* those
3] that *believe.*

D&C 63:9 **Analysis 63B**

3a/3b	Parallel concepts:	**3a-** faith **3b-** believe.
2a/2b	Parallel concepts:	**2a-** cometh **2b-** follow
1a/1b	Identical word:	**1-** signs

D&C 64:23-25 **Chiasmus 96, 64C**

3] 23 Behold, *now it is called today* until the coming of the Son of Man,
2] *and verily it is a day of sacrifice, and a day for the tithing of my people*;
1] *for he that is tithed shall not be burned at his coming.*
1] 24 *For after today cometh the burning*—this is speaking after the manner of the Lord—

2] *for verily I say, tomorrow all the proud and they that do wickedly shall be as stubble; and I will burn them up, for I am the Lord of Hosts; and I will not spare any that remain in Babylon.*

3] 25 Wherefore, if ye believe me, ye will labor *while it is called today.*

D&C 64:23-25 **Analysis 64C**

3a/3b	Identical words:	**3-** now/while it is called today
2a/2b	Positive to negative:	**2a-** and verily it is a day of sacrifice, and a day for the tithing of my people; **2b-** for verily I say, tomorrow all the proud and they that do wickedly shall be as stubble; and I will burn them up, for I am the Lord of Hosts; and I will not spare any that remain in Babylon.
1a/1b	Parallel concepts:	**1a-** for he that is tithed shall not be burned at his coming. **1b-** For after today cometh the burning—

D&C 68:25-31 **Chiasmus 100, 68B**

3] 25 *And again, inasmuch as parents have children in Zion, or in any of her stakes which are organized, that teach them not to understand the doctrine of repentance, faith in Christ the Son of the living God, and of baptism and the gift of the Holy Ghost by the laying on of the hands, when eight years old, the sin be upon the heads of the parents.*

2] 26 *For this shall be a law unto the inhabitants of Zion, or in any of her stakes which are organized.*

1] 27 *And their children shall be baptized for the remission of their sins when eight years old, and receive the laying on of the hands.*

1] 28 *And they shall also teach their children to pray, and to walk uprightly before the Lord.*

2] 29 *And the inhabitants of Zion shall also observe the Sabbath day to keep it holy.*

30 *And the inhabitants of Zion also shall remember their labors, inasmuch as they are appointed to labor, in all faithfulness; for the idler shall be had in remembrance before the Lord.*

3] 31 *Now, I, the Lord, am not well pleased with the inhabitants of Zion, for there are idlers among them; and their children are also growing up in wickedness*; they also seek not earnestly the riches of eternity, but their eyes are full of greediness.

D&C 68:25-31 **Analysis 68B**

3a/3b Parallel concepts: **3a-** And again, inasmuch as parents have children in Zion, or in any of her stakes which are organized, that teach them not to understand the doctrine of repentance, faith in Christ the Son of the living God, and of baptism and the gift of the Holy Ghost by the laying on of the hands, when eight years old, the sin be upon the heads of the parents.

3b- Now, I, the Lord, am not well pleased with the inhabitants of Zion, for there are idlers among them; and their children are also growing up in wickedness;

2a/2b Parallel concepts: **2a-** For this shall be a law unto the inhabitants of Zion, or in any of her stakes which are organized.

2b- And the inhabitants of Zion shall also observe the Sabbath day to keep it holy. And the inhabitants of Zion also shall remember their labors, inasmuch as they are appointed to labor, in all faithfulness; for the idler shall be had in remembrance before the Lord.

1a/1b Parallel concepts: **1a-** And their children shall be baptized for the remission of their sins when eight years old, and receive the laying on of the hands.

1b- And they shall also teach their children to pray, and to walk uprightly before the Lord.

D&C 72:2-5 **Chiasmus 103, 72A**

3] 2 For verily thus saith the Lord, *it is expedient in me for a bishop to be appointed unto you, or of you, unto the church in this part of the Lord's vineyard.*

2] 3 And verily in this thing ye have done wisely, *for it is required of the Lord, at the hand of every steward, to render an account of his stewardship,*

1] *both in time and in eternity.*
1] 4 *For he who is faithful and wise in time is accounted worthy to inherit the mansions prepared for him of my Father.*
2] 5 Verily I say unto you, *the elders of the church in this part of my vineyard shall render an account of their stewardship*
3] *unto the bishop, who shall be appointed of me in this part of my vineyard.*

D&C 72:2-5 — Analysis 72A

3a/3b	Parallel concepts:	**3a-** it is expedient in me for a bishop to be appointed unto you, or of you, unto the church in this part of the Lord's vineyard. **3b-** unto the bishop, who shall be appointed of me in this part of my vineyard.
2a/2b	Parallel concepts:	**2a-** for it is required of the Lord, at the hand of every steward, to render an account of his stewardship, both in time and in eternity. **2b-** the elders of the church in this part of my vineyard shall render an account of their stewardship
1a/1b	Parallel concepts:	**1a-** both in time and in eternity. **1b-** For he who is faithful and wise in time is accounted worthy to inherit the mansions prepared for him of my Father.

D&C 76:13 — Chiasmus 110, 76C

13 Even those things
a3] which were *from the beginning* before the world was,
a2] which were ordained *of the Father,*
a1] through his Only Begotten Son,
a2] who was in the bosom *of the Father,*
a3] even *from the beginning;*

D&C 76:13 — Analysis 76C

3a/3b	Identical words:	**3-** from the beginning
2a/2b	Identical words:	**2-** of the Father,
1	Central theme:	**1-** through his Only Begotten Son,

D&C 76:28-30 **Chiasmus 112, 76E**

3] 28 And while we were yet in the Spirit, *the Lord commanded us that we should write the vision*;
2] *for we beheld Satan, that old serpent, even the devil, who rebelled against God,*
1] *and sought to take the kingdom of our God and his Christ—*
1] 29 *Wherefore, he maketh war with the saints of God, and encompasseth them round about.*
2] 30 *And we saw a vision of the sufferings of those with whom he made war and overcame,*
3] *for thus came the voice of the Lord unto us*:

D&C 76:28-30 **Analysis 76E**

3a/3b	Parallel concepts:	**3a-** the Lord commanded us that we should write the vision; **3b-** for thus came the voice of the Lord unto us:
2a/2b	Parallel concepts:	**2a-** for we beheld Satan, that old serpent, even the devil, who rebelled against God, **2b-** And we saw a vision of the sufferings of those with whom he made war and overcame,
1a/1b	Parallel concepts:	**1a-** and sought to take the kingdom of our God and his Christ— **1b-** Wherefore, he maketh war with the saints of God, and encompasseth them round about.

D&C 76:45-48 **Chiasmus 115, 76H**

3] 45 *And the end thereof, neither the place thereof, nor their torment, no man knows*;
2] 46 *Neither was it revealed, neither is, neither will be revealed unto man,*
1] *except to them who are made partakers thereof*;
1] 47 *Nevertheless, I, the Lord, show it by vision unto many,*
2] *but straightway shut it up again*;
3] 48 *Wherefore, the end, the width, the height, the depth, and the misery thereof, they understand not, neither any man except those who are ordained unto this condemnation.*

D&C 76:45-48 **Analysis 76H**

3a/3b Parallel concepts: **3a-** And the end thereof, neither the place thereof, nor their torment, no man knows;
3b- Wherefore, the end, the width, the height, the depth, and the misery thereof, they understand not, neither any man except those who are ordained unto this condemnation.

2a/2b Parallel concepts: **2a-** Neither was it revealed, neither is, neither will be revealed unto man,
2b- but straightway shut it up again;

1a/1b Parallel concepts: **1a-** except to them who are made partakers thereof;
1b- Nevertheless, I, the Lord, show it by vision unto many,

D&C 76:89-98 **Chiasmus 118, 76K**

3] 89 And thus we saw, in the heavenly vision, *the glory of the telestial*, which surpasses all understanding;
90 And no man knows it except him to whom God has revealed it.

2] 91 And thus we saw *the glory of the terrestrial* which excels in all things the glory of the telestial, even in glory, and in power, and in might, and in dominion.

1] 92 And thus we saw *the glory of the celestial*, which excels in all things—where God, even the Father, reigns upon his throne forever and ever;
93 Before whose throne all things bow in humble reverence, and give him glory forever and ever.
94 They who dwell in his presence are the church of the Firstborn; and they see as they are seen, and know as they are known, having received of his fullness and of his grace;
95 And he makes them equal in power, and in might, and in dominion.

1] 96 And *the glory of the celestial* is one, even as the glory of the sun is one.

2] 97 And *the glory of the terrestrial* is one, even as the glory of the moon is one.

3] 98 And *the glory of the telestial* is one, even as the glory of the stars is one; for as one star differs from another star in glory, even so differs one from another in glory in the telestial world;

D&C76:89-98 — Analysis 76K

(Which forms element 3b of chiasmus 76J. See Chapter 10)

3a/3b	Identical words:	**3-** the glory of the telestial
2a/2b	Identical words:	**2-** the glory of the terrestrial
1a/1b	Identical words:	**1-** the glory of the celestial

D&C 78:5,6 — Chiasmus 120, 78A

3] 5 *That you may be equal in the bonds of heavenly things,*
2] yea, *and earthly things also,*
1] for the obtaining of heavenly things.
2] 6 For *if ye are not equal in earthly things*
3] *ye cannot be equal in obtaining heavenly things;*

D&C 78:5,6 — Analysis 78A

3a/3b	Positive to negative:	**3a-** That you may be equal in the bonds of heavenly things, **3b-** ye cannot be equal in obtaining heavenly things;
2a/2b	Positive to negative:	**2a-** and earthly things also, **2b-** if ye are not equal in earthly things
1	Central theme:	**1-** for the obtaining of heavenly things.

D&C 78:11-13 — Chiasmus 121, 78B

3] 11 Wherefore, *a commandment I give unto you,*
2] *to prepare and organize yourselves*
1] *by a bond or everlasting covenant that cannot be broken.*
1] 12 *And he who breaketh it* shall lose his office and standing in the church, and shall be delivered over to the buffetings of Satan until the day of redemption.
2] 13 Behold, *this is the preparation wherewith I prepare you,* and the foundation, and the ensample which I give unto you,
3] whereby you may accomplish *the commandments which are given you;*

D&C 78:11-13 **Analysis 78B**

3a/3b	Parallel concepts:	**3a-** a commandment I give unto you, **3b-** the commandments which are given you;
2a/2b	Parallel concepts:	**2a-** to prepare and organize yourselves **2b-** this is the preparation wherewith I prepare you,
1/1b	Positive to negative:	**1a-** by a bond or everlasting covenant that cannot be broken. **1b-** And he who breaketh it

D&C 84:45,46 **Chiasmus 126, 84A**

45 For the word of the Lord is truth, and whatsoever is truth is light,
3] and whatsoever is *light*
2] is *Spirit*,
1] even the Spirit of Jesus Christ.
2] 46 And the *Spirit*
3] giveth *light*

D&C 84:45,46 **Analysis 84A**

3a/3b	Identical words:	**3-** light
2a/2b	Identical words:	**2-** Spirit
1	Central theme:	**1-** even the Spirit of Jesus Christ.

D&C 84:55-56 **Chiasmus 128, 84C**

54 And your minds in times past have been darkened because of unbelief, and because you have treated lightly the things you have received—
3] 55 Which vanity and unbelief have brought *the whole*
2] *church*
1] under *condemnation*.
1] 56 And this *condemnation*
2] resteth upon *the children of Zion*,
3] *even all.*

D&C 84:55-56 **Analysis 84C**

3a/3b	Parallel concepts:	**3a-** the whole **3b-** even all.
2a/2b	Parallel concepts:	**2a-** church **2b-** children of Zion,
1a/1b	Identical word:	**1-** condemnation

D&C 85:3-9 — Chiasmus 131, 85A

3] 3 *It is contrary to the will and commandment of God that those who receive not their inheritance by consecration, agreeable to his law, which he has given, that he may tithe his people, to prepare them against the day of vengeance and burning, should have their names enrolled with the people of God.*

4 Neither is their genealogy to be kept, or to be had where it may be found on any of the records or history of the church.

2] 5 *Their names shall not be found, neither the names of the fathers, nor the names of the children written in the book of the law of God, saith the Lord of Hosts.*

1] 6 Yea, thus saith the still small voice, which whispereth through and pierceth all things, and often times it maketh my bones to quake while it maketh manifest, saying:

7 And it shall come to pass that *I, the Lord God, will send one mighty and strong, holding the scepter of power in his hand, clothed with light for a covering, whose mouth shall utter words, eternal words; while his bowels shall be a fountain of truth, to set in order the house of God,* and to arrange by lot the inheritances of the saints

2] *whose names are found, and the names of their fathers, and of their children, enrolled in the book of the law of God;*

8 While that man, who was called of God and appointed, that putteth forth his hand to steady the ark of God, shall fall by the shaft of death, like as a tree that is smitten by the vivid shaft of lightning.

3] 9 *And all they who are not found written in the book of remembrance shall find none inheritance in that day, but they shall be cut asunder, and their portion shall be appointed them among unbelievers, where are wailing and gnashing of teeth.*

D&C 85:3-9 — Analysis 85A

3a/3b	Parallel concepts:	**3a-** It is contrary to the will and commandment of God that those who receive not their inheritance by consecration, agreeable to his law, which he has given, that he may tithe his people, to prepare them against the day of vengeance and burning, should have their names enrolled with the people of God.

		3b- And all they who are not found written in the book of remembrance shall find none inheritance in that day, but they shall be cut asunder, and their portion shall be appointed them among unbelievers, where are wailing and gnashing of teeth.
2a/2b	Negative to positive:	**2a-** Their names shall not be found, neither the names of the fathers, nor the names of the children written in the book of the law of God, saith the Lord of Hosts.
		2b- whose names are found, and the names of their fathers, and of their children, enrolled in the book of the law of God;
1	Central theme:	**1-** I, the Lord God, will send one mighty and strong, holding the scepter of power in his hand, clothed with light for a covering, whose mouth shall utter words, eternal words; while his bowels shall be a fountain of truth, to set in order the house of God,

D&C 88:42-44 — Chiasmus 137, 88E

3] 42 And again, verily I say unto you, he hath given a law unto all things, by which they move *in their times and seasons;*
2] 43 And their courses are fixed, even the courses of *the heavens*
1] and *the earth,*
1] which comprehend *the earth*
2] *and all the planets.*
3] 44 And they give light to each other *in their times and in their seasons,* in their minutes, in their hours, in their days, in their weeks, in their months, in their years—all these are but one year with God, but not with man.

D&C 88:42-44 — Analysis 88E

3a/3b	Identical words:	**3-** in their times and in their seasons,
2a/2b	Parallel concepts:	**2a-** the heavens
		2b- all the planets.
1a/1b	Identical words:	**1-** the earth

D&C 88:62,63 — Chiasmus 140, 88H

3] *ye shall call upon me*
2] *while I am near—*
1] 63 *Draw near unto me*
1] *and I will draw near unto you;*
2] *seek me diligently and ye shall find me;*
3] *ask, and ye shall receive; knock, and it shall be opened unto you.*

D&C 88:62,63 — Analysis 88H

3a/3b	Parallel concepts:	**3a-** ye shall call upon me **3b-** ask, and ye shall receive; knock, and it shall be opened unto you.
2a/2b	Parallel concepts:	**2a-** while I am near— **2b-** seek me diligently and ye shall find me;
1a/1b	Parallel concepts:	**1a-** Draw near unto me **1b-** and I will draw near unto you;

D&C 88:77-81 — Chiasmus 143, 88K

3] 77 *And I give unto you a commandment that you shall teach one another the doctrine of the kingdom.*
2] 78 *Teach ye diligently and my grace shall attend you,*
1] *that you may be instructed more perfectly in theory, in principle, in doctrine, in the law of the gospel, in all things that pertain unto the kingdom of God, that are expedient for you to understand;*
79 *Of things both in heaven and in the earth, and under the earth; things which have been, things which are, things which must shortly come to pass; things which are at home, things which are abroad; the wars and the perplexities of the nations, and the judgments which are on the land; and a knowledge also of countries and of kingdoms—*
1] 80 *That ye may be prepared in all things*
2] when I shall send you again to *magnify the calling whereunto I have called you, and the mission with which I have commissioned you.*
3] 81 Behold, *I sent you out to testify and warn the people, and it becometh every man who hath been warned to warn his neighbor.*

D&C 88:77-81 — Analysis 88K

3a/3b	Parallel concepts:	**3a-** And I give unto you a commandment that you shall teach one another the doctrine of the kingdom. **3b-** Behold, I sent you out to testify and warn the people, and it becometh every man who hath been warned to warn his neighbor.
2a/2b	Parallel concepts:	**2a-** Teach ye diligently and my grace shall attend you, **2b-** magnify the calling whereunto I have called you, and the mission with which I have commissioned you.
1/1b	Specific to general:	**1a-** that you may be instructed more perfectly in theory, in principle, in doctrine, in the law of the gospel, in all things that pertain unto the kingdom of God, that are expedient for you to understand; Of things both in heaven and in the earth, and under the earth; things which have been, things which are, things which must shortly come to pass; things which are at home, things which are abroad; the wars and the perplexities of the nations, and the judgments which are on the land; and a knowledge also of countries and of kingdoms— **1b-** That ye may be prepared in all things

D&C 90:28-30 — Chiasmus 146, 90A

3] 28 And again, verily I say unto you, it is my will that *my handmaid Vienna Jaques should receive money to bear her expenses,*
2] and *go up unto the land of Zion;*
1] *29 And the residue of the money may be consecrated unto me,*
1] *and she be rewarded in mine own due time.*
2] 30 Verily I say unto you, that it is meet in mine eyes that she should *go up unto the land of Zion,*
3] *and receive an inheritance from the hand of the bishop;*

D&C 90:28-30 **Analysis 90A**

3a/3b	Parallel concepts:	**3a-** should receive money to bear her expenses, **3b-** and receive an inheritance from the hand of the bishop;
2a/2b	Identical words:	**2-** go up unto the land of Zion,
1a/1b	Parallel concepts:	**1a-** And the residue of the money may be consecrated unto me, **1b-** and she be rewarded in mine own due time.

D&C 93:8 **Chiasmus 151, 93C**

3] *the Word*
2] *was,*
1] for he
2] *was*
3] *the Word,*

D&C 93:8 **Analysis 93C**

3a/3b	Identical words:	**3-** the Word
2a/2b	Identical word:	**2-** was
1	Central theme:	**1-** he

D&C 93:12,13 **Chiasmus 152, 93D**

3] 12 And I, John, saw that *he received not of the fullness* at first,
2] *but received grace for grace.*
1] 13 And he received not of the fullness at first,
2] *but continued from grace to grace,*
3] until *he received a fullness;*

D&C 93:12,13 **Analysis 93D**

3a/3b	Negative to positive:	**3a-** he received not of the fullness **3b-** he received a fullness;
2a/2b	Parallel concepts:	**2a-** but received grace for grace. **2b-** but continued from grace to grace,
1	Central theme:	**1-** And he received not of the fullness at first,

D&C 93:39-42 **Chiasmus 156, 93H**

3] 39 *And that wicked one cometh and taketh away light and truth, through disobedience, from the children of men, and because of the tradition of their fathers.*

2] 40 *But I have commanded you to bring up your children in light and truth.*

1] 41 But verily I say unto you, my servant Frederick G. Williams, you have continued under this condemnation;

2] 42 *You have not taught your children light and truth,* according to the commandments;

3] *and that wicked one hath power, as yet, over you,* and this is the cause of your affliction.

D&C 93:39-42 **Analysis 93H**

3a/3b	Parallel concepts:	**3a-** And that wicked one cometh and taketh away light and truth, through disobedience, from the children of men, and because of the tradition of their fathers. **3b-** and that wicked one hath power, as yet, over you,
2a/2b	Positive to negative:	**2a-** But I have commanded you to bring up your children in light and truth. **2b-** You have not taught your children light and truth,
1	Central theme:	**1-** But verily I say unto you, my servant Frederick G. Williams, you have continued under this condemnation;

D&C 97:2-6 **Chiasmus 160, 97A**

3] 2 Verily, verily I say unto you, blessed are such, for they shall obtain; *for I, the Lord, show mercy* unto all the meek, and upon all whomsoever I will, that I may be justified when I shall bring them unto judgement.

2] 3 Behold, I say unto you, concerning the school in Zion, *I, the Lord, am well pleased that there should be a school in Zion,*

1] and also with my servant Parley P. Pratt, for *he abideth in me.*

1] 4 And inasmuch as *he continueth to abide in me*

2] *he shall continue to preside over the school in the land of Zion* until I shall give unto him other commandments.

5 And I will bless him with a multiplicity of blessings, in expounding all scriptures and mysteries to the edification of the school, and of the church in Zion.

3] 6 And to the residue of the school, *I, the Lord, am willing to show mercy;* nevertheless, there are those that must needs be chastened, and their works shall be made known.

D&C 97:2-6 **Analysis 97A**

3a/3b	Parallel concepts:	**3a-** I, the Lord, show mercy **3b-** I, the Lord, am willing to show mercy;
2a/2b	Parallel concepts:	**2a-** I, the Lord, am well pleased that there should be a school in Zion, **2b-** he shall continue to preside over the school in the land of Zion
1a/1b	Parallel concepts:	**1a-** he abideth in me. **1b-** he continueth to abide in me

D&C 97:10-12 **Chiasmus 161, 97B**

3] 10 Verily I say unto you, that it is my will *that a house should be built unto me in the land of Zion,* like unto the pattern which I have given you.
2] 11 *Yea, let it be built speedily,*
1] by *the tithing* of my people.
1] 12 Behold, this is *the tithing*
2] and *the sacrifice which I, the Lord, require at their hands,*
3] *that there may be a house built unto me for the salvation of Zion—*

D&C 97:10-12 **Analysis 97B**

3a/3b	Parallel concepts:	**3a-** that a house should be built unto me in the land of Zion, **3b-** that there may be a house built unto me for the salvation of Zion—
2a/2b	Parallel concepts:	**2a-** Yea, let it be built speedily, **2b-** the sacrifice which I, the Lord, require at their hands,
1a/1b	Identical words:	**1-** the tithing

D&C 97:24-27 **Chiasmus 164, 97E**

3] 24 *For the indignation of the Lord is kindled against their abominations and all their works.*
2] 25 *Nevertheless, Zion shall escape if she observe to do all things whatsoever I have commanded her.*
1] 26 But if she observe not to do whatsoever I have commanded her, I will visit her according to all her works, with sore affliction, with pestilence, with plague, with sword, with vengeance, with devouring fire.
2] 27 *Nevertheless, let it be read this once to her ears, that I, the Lord, have accepted her offering;*
3] *and if she sin no more none of these things shall come upon her;*

D&C 97:24-27 **Analysis 97E**

3a/3b	Negative to positive:	**3a-** For the indignation of the Lord is kindled against their abominations and all their works. **3b-** and if she sin no more none of these things shall come upon her;
2a/2b	Parallel concepts:	**2a-** Nevertheless, Zion shall escape if she observe to do all things whatsoever I have commanded her. **2b-** Nevertheless, let it be read this once to her ears, that I, the Lord, have accepted her offering;
1	Central theme:	**1-** But if she observe not to do whatsoever I have commanded her, I will visit her according to all her works, with sore affliction, with pestilence, with plague, with sword, with vengeance, with devouring fire.

D&C 104:49 **Chiasmus 181, 104C**

3] 49 And they shall be organized *in their own names,*
2] and *in their own name;*
1] and they shall do their business
2] *in their own name,*
3] and *in their own names;*

D&C 104:49 — Analysis 104C

3a/3b	Identical words:	**3-** in their own names,
2a/2b	Identical words:	**2-** in their own name;
1	Central theme:	**1-** and they shall do their business

D&C 105:9-13 — Chiasmus 185, 105A

9 Therefore, in consequence of the transgressions of my people,
3] *it is expedient in me that mine elders should wait for a little season for the redemption of Zion—*
2] 10 *That they themselves may be prepared,* and that my people may be taught more perfectly, and have experience, and know more perfectly concerning their duty, and the things which I require at their hands.
1] 11 And this cannot be brought to pass until mine elders are endowed with power from on high.
2] 12 *For behold, I have prepared a great endowment and blessing to be poured out upon them*, inasmuch as they are faithful and continue in humility before me.
3] 13 Therefore *it is expedient in me that mine elders should wait for a little season, for the redemption of Zion.*

D&C 105:9-13 — Analysis 105A

3a/3b	Identical words:	**3-** it is expedient in me that mine elders should wait for a little season for the redemption of Zion
2a/2b	Parallel concepts:	**2a-** That they themselves may be prepared, **2b-** For behold, I have prepared a great endowment and blessing to be poured out upon them
1	Central theme:	**1-** and this cannot be brought to pass until mine elders are endowed with power from on high.

D&C 107:1-6 — Chiasmus 187, 107A

3] 1 *There are, in the church, two priesthoods, namely, the Melchizedek and Aaronic, including the Levitical Priesthood.*
2] 2 *Why the first is called the Melchizedek Priesthood is because Melchizedek was such a great high priest.*
1] 3 Before his day it was called the Holy Priesthood, after the Order of the Son of God.

4 But out of respect or reverence to the name of the Supreme Being, to avoid the too frequent repetition of his name,
2] *they, the church, in ancient days, called that priesthood after Melchizedek, or the Melchizedek Priesthood.*
5 All other authorities or offices in the church are appendages to this priesthood.
3] 6 *But there are two divisions or grand heads—one is the Melchizedek Priesthood, and the other is the Aaronic or Levitical Priesthood.*

D&C 107:1-6 — Analysis 107A

3a/3b	Parallel concepts:	**3a-** There are, in the church, two priesthoods, namely, the Melchizedek and Aaronic, including the Levitical Priesthood. **3b-** But there are two divisions or grand heads—one is the Melchizedek Priesthood, and the other is the Aaronic or Levitical Priesthood.
2a/2b	Parallel concepts:	**2a-** Why the first is called the Melchizedek Priesthood is because Melchizedek was such a great high priest. **2b-** they, the church, in ancient days, called that priesthood after Melchizedek, or the Melchizedek Priesthood.
1	Central theme:	**1-** Before his day it was called the Holy Priesthood, after the Order of the Son of God. But out of respect or reverence to the name of the Supreme Being, to avoid the too frequent repetition of his name,

D&C 107:34-38 — Chiasmus 190, 107D

3] 34 *The Seventy are to act in the name of the Lord,*
2] *under the direction of the Twelve or the traveling high council,* in building up the church and regulating all the affairs of the same in all nations, first unto the Gentiles and then to the Jews;
35 The Twelve being sent out, holding the keys, to open the door by the proclamation of the gospel of Jesus Christ, and first unto the Gentiles and then unto the Jews.

1] 36 *The standing high councils, at the stakes of Zion, form a quorum equal in authority in the affairs of the church, in all their decisions, to the quorum of the presidency, or to the traveling high council.*
1] 37 *The high council in Zion form a quorum equal in authority in the affairs of the church, in all their decisions, to the councils of the Twelve at the stakes of Zion.*
2] 38 *It is the duty of the traveling high council*
3] *to call upon the Seventy*, when they need assistance, to fill the several calls for preaching and administering the gospel, instead of any others.

D&C 107:34-38 Analysis 107D

3a/3b	Parallel concepts:	**3a-** The Seventy are to act in the name of the Lord, **3b-** to call upon the Seventy,
2a/2b	Parallel concepts:	**2a-** under the direction of the Twelve or the traveling high council, **2b-** It is the duty of the traveling high council
1a1b	Parallel concepts:	**1a-** The standing high councils, at the stakes of Zion, form a quorum equal in authority in the affairs of the church, in all their decisions, to the quorum of the presidency, or to the traveling high council. **1b-** The high council in Zion form a quorum equal in authority in the affairs of the church, in all their decisions, to the councils of the Twelve at the stakes of Zion.

D&C 107:68-71 Chiasmus 194, 107H

3] 68 Wherefore, the office of a bishop is not equal unto it; for the office of a bishop is *in administering all temporal things*;
2] 69 *Nevertheless a bishop must be chosen from the High Priesthood,*
1] *unless he is a literal descendant of Aaron*;
1] 70 *For unless he is a literal descendant of Aaron* he cannot hold the keys of that priesthood.
2] 71 *Nevertheless, a high priest, that is, after the order of Melchizedek,*
3] may be set apart *unto the ministering of temporal things*, having a knowledge of them by the Spirit of truth;

D&C 107:68-71 **Analysis 107H**

3a/3b	Parallel concepts:	**3a-** in administering all temporal things; **3b-** unto the ministering of temporal things,
2a/2b	Parallel concepts:	**2a-** Nevertheless a bishop must be chosen from the High Priesthood, **2b-** Nevertheless, a high priest, that is, after the order of Melchizedek,
1a/1b	Identical words:	**1-** unless he is a literal descendant of Aaron

D&C 109:24-29 **Chiasmus 199, 109C**

3] 24 *We ask thee, Holy Father, to establish the people that shall worship, and honorably hold a name and standing in this thy house, to all generations and for eternity;*

2] 25 *That no weapon formed against them shall prosper; that he who diggeth a pit for them shall fall into the same himself;*

1] 26 *That no combination of wickedness shall have power to rise up and prevail over thy people upon whom thy name shall be put in this house;*

1] 27 *And if any people shall rise against this people, that thine anger be kindled against them;*

2] 28 *And if they shall smite this people thou wilt smite them; thou wilt fight for thy people as thou didst in the day of battle, that they may be delivered from the hands of all their enemies.*

3] 29 *We ask thee, Holy Father, to confound, and astonish, and to bring to shame and confusion, all those who have spread lying reports abroad, over the world, against thy servant or servants,*

D&C 109:24-29 **Analysis 109C**

3a/3b	Positive to negative:	**3a-** We ask thee, Holy Father, to establish the people that shall worship, and honorably hold a name and standing in this thy house, to all generations and for eternity; **3b-** We ask thee, Holy Father, to confound, and astonish, and to bring to shame and confusion, all those who have spread lying reports abroad, over the world, against thy servant or servants,

2a/2b Parallel concepts: **2a-** That no weapon formed against them shall prosper; that he who diggeth a pit for them shall fall into the same himself;
2b- And if they shall smite this people thou wilt smite them; thou wilt fight for thy people as thou didst in the day of battle, that they may be delivered from the hands of all their enemies.

1a/1b Parallel concepts: **1a-** That no combination of wickedness shall have power to rise up and prevail over thy people upon whom thy name shall be put in this house;
1b- And if any people shall rise against this people, that thine anger be kindled against them;

D&C 110:14-16 Chiasmus 202, 110B

3] 14 Behold, the time has fully come, which was spoken of by the mouth of Malachi—testifying that he [Elijah] should be sent, *before the great and dreadful day of the Lord come—*
2] 15 To turn the hearts of *the fathers*
1] to *the children,*
1] and *the children*
2] to *the fathers*, lest the whole earth be smitten with a curse—
3] 16 Therefore, the keys of this dispensation are committed into your hands; and by this ye may know *that the great and dreadful day of the Lord is near, even at the doors.*

D&C 110:14-16 Analysis 110B

3a/3b Parallel concepts: **3a-** before the great and dreadful day of the Lord come—
3b- that the great and dreadful day of the Lord is near, even at the doors.

2a/2b Identical words: **2-** the fathers

1a/1b Identical words: **1-** the children

D&C 112:1-4 **Chiasmus 204, 112A**

3] 1 Verily thus saith the Lord unto you my servant Thomas: I have heard thy prayers; and thine alms have come up as a memorial before me, in behalf of those, thy brethren, who were chosen *to bear testimony of my name and to send it abroad among all nations, kindreds, tongues, and people,* and ordained through the instrumentality of my servants.

2] 2 Verily I say unto you, *there have been some few things in thine heart and with thee with which I, the Lord, was not well pleased.*

1] 3 Nevertheless, inasmuch as thou hast abased thyself thou shalt be exalted; therefore, all thy sins are forgiven thee.

2] 4 *Let thy heart be of good cheer before my face;*

3] *and thou shalt bear record of my name, not only unto the Gentiles, but also unto the Jews; and thou shalt send forth my word unto the ends of the earth.*

D&C 112:1-4 **Analysis 112A**

3a/3b	Parallel concepts:	**3a-** to bear testimony of my name and to send it abroad among all nations, kindreds, tongues, and people, **3b-** and thou shalt bear record of my name, not only unto the Gentiles, but also unto the Jews; and thou shalt send forth my word unto the ends of the earth.
2a/2b	Negative to positive:	**2a-** there have been some few things in thine heart and with thee with which I, the Lord, was not well pleased. **2b-** Let thy heart be of good cheer before my face;
1	Central theme:	**1-** Nevertheless, inasmuch as thou hast abased thyself thou shalt be exalted; therefore, all thy sins are forgiven thee.

D&C 121:3-5 **Chiasmus 211, 121B**

3] 3 Yea, O Lord, how *long shall they suffer these wrongs* and unlawful oppressions,

2] *before thine heart shall be softened toward them, and thy bowels be moved with compassion toward them?*

1] 4 O Lord God Almighty, maker of heaven, earth, and seas, and of all things that in them are, and who controllest and subjectest the devil, and the dark and benighted dominion of Sheol—stretch forth thy hand; let thine eye pierce; let thy pavilion be taken up; let thy hiding place no longer be covered; let thine ear be inclined;

2] *let thine heart be softened, and thy bowels moved with compassion toward us.*

3] 5 Let thine anger be kindled against our enemies; and, in the fury of thine heart, with thy sword *avenge us of our wrongs.*

D&C 121:3-5 — Analysis 121B

3a/3b	Parallel concepts:	**3a-** how long shall they suffer these wrongs **3b-** avenge us of our wrongs.
2a/2b	Parallel concepts:	**2a-** before thine heart shall be softened toward them, and thy bowels be moved with compassion toward them? **2b-** let thine heart be softened, and thy bowels moved with compassion toward us.
1	Central theme:	**1-** O Lord God Almighty, maker of heaven, earth, and seas, and of all things that in them are, and who controllest and subjectest the devil, and the dark and benighted dominion of Sheol—stretch forth thy hand; let thine eye pierce; let thy pavilion be taken up; let thy hiding place no longer be covered; let thine ear be inclined;

D&C 124:30-32 — Chiasmus 212, 124A

3] 30 For this ordinance belongeth to my house, and *cannot be acceptable to me,*

2] *only in the days of your poverty, wherein ye are not able to build a house unto me.*

1] 31 But *I command you, all ye my saints, to build a house unto me;*

1] and *I grant unto you a sufficient time to build a house unto me;*

2] *and during this time your baptisms shall be acceptable unto me.*

3] 32 But behold, at the end of this appointment your baptisms for your dead *shall not be acceptable unto me;* and if you do not these things at the end of the appointment ye shall be rejected as a church, with your dead, saith the Lord your God.

D&C 124:30-32 **Analysis 124A**

3a/3b Parallel concepts: **3a-** cannot be acceptable to me
3b- shall not be acceptable unto me;

2a/2b Parallel concepts: **2a-** only in the days of your poverty, wherein ye are not able to build a house unto me.
2b- and during this time your baptisms shall be acceptable unto me.

1a/1b Parallel concepts: **1a-** I command you, all ye my saints, to build a house unto me;
1b- I grant unto you a sufficient time to build a house unto me;

D&C 124:33-36 **Chiasmus 213, 124B**

3] 33 For verily I say unto you, that after you have had sufficient time *to build a house to me, wherein the ordinance of baptizing for the dead belongeth,* and for which the same was instituted from before the foundation of the world,
2] *your baptisms for your dead cannot be acceptable unto me;*
1] 34 For therein are the keys of the holy priesthood ordained, that you may receive honor and glory.
2] 35 And after this time, *your baptisms for the dead, by those who are scattered abroad, are not acceptable unto me,* saith the Lord.
3] 36 *For it is ordained that in Zion, and in her stakes, and in Jerusalem, those places which I have appointed for refuge, shall be the places for your baptisms for your dead.*

D&C 124:33-36 **Analysis 124B**

3a/3b Parallel concepts: **3a-** to build a house to me, wherein the ordinance of baptizing for the dead belongeth,
3b- For it is ordained that in Zion, and in her stakes, and in Jerusalem, those places which I have appointed for refuge, shall be the places for your baptisms for your dead.

2a/2b Parallel concepts: **2a-** your baptisms for your dead cannot be acceptable unto me;
2b- your baptisms for the dead, by those who are scattered abroad, are not acceptable unto me,

1 Central theme: **1-** For therein are the keys of the holy priesthood ordained, that you may receive honor and glory.

D&C 132:4-6 **Chiasmus 219, 132A**

3] 4 For behold, I reveal unto you a new and an everlasting covenant; *and if ye abide not that covenant, then are ye damned*;
2] *for no one can reject this covenant and be permitted to enter into my glory.*
1] 5 For all who will have a blessing at my hands shall abide the law which was appointed for that blessing, and the conditions thereof, as were instituted from before the foundation of the world.
2] 6 *And as pertaining to the new and everlasting covenant, it was instituted for the fullness of my glory*;
3] *and he* that receiveth a fullness thereof *must and shall abide the law, or he shall be damned*, saith the Lord God.

D&C 132:4-6 **Analysis 132A**

3a/3b Parallel concepts: **3a-** and if ye abide not that covenant, then are ye damned;
3b- and he...must and shall abide the law, or he shall be damned,

2a/2b Negative to positive: **2a-** for no one can reject this covenant and be permitted to enter into my glory.
2b- And as pertaining to the new and everlasting covenant, it was instituted for the fullness of my glory;

1 Central theme: **1-** For all who will have a blessing at my hands shall abide the law which was appointed for that blessing, and the conditions thereof, as were instituted from before the foundation of the world.

D&C 132:21-24 **Chiasmus 222, 132D**

3] 21 Verily, verily, I say unto you, *except ye abide my law* ye cannot attain to this glory.
2] 22 *For strait is the gate, and narrow the way that leadeth unto the exaltation and continuation of the lives, and few there be that find it,*
1] *because ye receive me not in the world neither do ye know me.*

1] 23 *But if ye receive me in the world, then shall ye know me,* and
shall receive your exaltation; that where I am ye shall be also.
2] 24 *This is eternal lives—to know the only wise and true God, and Jesus*
Christ, whom he hath sent. I am he.
3] *Receive ye, therefore, my law.*

D&C 132:21-24 — Analysis 132D

3a/3b	Negative to positive:	**3a-** except ye abide my law **3b-** Receive ye, therefore, my law.
2a/2b	General to specific:	**2a-** For strait is the gate, and narrow the way that leadeth unto the exaltation and continuation of the lives, and few there be that find it, **2b-** This is eternal lives—to know the only wise and true God, and Jesus Christ, whom he hath sent.
1a/1b	Negative to positive:	**1a-** because ye receive me not in the world neither do ye know me. **1b-** But if ye receive me in the world, then shall ye know me,

7

THE SIMPLE CHIASTIC FORM IN THE DOCTRINE AND COVENANTS—MULTIPLE-ELEMENT CHIASMA

Four-Element Chiasma

D&C 10:23-29 Chiasmus 13, 10C

4] 23 *And thus he has laid a cunning plan, thinking to destroy the work of God*; but I will require this at their hands, and it shall turn to their shame and condemnation in the day of judgment.
24 Yea, he stirreth up their hearts to anger against this work.
3] 25 *Yea, he saith unto them: Deceive and lie in wait to catch, that ye may destroy*; behold, this is no harm. And thus he flattereth them, and telleth them that it is no sin to lie that they may catch a man in a lie, that they may destroy him.
2] 26 *And thus he* flattereth them, and *leadeth them along until he draggeth their souls down to hell*;
1] *and thus he causeth them to catch themselves in their own snare.*
1] 27 *And thus he goeth up and down, to and fro in the earth,*
2] *seeking to destroy the souls of men.*
3] 28 *Verily, verily, I say unto you, wo be unto him that lieth to deceive because he supposeth that another lieth to deceive*, for such are not exempt from the justice of God.
4] 29 *Now, behold, they have altered these words, because Satan saith unto them: He hath deceived you—and thus he flattereth them away to do iniquity, to get thee to tempt the Lord thy God.*

D&C 10:23-29 Analysis 10C

4a/4b	General to specific:	**4a-** And thus he has laid a cunning plan, thinking to destroy the work of God **4b-** Now, behold, they have altered these words, because Satan saith unto them: He hath deceived you—and thus he flattereth them away to do iniquity, to get thee to tempt the Lord thy God.

3a/3b	Satan's commands vs the Lord's counsel:	**3a-** Yea, he saith unto them: Deceive and lie in wait to catch, that ye may destroy **3b-** Verily, verily, I say unto you, wo be unto him that lieth to deceive because he supposeth that another lieth to deceive
2a/2b	Parallel concepts:	**2a-** And thus he . . . leadeth them along until he draggeth their souls down to hell; **2b-** seeking to destroy the souls of men.
1a/1b	Specific to general:	**1a-** and thus he causeth them to catch themselves in their own snare. **1b-** And thus he goeth up and down, to and fro in the earth,

D&C 18:15,16 — Chiasmus 28, 18D

4] And *if it so be that you should* labor all your days in crying repentance unto this people, and *bring, save it be one soul unto me,*
3] *how great shall be your joy* with him
2] *in the kingdom of my Father!*
1] 16 And now, if your joy will be great with one soul that you have brought unto me
2] *into the kingdom of my Father,*
3] *how great will be your joy*
4] *if you should bring many souls unto me!*

D&C 18:15,16 — Analysis 18D

4a/4b	Parallel concepts:	**4a-** if it so be that you should . . . bring, save it be one soul unto me, **4b-** if you should bring many souls unto me!
3a/3b	Identical words:	**3-** how great shall/will be your joy
2a/2b	Identical words:	**2-** in/into the kingdom of my Father
1	Central theme:	**1-** and now, if your joy will be great with one soul that you have brought unto me

D&C 18:26-32 — Chiasmus 30, 18F

4] 26 And now, behold, *there are others who are called to declare my gospel, both unto Gentile and unto Jew;*

3] 27 Yea, even twelve; *and the Twelve shall be my disciples, and they shall take upon them my name; and the Twelve are they who shall desire to take upon them my name with full purpose of heart.*

2] 28 And if they desire to take upon them my name with full purpose of heart, *they are called to go into all the world to preach my gospel unto every creature.*

1] 29 And they are they who are ordained of me to baptize in my name, *according to that which is written;*

1] 30 *And you have that which is written before you;*

2] wherefore, *you must perform it according to the words which are written.*

3] 31 *And now I speak unto you, the Twelve—Behold, my grace is sufficient for you; you must walk uprightly before me and sin not.*

4] 32 *And, behold, you are they who are ordained of me to ordain priests and teachers; to declare my gospel, according to the power of the Holy Ghost which is in you, and according to the callings and gifts of God unto men;*

D&C 18:26-32 — Analysis 18F

4a/4b	General to specific:	**4a-** there are others who are called to declare my gospel, both unto Gentile and unto Jew; **4b-** And, behold, you are they who are ordained of me to ordain priests and teachers; to declare my gospel, according to the power of the Holy Ghost which is in you, and according to the callings and gifts of God unto men;
3a/3b	Parallel concepts:	**3a-** and the Twelve shall be my disciples, and they shall take upon them my name; and the Twelve are they who shall desire to take upon them my name with full purpose of heart. **3b-** And now I speak unto you, the Twelve—Behold, my grace is sufficient for you; you must walk uprightly before me and sin not.
2a/2b	Parallel concepts:	**2a-** they are called to go into all the world to preach my gospel unto every creature.

		2b- you must perform it according to the words which are written.
1a/1b	Parallel concepts:	**1a-** according to that which is written; **1b-** And you have that which is written before you;

DC 20:46-52 Chiasmus 39, 20B

4] 46 *The priest's duty is to preach, teach, expound, exhort, and baptize, and administer the sacrament,*
3] 47 *And visit the house of each member, and exhort them to pray vocally and in secret and attend to all family duties.*
2] 48 *And he may also ordain other priests, teachers, and deacons.*
49 *And he is to take the lead of meetings*
1] *when there is no elder present;*
1] 50 But *when there is an elder present,*
2] *he is only to preach, teach, expound, exhort, and baptize,*
3] 51 *And visit the house of each member, exhorting them to pray vocally and in secret and attend to all family duties.*
4] 52 *In all these duties the priest is to assist the elder if occasion requires.*

DC 20:46-52 Analysis 20B

4a/4b	Parallel concepts:	**4a-** The priest's duty is to preach, teach, expound, exhort, and baptize, and administer the sacrament, **4b-** In all these duties the priest is to assist the elder if occasion requires.
3a/3b	Identical words:	**3-** And visit the house of each member, and exhort/exhorting them to pray vocally and in secret and attend to all family duties.
2a/2b	Permissive to restrictive:	**2a-** And he may also ordain other priests, teachers, and deacons. And he is to take the lead of meetings **2b-** he is only to preach, teach, expound, exhort, and baptize,
1a/1b	Negative to positive:	**1a-** when there is no elder present; **1b-** when there is an elder present,

D&C 22:1-4 **Chiasmus 40, 22A**

4] 1 Behold, I say unto you that all old covenants have I caused to be done away in this thing; and *this is a new and an everlasting covenant,*
3] *even that which was from the beginning.*
2] 2 Wherefore, although a man should be baptized an hundred times it availeth him nothing, *for you cannot enter in at the strait gate by the law of Moses,*
1] *neither by your dead works.*
1] 3 For it is *because of your dead works*
2] that *I have caused this last covenant and this church to be built up unto me,*
3] *even as in days of old.*
4] 4 *Wherefore, enter ye in at the gate,* as I have commanded, and seek not to counsel your God. Amen.

D&C 22:1-4 **Analysis 22A**

4a/4b	General to specific:	**4a-** this is a new and an everlasting covenant, **4b-** Wherefore, enter ye in at the gate,
3a/3b	Parallel concepts:	**3a-** even that which was from the beginning. **3b-** even as in days of old.
2a/2b	Old vs new:	**2a-** for you cannot enter in at the strait gate by the law of Moses, **2b-** I have caused this last covenant and this church to be built up unto me,
1a/1b	Identical words:	**1-** (neither by)/(because of) your dead works.

D&C 24:1-8 **Chiasmus 41, 24A**

4] 1 Behold, thou wast called and chosen to write the Book of Mormon, and to my ministry; and *I have lifted thee up out of thine afflictions, and have counseled thee, that thou hast been delivered from all thine enemies, and thou hast been delivered from the powers of Satan and from darkness!*
3] 2 Nevertheless, thou art not excusable in thy transgressions; nevertheless, go thy way and sin no more.
3 *Magnify thine office; and after thou hast sowed thy fields and secured them, go speedily unto the church which is in Colesville, Fayette, and*

Manchester, and they shall support thee; and I will bless them both spiritually and temporally;

2] 4 But if they receive thee not, *I will send upon them a cursing instead of a blessing.*

1] 5 And thou shalt continue in calling upon God in my name, and writing the things which shall be given thee by the Comforter, and expounding all scriptures unto the church.

2] 6 And it shall be given thee in the very moment what thou shalt speak and write, and they shall hear it, or *I will send unto them a cursing instead of a blessing.*

3] 7 *For thou shalt devote all thy service in Zion; and in this thou shalt have strength.*

4] 8 *Be patient in afflictions, for thou shalt have many; but endure them, for, lo, I am with thee, even unto the end of thy days.*

D&C 24:1-8 — Analysis 24A

4a/4b	Past to future:	**4a-** and I have lifted thee up out of thine afflictions, and have counseled thee, that thou hast been delivered from all thine enemies, and thou hast been delivered from the powers of Satan and from darkness! **4b-** Be patient in afflictions, for thou shalt have many; but endure them, for, lo, I am with thee, even unto the end of thy days.
3a/3b	Specific to general:	**3a-** Magnify thine office; and after thou hast sowed thy fields and secured them, go speedily unto the church which is in Colesville, Fayette, and Manchester, **3b-** For thou shalt devote all thy service in Zion; and in this thou shalt have strength.
2a/2b	Identical words:	**2-** I will send upon/unto them a cursing instead of a blessing.
1	Central theme:	**1-** And thou shalt continue in calling upon God in my name, and writing the things which shall be given thee by the Comforter, and expounding all scriptures unto the church.

D&C 27:6,7 **Chiasmus 43, 27A**

4] 6 And also with *Elias*, to whom I have committed the keys of bringing to pass the restoration of all things spoken by the mouth of all the holy prophets since the world began, concerning the last days;
3] 7 And also *John*
2] *the son*
1] of *Zacharias,*
1] which *Zacharias*
2] he (Elias) visited and gave promise that he should have *a son*,
3] and his name should be *John,*
4] and he should be filled with the spirit of *Elias;*

D&C 27:6,7 **Analysis 27A**

4a/4b	Same person:	**4-** Elias
3a/3b	Same person:	**3-** John
2b/2b	Same person:	**2-** son
1a/1b	Same person:	**1-** Zacharias

D&C 29:30-31 **Chiasmus 47, 29C**

4] in *all things whatsoever*
3] *I*
2] have *created* by the word of my power,
1] which is *the power of my Spirit.*
1] 31 For by *the power of my Spirit*
2] *created*
3] *I* them;
4] yea, *all things both spiritual and temporal—*

D&C 29:30-31 **Analysis 29C**

4a/4b	Parallel concepts:	**4a-** all things whatsoever
		4b- all things both spiritual and temporal
3a/3b	Identical word:	**3-** I
2a/2b	Identical word:	**2-** created
1a/1b	Identical word:	**1-** the power of my Spirit.

D&C 33:2-11 **Chiasmus 50, 33A**

4] 2 For verily, verily, I say unto you that *ye are called to lift up your voices as with the sound of a trump, to declare my gospel unto a crooked and perverse generation.*

3] 3 For behold, *the field is white already to harvest;*

2] *and it is the eleventh hour, and the last time that I shall call laborers into my vineyard.*

1] 4 *And my vineyard has become corrupted every whit; and there is none which doeth good save it be a few; and they err in many instances because of priestcrafts, all having corrupt minds.*

1] 5 *And verily, verily, I say unto you, that this church have I established and called forth out of the wilderness.*

2] 6 *And even so will I gather mine elect from the four quarters of the earth, even as many as will believe in me, and hearken unto my voice.*

3] 7 Yea, verily, verily, I say unto you, that *the field is white already to harvest*; wherefore, thrust in your sickles, and reap with all your might, mind, and strength.

4] 8 *Open your mouths and they shall be filled*, and you shall become even as Nephi of old, who journeyed from Jerusalem in the wilderness.
9 *Yea, open your mouths and spare not*, and you shall be laden with sheaves upon your backs, for lo, I am with you.
10 *Yea, open your mouths and they shall be filled, saying: Repent, repent, and prepare ye the way of the Lord, and make his paths straight; for the kingdom of heaven is at hand;*
11 Yea, repent and be baptized, every one of you, for a remission of your sins; yea, be baptized even by water, and then cometh the baptism of fire and of the Holy Ghost.

D&C 33:2-11 **Analysis 33A**

4a/4b Parallel concepts: **4a-** ye are called to lift up your voices as with the sound of a trump, to declare my gospel unto a crooked and perverse generation
4b- Open your mouths and they shall be filled,—Yea, open your mouths and spare not—Yea, open your mouths and they shall be filled, saying: Repent, repent, and prepare ye the way of the Lord, and make

		his paths straight; for the kingdom of heaven is at hand;—Yea, repent and be baptized, every one of you, for a remission of your sins; yea, be baptized even by water, and then cometh the baptism of fire and of the Holy Ghost.
3a/3b	Identical words:	**3-** the field is white already to harvest
2a/2b	Parallel concepts:	**2a-** and it is the eleventh hour, and the last time that I shall call laborers into my vineyard **2b-** And even so will I gather mine elect from the four quarters of the earth, even as many as will believe in me, and hearken unto my voice
1a/1b	Negative to positive:	**1a-** And my vineyard has become corrupted every whit; and there is none which doeth good save it be a few; and they err in many instances because of priestcrafts, all having corrupt minds **1b-** And verily, verily, I say unto you, that this church have I established and called forth out of the wilderness.

D&C 38:16-22 — Chiasmus 54, 38B

4] 16 And for your salvation I give unto you a commandment, for *I have heard your prayers,* and the poor have complained before me, and the rich have I made,

3] *and all flesh is mine, and I am no respecter of persons.*

2] 17 And I have made the earth rich, and behold it is my footstool, wherefore, again I will stand upon it.
18 *And I hold forth and deign to give unto you greater riches, even a land of promise, a land flowing with milk and honey, upon which there shall be no curse when the Lord cometh;*

1] 19 *And I will give it unto you for the land of your inheritance,* if you seek it with all your hearts.

1] 20 And this shall be my covenant with you, *ye shall have it for the land of your inheritance,* and for the inheritance of your children forever, while the earth shall stand,

2] *and ye shall possess it again in eternity, no more to pass away.*

3] 21 But, verily I say unto you that in time ye shall have no king nor ruler, for *I will be your king and watch over you.*

4] 22 Wherefore, *hear my voice and follow me,* and you shall be a free people, and ye shall have no laws but my laws when I come, for I am your lawgiver, and what can stay my hand?

D&C 38:16-22 — Analysis 38B

4a/4b	Past to future:	**4a-** I have heard your prayers, **4b-** hear my voice and follow me,
3a/3b	Parallel concepts:	**3a-** and all flesh is mine, and I am no respecter of persons. **3b-** I will be your king and watch over you.
2a/2b	Parallel concepts:	**2a-** And I hold forth and deign to give unto you greater riches, even a land of promise, a land flowing with milk and honey, upon which there shall be no curse when the Lord cometh; **2b-** and ye shall possess it again in eternity, no more to pass away.
1a/1b	Parallel concepts:	**1a-** And I will give it unto you for the land of your inheritance, **1b-** ye shall have it for the land of your inheritance,

D&C 39:10-15 — Chiasmus 55, 39A

4] 10 *But, behold, the days of thy deliverance are come,* if thou wilt hearken to my voice, which saith unto thee:

3] Arise and be baptized, and wash away your sins, calling on my name, *and you shall receive my Spirit, and a blessing so great as you never have known.*

2] 11 And if thou do this, I have prepared thee for a greater work. *Thou shalt preach the fulness of my gospel, which I have sent forth in these last days,* the covenant which I have sent forth to recover my people, which are of the house of Israel.

1] 12 *And it shall come to pass that power shall rest upon thee;* thou shalt have great faith, and I will be with thee and go before thy face.

1] 13 *Thou art called to labor in my vineyard, and to build up my church, and to bring forth Zion,* that it may rejoice upon the hills and flourish.

2] 14 *Behold, verily, verily, I say unto thee, thou art not called to go into the eastern countries, but thou art called to go to the Ohio.*

3] 15 And inasmuch as my people shall assemble themselves at the Ohio, *I have kept in store a blessing such as is not known among the children of men,* and it shall be poured forth upon their heads.

4] *And from thence men shall go forth into all nations.*

D&C 39:10-15 — Analysis 39A

4a/4b	Parallel concepts:	**4a-** But, behold, the days of thy deliverance are come, **4b-** And from thence men shall go forth into all nations.
3a/3b	Parallel concepts:	**3a-** and you shall receive my Spirit, and a blessing so great as you never have known. **3b-** I have kept in store a blessing such as is not known among the children of men,
2a/2b	General to specific:	**2a-** Thou shalt preach the fulness of my gospel, which I have sent forth in these last days, **2b-** Behold, verily, verily, I say unto thee, thou art not called to go into the eastern countries, but thou art called to go to the Ohio.
1a/1b	Parallel concepts:	**1a-** And it shall come to pass that power shall rest upon thee; **1b-** Thou art called to labor in my vineyard, and to build up my church, and to bring forth Zion,

D&C 39:19-23 — Chiasmus 56, 39B

4] 19 Wherefore, go forth, crying with a loud voice, saying: *The kingdom of heaven is at hand;* crying: Hosanna! blessed be the name of the Most High God.

3] 20 *Go forth baptizing with water,*

2] *preparing the way before my face for the time of my coming;*

1] 21 For the time is at hand; the day or the hour no man knoweth; but it surely shall come.

2] 22 And he that receiveth these things receiveth me; *and they shall be gathered unto me in time and in eternity.*

3] 23 And again, it shall come to pass that *on as many as ye shall baptize with water,* ye shall lay your hands, and they shall receive the gift of the Holy Ghost,

4] *and shall be looking forth for the signs of my coming,* and shall know me.

D&C 39:19-23 **Analysis 39B**

4a/4b	Parallel concepts:	**4a-** The kingdom of heaven is at hand; **4b-** and shall be looking forth for the signs of my coming,
3a/3b	Parallel concepts:	**3a-** Go forth baptizing with water, **3b-** on as many as ye shall baptize with water,
2a/2b	Cause to effect:	**2a-** preparing the way before my face for the time of my coming; **2b-** and they shall be gathered unto me in time and in eternity.
1	Central theme:	**1-** For the time is at hand; the day or the hour no man knoweth; but it surely shall come.

D&C 45:67-70 Chiasmus 71, 45E

4] 67 *And the glory of the Lord shall be there, and the terror of the Lord also shall be there,*

3] insomuch that *the wicked will not come unto it,* and it shall be called Zion.

2] 68 *And it shall come to pass among the wicked, that every man that will not take his sword against his neighbor must needs flee unto Zion for safety.*

1] 69 And there shall be gathered unto it out of every nation under heaven;

2] *and it shall be the only people that shall not be at war one with another.*

3] 70 *And it shall be said among the wicked: Let us not go up to battle against Zion,*

4] *for the inhabitants of Zion are terrible; wherefore we cannot stand.*

D&C 45:67-70 **Analysis 45E**

4a/4b	Parallel concepts:	**4a-** And the glory of the Lord shall be there, and the terror of the Lord also shall be there, **4b-** for the inhabitants of Zion are terrible; wherefore we cannot stand.
3a/3b	Parallel concepts:	**3a-** the wicked will not come unto it, **3b-** And it shall be said among the wicked: Let us not go up to battle against Zion,
2a/2b	Parallel concepts:	**2a-** And it shall come to pass among the wicked, that every man that will not take his sword against his neighbor must needs flee unto Zion for safety. **2b-** and it shall be the only people that shall not be at war one with another.
1	Central theme:	**1-** And there shall be gathered unto it out of every nation under heaven;

D&C 50:32-35 **Chiasmus 76, 50C**

4] 32 *And it shall be given unto you, power over that spirit;*
3] *and you shall proclaim against that spirit with a loud voice that it is not of God—*
33 Not with railing accusation, that ye be not overcome, neither with boasting nor rejoicing, lest you be seized therewith.
2] 34 *He that receiveth of God,*
1] *let him account it of God;*
1] and let him rejoice that *he is accounted of God*
2] *worthy to receive.*
3] 35 *And by giving heed and doing these things which ye have received,* and which ye shall hereafter receive—
4] *and the kingdom is given you of the Father, and power to overcome all things which are not ordained of him—*

D&C 50:32-35 **Analysis 50C**

4a/4b	Parallel concepts:	**4a-** And it shall be given unto you, power over that spirit; **4b-** and the kingdom is given you of the Father, and power to overcome all things which are not ordained of him—

3a/3b	Specific to general:	**3a-** and you shall proclaim against that spirit with a loud voice that it is not of God— **3b-** And by giving heed and doing these things which ye have received,
2a/2b	Parallel concepts:	**2a-** He that receiveth of God, **2b-** worthy to receive.
1a/1b	Parallel concepts:	**1a-** let him accout it of God; **1b-** he is accounted of God

D&C 51:3-7 — Chiasmus 79, 51A

4] 3 Wherefore, let my servant Edward Partridge, and those whom he has chosen, in whom I am well pleased, *appoint unto this people their portions,* every man equal according to his family, according to his circumstances and his wants and needs.

3] 4 And let my servant Edward Partridge, when he shall appoint a man his portion, *give unto him a writing that shall secure unto him*

2] *his portion,* that he shall hold it, even this right and this inheritance in the church,

1] *until he transgresses and is not accounted worthy by the voice of the church,* according to the laws and covenants of the church, to belong to the church.

1] 5 And *if he shall transgress and is not accounted worthy to belong to the church,*

2] he shall not have power to claim *that portion* which he has consecrated unto the bishop for the poor and needy of my church;

3] therefore, he shall not retain the gift, *but shall only have claim on that portion that is deeded unto him.*
6 And thus all things shall be made sure, according to the laws of the land.

4] 7 *And let that which belongs to this people be appointed unto this people.*

D&C 51:3-7 — Analysis 51A

4a/4b	Parallel concepts:	**4a-** appoint unto this people their portions, **4b-** And let that which belongs to this people be appointed unto this people.
3a/3b	Parallel concepts:	**3a-** give unto him a writing that shall secure unto him

		3b- but shall only have claim on that portion that is deeded unto him.
2a/2b	Parallel concepts:	**2a-** his portion, **2b-** that portion
1a/1b	Parallel concepts:	**1a-** until he transgresses and is not accounted worthy by the voice of the church, **1b-** if he shall transgress and is not accounted worthy to belong to the church,

D&C 54:1-8 — Chiasmus 81, 54A

1 Behold, thus saith the Lord, even Alpha and Omega, the beginning and the end, even he who was crucified for the sins of the world—

4] 2 Behold, verily, verily, I say unto you, my servant Newel Knight, *you shall stand fast in the office whereunto I have appointed you.*

3] 3 *And if your brethren desire to escape their enemies*, let them repent of all their sins, and become truly humble before me and contrite.

2] 4 *And as the covenant which they made unto me has been broken, even so it has become void and of none effect.*

1] 5 And wo to him by whom this offense cometh, for it had been better for him that he had been drowned in the depth of the sea.

2] 6 *But blessed are they who have kept the covenant and observed the commandment, for they shall obtain mercy.*

3] 7 Wherefore, *go to now and flee the land, lest your enemies come upon you*; and take your journey, and appoint whom you will to be your leader, and to pay moneys for you.

4] 8 And thus *you shall take your journey into the regions westward, unto the land of Missouri, unto the borders of the Lamanites.*

D&C 54:1-8 — Analysis 54A

4a/4b	Parallel concepts:	**4a-** you shall stand fast in the office where-unto I have appointed you. **4b-** you shall take your journey into the regions westward, unto the land of Missouri, unto the borders of the Lamanites.
3a/3b	Parallel concepts:	**3a-** And if your brethren desire to escape their enemies, **3b-** go to now and flee the land, lest your enemies come upon you;

2a/2b	Negative to positive:	**2a-** And as the covenant which they made unto me has been broken, even so it has become void and of none effect. **2b-** But blessed are they who have kept the covenant and observed the commandment, for they shall obtain mercy.
1	Central theme:	**1-** And wo to him by whom this offense cometh, for it had been better for him that he had been drowned in the depth of the sea.

D&C 64:2-4 — Chiasmus 95, 64B

4] 2 For verily I say unto you, *I will that ye should overcome the world*;
3] wherefore *I will have compassion upon you.*
2] 3 *There are those among you who have sinned*;
1] but verily I say, for this once, for mine own glory, and for the salvation of souls,
2] *I have forgiven you your sins.*
3] 4 *I will be merciful unto you,*
4] for *I have given unto you the kingdom.*

D&C 64:2-4 — Analysis 64B

4a/4b	Parallel concepts:	**4a-** I will that you should overcome the world; **4b-** I have given unto you the kingdom.
3a/3b	Parallel concepts:	**3a-** I will have compassion upon you, **3b-** I will be merciful unto you,
2a/2b	Negative to positive:	**2a-** There are those among you who have sinned; **2b-** I have forgiven you your sins.
1	Central theme:	**1-** but verily I say, for this once, for mine own glory, and for the salvation of souls, (I have forgiven you your sins.)

D&C 76:11-27 — Chiasmus 109, 76B

4] 11 We, Joseph Smith, Jun., and Sidney Rigdon, being in the Spirit on the sixteenth day of February, in the year of our Lord one thousand eight hundred and thirty-two—

12 By the power of the Spirit *our eyes were opened and our understandings were enlightened, so as to see and understand the things of God—*

D&C 76:13[1] **Chiasmus 110, 76C**

13 Even those things
a3] which were *from the beginning* before the world was,
a2] which were ordained *of the Father,*
a1] through his Only Begotten Son,
a2] who was in the bosom *of the Father,*
a3] even *from the beginning;*
3] 14 *Of whom we bear record; and the record which we bear is the fulness of the gospel of Jesus Christ, who is the Son,*
2] *whom we saw and with whom we conversed in the heavenly vision.*
1] 15 For while we were doing the work of translation, which the Lord had appointed unto us, we came to the twenty-ninth verse of the fifth chapter of John, which was given unto us as follows:
16 Speaking of the resurrection of the dead, concerning those who shall hear the voice of the Son of Man, and shall come forth—
17 They who have done good in the resurrection of the just, and they who have done evil in the resurrection of the unjust—
18 Now this caused us to marvel, for it was given unto us of the Spirit.
19 *And while we meditated upon these things, the Lord touched the eyes of our understandings and they were opened, and the glory of the Lord shone round about.*
20 *And we beheld the glory of the Son, on the right hand of the Father, and received of his fulness;*
21 *And saw the holy angels, and them who are sanctified before his throne, worshiping God, and the Lamb, who worship him forever and ever.*
22 And now, after the many testimonies which have been given of him, this is the testimony, last of all, which we give of him: That he lives!

---

hapter 6, p. 96.

2] *For we saw him, even on the right hand of God;*
3] 23 *and we heard the voice bearing record that he is the Only Begotten of the Father—*
24 *That by him, and through him, and of him, the worlds are and were created, and the inhabitants thereof are begotten sons and daughters unto God.*
4] 25 *And this we saw also,* and bear record, that an angel of God who was in authority in the presence of God, who rebelled against the Only Begotten Son whom the Father loved and who was in the bosom of the Father, was thrust down from the presence of God and the Son,
26 And was called Perdition, for the heavens wept over him—he was Lucifer,

D&C 76:11-27 **Analysis 76B**

4a/4b	Parallel concepts:	**4a-** our eyes were opened and our understandings were enlightened, so as to see and understand the things of God— **4b-** And this we saw also,
3a/3b	Parallel concepts:	**3a-** Of whom we bear record; and the record which we bear is the fulness of the gospel of Jesus Christ, who is the Son, **3b-** and we heard the voice bearing record that he is the Only Begotten of the Father— That by him, and through him, and of him, the worlds are and were created, and the inhabitants thereof are begotten sons and daughters unto God.
2a/2b	Parallel concepts:	**2a-** whom we saw and with whom we conversed in the heavenly vision. **2b-** For we say him, even on the right hand of God;
1	Central theme:	**1-** And while we meditated upon these things, the Lord touched the eyes of our understandings and they were opened, and the glory of the Lord shone round about. And we beheld the glory of the Son, on the right hand of the Father, and received of his fulness; And saw the holy angels, and them who are sanctified before his

throne, worshiping God, and the Lamb, who worship him forever and ever.

NOTE: A three-element chiasmus exists in element 4a of Chiasmus 76B, the analysis of which follows:

D&C 76:13 **Analysis 76C**

a3	Identical words:	**3-** from the beginning
a2	Identical words:	**2-** of the Father,
a1	Central theme:	**1-** through his Only Begotten Son,

D&C 84:62-64 **Chiasmus 129, 84D**

x4] 62 *Therefore, go ye into all the world; and unto whatsoever place ye cannot go ye shall send, that the testimony may go from you into all the world unto every creature.*
3] 63 And *as I said unto mine apostles*, even so *I say unto you,*
2] *for you are mine apostles,* even God's high priests;
1] ye are they whom my Father hath given me;
2] *ye are my friends;*
3] 64 Therefore, *as I said unto mine apostles I say unto you* again,
4] *that every soul who believeth on your words, and is baptized by water for the remission of sins, shall receive the Holy Ghost.*

D&C 84:62-64 **Analysis 84D**

4a/4b	Cause to effect:	**4a-** Therefore, go ye into all the world; and unto whatsoever place ye cannot go ye shall send, that the testimony may go from you into all the world unto every creature. **4b-** that every soul who believeth on your words, and is baptized by water for the remission of sins, shall receive the Holy Ghost.
3a/3b	Identical words:	**3-** as I said unto mine apostles . . . I say unto you,
2a/2b	Parallel concepts:	**2a-** for you are mine apostles, **2b-** ye are my friends;
1	Central theme:	**1-** ye are they whom my Father hath given me;

D&C 89:13-15 **Chiasmus 145, 89A**

4] 13 And it is pleasing unto me that they should not be used, *only in times of winter, or of cold,*

3] or *famine.*

2] 14 All grain is ordained *for the use of man* and of beasts,

1] to be the staff of life, not only for man but for the beasts of the field, and the fowls of heaven, and all wild animals that run or creep on the earth;

2] 15 And these hath God made *for the use of man*

3] only in times of *famine*

4] *and excess of hunger.*

D&C 89:13-15 **Analysis 89A**

4a/4b	Parallel concepts:	**4a-** only in times of winter, or of cold, **4b-** and excess of hunger.
3a/3b	Identical word:	**3-** famine
2a/2b	Identical words:	**2-** for the use of man
1	Central theme:	**1-** to be the staff of life, not only for man but for the beasts of the field, and the fowls of heaven, and all wild animals that run or creep on the earth;

D&C 97:18-23 **Chiasmus 163, 97D**

4] 18 *And, now, behold, if Zion do these things she shall prosper, and spread herself and become very glorious, very great, and very terrible.*

3] 19 *And the nations of the earth shall honor her, and shall say: Surely Zion is the city of our God, and surely Zion cannot fall, neither be moved out of her place, for God is there, and the hand of the Lord is there;*

20 And he hath sworn by the power of his might to be her salvation and her high tower.

2] 21 *Therefore, verily, thus saith the Lord, let Zion rejoice,*

1] for this is Zion—THE PURE IN HEART;

2] *therefore, let Zion rejoice,* while all the wicked shall mourn.

3] 22 *For behold, and lo, vengeance cometh speedily upon the ungodly as the whirlwind; and who shall escape it?*

4] 23 *The Lord's scourge shall pass over by night and by day, and the report thereof shall vex all people;* yea, it shall not be stayed until the Lord come;

D&C 97:18-23 **Analysis 97D**

4a/4b	Positive to negative:	**4a-** And, now, behold, if Zion do these things she shall prosper, and spread herself and become very glorious, very great, and very terrible. **4b-** The Lord's scourge shall pass over by night and by day, and the report thereof shall vex all people;
3a/3b	Positive to negative:	**3a-** And the nations of the earth shall honor her, and shall say: Surely Zion is the city of our God, and surely Zion cannot fall, neither be moved out of her place, for God is there, and the hand of the Lord is there; **3b-** For behold, and lo, vengeance cometh speedily upon the ungodly as the whirlwind; and who shall escape it?
2a/2b	Identical words:	**2-** Therefore, (verily, thus saith the Lord,) let Zion rejoice,
1	Central theme:	**1-** for this is Zion—THE PURE IN HEART;

D&C 101:2-6 **Chiasmus 169, 101A**

4] 2 *I, the Lord, have suffered the affliction to come upon them, wherewith they have been afflicted,*
3] *in consequence of their transgressions;*
2] 3 *Yet I will own them, and they shall be mine in that day when I shall come to make up my jewels.*
1] 4 Therefore, they must needs be chastened and tried, even as Abraham, who was commanded to offer up his only son.
2] 5 *For all those who will not endure chastening, but deny me, cannot be sanctified.*
3] 6 *Behold, I say unto you, there were jarrings, and contentions, and envyings, and strifes, and lustful and covetous desires among them;*
4] *therefore by these things they polluted their inheritances.*

D&C 101:2-6 **Analysis 101A**

4a/4b	Effect to cause:	**4a-** I, the Lord, have suffered the affliction to come upon them, wherewith they have been afflicted, **4b-** therefore by these things they polluted their inheritances
3a/3b	General to specific:	**3a-** in consequence of their transgressions; **3b-** Behold, I say unto you, there were jarrings, and contentions, and envyings, and strifes, and lustful and covetous desires among them;
2a/2b	Positive to negative:	**2a-** Yet I will own them, and they shall be mine in that day when I shall come to make up my jewels **2b-** For all those who will not endure chastening, but deny me, cannot be sanctified.
1	Central theme:	**1-** Therefore, they must needs be chastened and tried, even as Abraham, who was commanded to offer up his only son.

D&C 104:54-57 **Chiasmus 182, 104D**

4] 54 *And again, a commandment I give unto you concerning your stewardship*
3] which *I have appointed unto you.*
2] 55 *Behold, all these properties are mine,*
1] or else your faith is vain, and ye are found hypocrites, and the covenants which ye have made unto me are broken;
2] 56 *And if the properties are mine,* then ye are stewards; otherwise ye are no stewards.
3] 57 But, verily I say unto you, *I have appointed unto you*
4] *to be stewards over mine house, even stewards indeed.*

D&C 104:54-57 **Analysis 104D**

4a/4b	Parallel concepts:	**4a-** And again, a commandment I give unto you concerning your stewardship **4b-** to be stewards over mine house, even stewards indeed.
3a/3b	Identical words:	**3-** I have appointed unto you

2a/2b	Parallel concepts:	**2a-** Behold, all these properties are mine, **2b-** And if the properties are mine,
1	Central theme:	**1-** or else your faith is vain, and ye are found hypocrites, and the covenants which ye have made unto me are broken;

D&C 105:14 — Chiasmus 186, 105B

4] For behold, I do not require at their hands to *fight the battles of Zion;* for as I said in a former commandment,
3] even so *will*
2] *I*
1] fulfil—
2] *I*
3] *will*
4] *fight your battles.*

D&C 105:14 — Analysis 105B

4a/4b	Parallel concepts:	**4a-** fight the battles of Zion; **4b-** fight your battles.
3a/3b	Identical word:	**3-** will
2a/2b	Identical word:	**2-** I
1	Central theme:	**1-** fulfill—

D&C 107:39-58 — Chiasmus 191, 107E

4] 39 *It is the duty of the Twelve*, in all large branches of the church, *to ordain evangelical ministers, as they shall be designated unto them by revelation—*
40 The order of this priesthood was confirmed to be handed down from father to son, and rightly belongs to the literal descendants of the chosen seed, to whom the promises were made.
41 This order was instituted in the days of Adam, and came down by lineage in the following manner:
3] 42 From Adam to Seth, who was ordained by Adam at the age of sixty-nine years, *and was blessed by him*
2] *three years previous to his (Adam's) death*, and received the promise of God by his father, that his posterity should be the chosen of the Lord, and that they should be preserved unto the end of the earth;
43 Because he (Seth) was a perfect man, and his likeness was the express likeness of his father, insomuch that he seemed to be like

unto his father in all things, and could be distinguished from him only by his age.

1] 44 Enos was ordained at the age of one hundred and thirty-four years and four months, by the hand of Adam.

45 God called upon Cainan in the wilderness in the fortieth year of his age; and he met Adam in journeying to the place Shedolamak. He was eighty-seven years old when he received his ordination.

46 Mahalaleel was four hundred and ninety-six years and seven days old when he was ordained by the hand of Adam, who also blessed him.

47 Jared was two hundred years old when he was ordained under the hand of Adam, who also blessed him.

48 Enoch was twenty-five years old when he was ordained under the hand of Adam; and he was sixty-five and Adam blessed him.

49 And he saw the Lord, and he walked with him, and was before his face continually; and he walked with God three hundred and sixty-five years, making him four hundred and thirty years old when he was translated.

50 Methuselah was one hundred years old when he was ordained under the hand of Adam.

51 Lamech was thirty-two years old when he was ordained under the hand of Seth.

52 Noah was ten years old when he was ordained under the hand of Methuselah.

2] 53 *Three years previous to the death of Adam*, he called Seth, Enos, Cainan, Mahalaleel, Jared, Enoch, and Methuselah, who were all high priests, with the residue of his posterity who were righteous, into the valley of Adam-ondi-Ahman,

3] *and there bestowed upon them his last blessing.*

54 And the Lord appeared unto them, and they rose up and blessed Adam, and called him Michael, the prince, the archangel.

55 And the Lord administered comfort unto Adam, and said unto him: I have set thee to be at the head; a multitude of nations shall come of thee, and thou art a prince over them forever.

56 And Adam stood up in the midst of the congregation; and, notwithstanding he was bowed down with age, being full of the Holy

Ghost, predicted whatsoever should befall his posterity unto the latest generation.
57 These things were all written in the book of Enoch, and are to be testified of in due time.
4] 58 *It is the duty of the Twelve, also, to ordain and set in order all the other officers of the church, agreeable to the revelation* which says:
59 To the church of Christ in the land of Zion, in addition to the church laws respecting church business—

D&C 107:39-58 — Analysis 107E

4a/4b	Parallel concepts:	**4a-** It is the duty of the Twelve...to ordain evangelical ministers, as they shall be designated unto them by revelation— **4b-** It is the duty of the Twelve, also, to ordain and set in order all the other officers of the church, agreeable to the revelation
3a/3b	Parallel concepts:	**3a-** and was blessed by him **3b-** and there bestowed upon them his last blessing.
2a/2b	Parallel concepts:	**2a-** three years previous to his (Adam's) death, **2b-** Three years previous to the death of Adam,
1	Central theme:	**1-** (The ordinations of the pre-deluvial prophets.)

D&C 107:60-63 — Chiasmus 192, 107F

4] 60 Verily, I say unto you, saith the Lord of Hosts, there must needs be presiding elders to preside over *those who are of the office of an elder;*
3] 61 And also *priests to preside over those who are of the office of a priest;*
2] 62 And also *teachers to preside over those who are of the office of a teacher,*
1] in like manner, and also the *deacons*—
1] 63 Wherefore, from *deacon*
2] *to teacher, and from teacher*
3] *to priest, and from priest*
4] *to elder*, severally as they are appointed, according to the covenants and commandments of the church.

D&C 107:60-63 **Analysis 107F**

4a/4b	Parallel concepts:	**4a-** those who are of the office of an elder; **4b-** to elder,
3a/3b	Parallel concepts:	**3a-** priests to preside over those who are of the office of a priest; **3b-** to priest, and from priest
2a/2b	Parallel concepts:	**2a-** teachers to preside over those who are of the office of a teacher, **2b-** to teacher, and from teacher
1a/1b	Identical word:	**1-** deacon(s)

D&C 107:64-67 **Chiasmus 193, 107G**

4] 64 *Then comes the High Priesthood, which is the greatest of all.*
3] 65 Wherefore, it must needs be that one be appointed of *the High Priesthood*
2] *to preside over the priesthood,*
1] and he shall be called President of the High Priesthood of the Church,
2] 66 *Or, in other words, the Presiding High Priest*
3] over *the High Priesthood* of the Church.
4] 67 *From the same comes the administering of ordinances and blessings upon the church, by the laying on of the hands.*

D&C 107:64-67 **Analysis 107G**

4a/4b	Parallel concepts:	**4a-** Then comes the High Priesthood, which is the greatest of all. **4b-** From the same comes the administering of ordinances and blessings upon the church, by the laying on of the hands.
3a/3b	Identical words:	**3-** the High Priesthood
2a/2b	Parallel concepts:	**2a-** to preside over the priesthood, **2b-** Or, in other words, the High Priesthood
1	Central theme:	**1-** and he shall be called President of the High Priesthood of the Church,

D&C 109:2-4 **Chiasmus 197, 109A**

4] 2 *Thou who hast commanded thy servants to build*
3] *a house to thy name* in this place [Kirtland].
3 And now thou beholdest, O Lord, that thy servants have done according to thy commandment.
2] 4 And now *we ask thee, Holy Father,*
1] in the name of Jesus Christ, the Son of thy bosom, in whose name alone salvation can be administered to the children of men,
2] *we ask thee, O Lord,*
3] *to accept of this house,* the workmanship of the hands of us, thy servants,
4] *which thou didst command us to build.*

D&C 109:2-4 **Analysis 109A**

4a/4b	Parallel concepts:	**4a-** Thou who hast commanded thy servants to build **4b-** which thou didst command us to build.
3a/3b	Parallel concepts:	**3a-** a house to thy name **3b-** to accept of this house,
2a/2b	Parallel concepts:	**2a-** we ask thee, Holy Father, **2b-** we ask thee, O Lord,
1	Central theme:	**1-** in the name of Jesus Christ, the Son of thy bosom, in whose name alone salvation can be administered to the children of men,

D&C 111:2-10 **Chiasmus 203, 111A**

4] 2 *I have much treasure in this city for you*, for the benefit of Zion, and many people in this city, whom I will gather out in due time for the benefit of Zion, through your instrumentality.
3] 3 *Therefore, it is expedient that you should form acquaintance with men in this city,*
2] *as you shall be led, and as it shall be given you.*
4 And it shall come to pass in due time that I will give this city into your hands, that you shall have power over it, insomuch that they shall not discover your secret parts; and its wealth pertaining to gold and silver shall be yours.

1] 5 *Concern not yourselves about your debts, for I will give you power to pay them.*
1] 6 *Concern not yourselves about Zion, for I will deal mercifully with her.*
7 Tarry in this place, and in the regions round about;
2] 8 And the place where it is my will that you should tarry, for the main, *shall be signalized unto you by the peace and power of my Spirit, that shall flow unto you.*
3] 9 This place you may obtain by hire. *And inquire diligently concerning the more ancient inhabitants and founders of this city;*
4] 10 *For there are more treasures than one for you in this city.*

D&C 111:2-10 — Analysis 111A

4a/4b	Parallel concepts:	**4a-** I have much treasure in this city for you, **4b-** For there are more treasures than one for you in this city.
3a/3b	Parallel concepts:	**3a-** Therefore, it is expedient that you should form acquaintance with men in this city, **3b-** And inquire diligently concerning the more ancient inhabitants and founders of this city;
2a/2b	Parallel concepts:	**2a-** as you shall be led, and as it shall be given you. **2b-** shall be signalized unto you by the peace and power of my Spirit, that shall flow unto you.
1a/1b	Parallel concepts:	**1a-** Concern not yourselves about your debts, for I will give you power to pay them. **1b-** Concern not yourselves about Zion, for I will deal mercifully with her.

D&C 112:10-12 — Chiasmus 207, 112D

4] 10 *Be thou humble*; and the Lord thy God shall lead thee by the hand, and give thee answer to thy prayers.
3] 11 *I* know thy heart, and *have heard thy prayers concerning thy brethren.*

2] *Be not partial towards them*
1] *in love* above many others,
1] but let *thy love*
2] *be for them as for thyself;* and let thy love abound unto all men, and unto all who love my name.
3] 12 *And pray for thy brethren of the Twelve.* Admonish them sharply for my name's sake, and let them be admonished for all their sins,
4] and *be ye faithful* before me unto my name.

D&C 112:10-12 — Analysis 112D

4a/4b	Parallel concepts:	**4a-** Be thou humble **4b-** be ye faithful
3a/3b	Parallel concepts:	**3a-** I...have heard thy prayers concerning thy brethren. **3b-** And pray for thy brethren of the Twelve.
2a/2b	Parallel concepts:	**2a-** Be not partial towards them **2b-** be for them as for thyself;
1a/1b	Parallel concepts:	**1a-** in love **1b-** thy love

D&C 124:49-51 — Chiasmus 215, 124D

4] 49 Verily, verily, I say unto you, that when I give a commandment to any of the sons of men to do a work unto my name, and those sons of men go with all their might and with all they have to perform that work, and cease not their diligence, and *their enemies* come upon them
3] *and hinder them* from performing that work,
2] behold, it behooveth me to require that work no more at the hands of those sons of men, *but to accept of their offerings.*
1] 50 And the iniquity and transgression of my holy laws and commandments I will visit upon the heads of those who hindered my work, unto the third and fourth generation, so long as they repent not, and hate me, saith the Lord God.
2] 51 Therefore, for this cause *have I accepted the offerings* of those whom I commanded to build up a city and a house unto my name, in Jackson county, Missouri,
3] *and were hindered*
4] by *their enemies*, saith the Lord your God.

D&C 124:49-51 **Analysis 124D**

4a/4b	Identical words:	**4a-** their enemies **4b-** their enemies
3a/3b	Parallel concepts:	**3a-** and hinder them **3b-** and were hindered
2a/2b	Parallel concepts:	**2a-** but to accept of their offerings. **2b-** have I accepted the offerings
1	Central theme:	**1-** And the iniquity and transgression of my holy laws and commandments I will visit upon the heads of those who hindered my work, unto the third and fourth generation, so long as they repent not, and hate me, saith the Lord God.

D&C 133:4-7 **Chiasmus 223, 133A**

4] *gather ye together, O ye people of my church, upon the land of Zion*, all you that have not been commanded to tarry.
3] 5 *Go ye out from Babylon.*
2] *Be ye clean that bear the vessels of the Lord.*
1] 6 Call your solemn assemblies, and speak often one to another.

2] *And let every man call upon the name of the Lord.*
7 Yea, verily I say unto you again, the time has come when the voice of the Lord is unto you:
3] *Go ye out of Babylon*;
4] *gather ye out from among the nations, from the four winds, from one end of heaven to the other.*

D&C 133:4-7 **Analysis 133A**

4a/4b	Parallel concepts:	**4a-** gather ye together, O ye people of my church, upon the land of Zion, **4b-** gather ye out from among the nations, from the four winds, from one end of heaven to the other.
3a/3b	Identical words:	go ye out from/of Babylon
2a/2b	Parallel concepts:	**2a-** Be ye clean that bear the vessels of the Lord. **2b-** And let every man call upon the name of the Lord.
1	Central theme:	**1-** Call your solemn assemblies, and speak often one to another.

D&C 133:8-14 **Chiasmus 224, 133B**

4] 8 *Send forth the elders of my church unto the nations which are afar off; unto the islands of the sea; send forth unto foreign lands;*
3] *call upon all nations,*
2] *first upon the Gentiles, and then upon the Jews.*
1] 9 *And behold, and lo, this shall be their cry, and the voice of the Lord unto all people: Go ye forth unto the land of Zion, that the borders of my people may be enlarged, and that her stakes may be strengthened, and that Zion may go forth unto the regions round about.*
1] 10 *Yea, let the cry go forth among all people: Awake and arise and go forth to meet the Bridegroom; behold and lo, the Bridegroom cometh; go ye out to meet him. Prepare yourselves for the great day of the Lord.*
11 Watch, therefore, for ye know neither the day nor the hour.
2] 12 *Let them, therefore, who are among the Gentiles flee unto Zion.*
13 *And let them who be of Judah flee unto Jerusalem,* unto the mountains of the Lord's house.
3] 14 *Go ye out from among the nations,*
4] *even from Babylon, from the midst of wickedness, which is spiritual Babylon.*

D&C 133:8-14 **Analysis 133B**

4a/4b	Positive to negative:	**4a-** Send forth the elders of my church unto the nations which are afar off; unto the islands of the sea; send forth unto foreign lands; **4b-** even from Babylon, from the midst of wickedness, which is spiritual Babylon.
3a/3b	Positive to negative:	**3a-** call upon all nations, **3b-** Go ye out from among the nations,
2a/2b	Parallel concepts:	**2a-** first upon the Gentiles, and then upon the Jews. **2b-** Let them, therefore, who are among the Gentiles flee unto Zion. And let them who be of Judah flee unto Jerusalem,
1a/1b	Parallel concepts:	**1a-** And behold, and lo, this shall be their cry, and the voice of the Lord unto all

people: Go ye forth unto the land of Zion, that the borders of my people may be enlarged, and that her stakes may be strengthened, and that Zion may go forth unto the regions round about.

1b- Yea, let the cry go forth among all people: Awake and arise and go forth to meet the Bridegroom; behold and lo, the Bridegroom cometh; go ye out to meet him. Prepare yourselves for the great day of the Lord.

Five-Element Chiasma

D&C 7:1-8 — Chiasmus 8, 7A

5] 1 And the Lord said unto me: John, my beloved, *what desirest thou*? For if you shall ask what you will, it shall be granted unto you.

4] 2 *And I said unto him: Lord, give unto me power over death*, that I may live and bring souls unto thee.

3] 3 *And the Lord said unto me: Verily, verily, I say unto thee, because thou desirest this thou shalt tarry until I come in my glory, and shalt prophesy before nations, kindreds, tongues and people.*
4 And for this cause the Lord said unto Peter: If I will that he tarry till I come, what is that to thee?

2] *For he desired of me that he might bring souls unto me,*

1] *but thou desiredst that thou mightest speedily come unto me in my kingdom.*

1] 5 *I say unto thee, Peter, this was a good desire;*

2] *but my beloved has desired that he might do more, or a greater work yet among men than what he has before done.*

3] 6 *Yea, he has undertaken a greater work; therefore I will make him as flaming fire and a ministering angel; he shall minister for those who shall be heirs of salvation who dwell on the earth.*

4] 7 And I will make thee to minister for him and for thy brother James; *and unto you three I will give this power* and the keys of this ministry until I come.

5] 8 Verily I say unto you, *ye shall both have according to your desires*, for ye both joy in that which ye have desired.

D&C 7:1-8 — Analysis 7A

5a/5b	Question/answer:	**5a-** what desirest thou? **5b-** ye shall both have according to your desires,
4a/4b	Parallel concepts:	**4a-** And I said unto him: Lord, give unto me power over death, **4b-** and unto you three I will give this power
3a/3b	Parallel concepts:	**3a-** And the Lord said unto me: Verily, verily, I say unto thee, because thou desirest this thou shalt tarry until I come in

		my glory, and shalt prophesy before nations, kindreds, tongues and people. **3b-** Yea, he has undertaken a greater work; therefore I will make him as flaming fire and a ministering angel; he shall minister for those who shall be heirs of salvation who dwell on the earth.
2a/2b	Parallel concepts:	**2a-** For he desired of me that he might bring souls unto me, **2b-** but my beloved has desired that he might do more, or a greater work yet among men than what he has before done.
1a/1b	Parallel concepts:	**1a-** but thou desiredst that thou mightest speedily come unto me in my kingdom. **1b-** I say unto thee, Peter, this was a good desire;

D&C 10:1-8 — Chiasmus 11, 10A

5] 1 Now, behold, I say unto you, *that because you delivered up those writings* which you had power given unto you to translate by the means of the Urim and Thummim, *into the hands of a wicked man, you have lost them.*

4] 2 *And you also lost your gift* at the same time, and your mind became darkened.

3] 3 *Nevertheless, it is now restored unto you again*;

2] therefore *see that you are faithful* and continue on unto the finishing of the remainder of the work of translation as you have begun.

1] 4 *Do not run faster or labor more than you have strength and means provided to enable you to translate; but be diligent unto the end.*
5 *Pray always, that you may come off conqueror;* yea, that you may conquer Satan, and that you may escape the hands of the servants of Satan that do uphold his work.
6 Behold, they have sought to destroy you; yea, even the man in whom you have trusted has sought to destroy you.

2] 7 And for this cause *I said that he is a wicked man,*

3] *for he has sought to take away the things wherewith you have been entrusted;*

4] *and he has also sought to destroy your gift.*

5] 8 *And because you have delivered the writings into his hands, behold, wicked men have taken them from you.*

D&C 10:1-8 **Analysis 10A**

5a/5b	Parallel concepts:	**5a-** because you delivered up those writings . . . into the hands of a wicked man, you have lost them. **5b-** because you have delivered the writings into his hands, behold, wicked men have taken them from you.
4a/4b	Parallel concepts:	**4a-** and you also lost your gift **4b-** and he has also sought to destroy your gift.
3a/3b	Positive to negative:	**3a-** Nevertheless, it is now restored unto you again; **3b-** for he has sought to take away the things wherewith you have been entrusted;
2a/2b	Positive to negative:	**2a-** see that you are faithful **2b-** I said that he is a wicked man,
1	Central theme:	**1-** Do not run faster or labor more than you have strength and means provided to enable you to translate; but be diligent unto the end. Pray always, that you may come off conqueror;

D&C 18:21-24 **Chiasmus 31, 18E**

5] 21 *Take upon you the name of Christ,* and speak the truth in soberness.
4] 22 *And as many as repent and are baptized*
3] *in my name,*
2] *which is Jesus Christ,*
1] and endure to the end, the same shall be saved.
2] 23 *Behold, Jesus Christ is the name which is given of the Father,*
3] and *there is none other name* given
4] *whereby man can be saved;*
5] 24 Wherefore, *all men must take upon them the name which is given of the Father,* for in that name shall they be called at the last day;

D&C 18:21-24 **Analysis 18E**

5a/5b	Parallel concepts:	**5a-** Take upon you the name of Christ, **5b-** all men must take upon them the name which is given of the Father,

4a/4b	Parallel concepts:	**4a-** And as many as repent and are baptized **4b-** whereby man can be saved;
3a/3b	Parallel concepts:	**3a-** in my name, **3b-** there is none other name
2a/2b	Parallel concepts:	**2a-** which is Jesus Christ, **2b-** Behold, Jesus Christ is the name which is given of the Father,
1	Central theme:	**1-** and endure to the end, the same shall be saved.

D&C 25:4-10 — Chiasmus 42, 25A

5] 4 *Murmur not because of the things which thou hast not seen, for they are withheld from thee and from the world*, which is wisdom in me in a time to come.

4] 5 And *the office of thy calling* shall be for a comfort unto my servant, Joseph Smith, Jun., thy husband, in his afflictions, with consoling words, in the spirit of meekness.

3] 6 And *thou shalt go with him at the time of his going*,

2] *and be unto him for a scribe*, while there is no one to be a scribe for him, that I may send my servant, Oliver Cowdery, whithersoever I will.

1] 7 *And thou shalt be ordained under his hand* to expound scriptures, and to exhort the church, according as it shall be given thee by my Spirit.

1] 8 *For he shall lay his hands upon thee*, and thou shalt receive the Holy Ghost,

2] *and thy time shall be given to writing*, and to learning much.

3] 9 And thou needest not fear, for *thy husband shall support thee in the church*;

4] *for unto them is his calling*, that all things might be revealed unto them, whatsoever I will, according to their faith.

5] 10 *And verily I say unto thee that thou shalt lay aside the things of this world*, and seek for the things of a better.

D&C 25:4-10 — Analysis 25A

5a/5b	Parallel counsel:	**5a-** Murmur not because of the things which thou hast not seen, for they are withheld from thee and from the world,

		5b- And verily I say unto thee that thou shalt lay aside the things of this world,
4a/4b	Parallel concepts:	**4a-** the office of thy calling
		4b- for unto them is his calling,
3a/3b	Reciprocal action:	**3a-** thou shalt go with him at the time of his going,
		3b- thy husband shall support thee in the church;
2a/2b	Parallel concepts:	**2a-** and be unto him for a scribe,
		2b- and thy time shall be given to writing,
1a/1b	Parallel concepts:	**1a-** And thou shalt be ordained under his hand
		1b- For he shall lay his hands upon thee,

D&C 29:1-5 — Chiasmus 45, 29A

5] 1 Listen to the voice of *Jesus Christ,*
4] *your Redeemer,*
3] *the Great I AM,* whose arm of mercy hath atoned for your sins;
2] 2 *Who will gather his people* even as a hen gathereth her chickens under her wings, even as many as will hearken to my voice and humble themselves before me, and call upon me in mighty prayer.
1] 3 Behold, verily, verily, I say unto you, that *at this time your sins are forgiven you,* therefore ye receive these things; but remember to sin no more, lest perils shall come upon you.
2] 4 Verily, I say unto you that *ye are chosen out of the world* to declare my gospel with the sound of rejoicing, as with the voice of a trump.
5 Lift up your hearts and be glad, for I am in your midst,
3] *and am*
4] *your advocate*
5] with *the Father*; and it is his good will to give you the kingdom.

D&C 29:1-5 — Analysis 29A

5a/5b	Parallel concepts:	**5a-** Jesus Christ,
		5b- the Father;
4a/4b	Parallel concepts:	**4a-** your Redeemer,
		4b- your advocate

3a/3b	Identical word:	**3a-** (I) AM **3b-** (and) am
2a/2b	Parallel concepts:	**2a-** Who will gather his people **2b-** ye are chosen out of the world
1	Central theme:	**1-** at this time your sins are forgiven you,

D&C 34:1-12 — Chiasmus 51, 34A

5] 1 My son Orson, hearken and hear and behold what I, the Lord God, shall say unto you, *even Jesus Christ your Redeemer;*
2 The light and the life of the world, a light which shineth in darkness and the darkness comprehendeth it not;
3 Who so loved the world that he gave his own life, that as many as would believe might become the sons of God. Wherefore you are my son;

4] 4 *And blessed are you because you have believed;*
5 And more blessed are you because you are called of me to preach my gospel—

3] 6 To *lift up your voice as with the sound of a trump, both long and loud, and cry repentance unto a crooked and perverse generation,* preparing the way of the Lord for his second coming.

2] 7 For behold, verily, verily, I say unto you, *the time is soon at hand* that I shall come in a cloud with power and great glory.

1] 8 And it shall be a great day at the time of my coming, for all nations shall tremble.

2] 9 *But before that great day shall come,* the sun shall be darkened, and the moon be turned into blood; and the stars shall refuse their shining, and some shall fall, and great destructions await the wicked.

3] 10 Wherefore, *lift up your voice and spare not,* for the Lord God hath spoken; therefore prophesy, and it shall be given by the power of the Holy Ghost.

4] 11 *And if you are faithful, behold, I am with you until I come—*

5] And verily, verily, I say unto you, I come quickly. *I am your Lord and your Redeemer.* Even so. Amen.

D&C 34:1-12 — Analysis 34A

5a/5b	Parallel concepts:	**5a-** even Jesus Christ your Redeemer; **5a-** I am your Lord and your Redeemer.

4a/4b	Parallel concepts:	**4a-** And blessed are you because you have believed; And more blessed are you because you are called of me to preach my gospel— **4b-** And if you are faithful, behold, I am with you until I come—
3a/3b	Parallel concepts:	**3a-** lift up your voice as with the sound of a trump, both long and loud, and cry repentance unto a crooked and perverse generation, **3b-** lift up your voice and spare not,
2a/2b	Parallel concepts:	**2a-** the time is soon at hand **2b-** But before that great day shall come,
1]	Central theme:	**1-** And it shall be a great day at the time of my coming, for all nations shall tremble.

D&C 35:2 — Chiasmus 52, 35A

2 I am Jesus Christ, the Son of God, who was crucified for the sins of the world, even as many as will believe on my name, that they may become the sons of God,

5] even *one*
4] in *me*
3] as *I*
2] am *one*
1] in *the Father,*
1] as *the Father*
2] is *one*
3] in *me*,
4] that *we*
5] may be *one*.

D&C 35:2 — Analysis 35A

5a/5b	Identical word:	**5-** one
4a/4b	Parallel concepts:	**4a-** me **4b-** we
3a/3b	Parallel concepts:	**3a-** I **3b-** me
2a/2b	Identical word:	**2-** one
1a/1b	Identical word:	**1-** the Father,

D&C 42:31-33 **Chiasmus 61, 42C**

5] 31 *And inasmuch as ye impart of your substance unto the poor, ye will do it unto me;* and they shall be laid before the bishop of my church and his counselors, two of the elders, or high priests, such as he shall appoint or has appointed and set apart for that purpose.

4] 32 And it shall come to pass, *that after they are laid before the bishop of my church,*

3] and after that he has received these testimonies *concerning the consecration of the properties of my church,*

2] *that they cannot be taken from the church,* agreeable to my commandments,

1] every man shall be made accountable unto me, a steward over his own property, or that which he has received by consecration, as much as is sufficient for himself and family.

2] 33 And again, *if there shall be properties in the hands of the church,* or any individuals of it, more than is necessary for their support

3] *after this first consecration,*

4] *which is a residue to be consecrated unto the bishop,*

5] *it shall be kept to administer to those who have not, from time to time, that every man who has need may be amply supplied and receive according to his wants.*

D&C 42:31-33 **Analysis 42C**

5a/5b	Parallel concepts:	**5a-** And inasmuch as ye impart of your substance unto the poor, ye will do it unto me; **5b-** it shall be kept to administer to those who have not, from time to time, that every man who has need may be amply supplied and receive according to his wants.
4a/4b	Parallel concepts:	**4a-** that after they are laid before the bishop of my church, **4b-** which is a residue to be consecrated unto the bishop,
3a/3b	Parallel concepts:	**3a-** concerning the consecration of the properties of my church, **3b-** after this first consecration,
2a/2b	Negative to positive:	**2a-** that they cannot be taken from the church,

2b- if there shall be properties in the hands of the church,

1 Central theme: **1-** every man shall be made accountable unto me, a steward over his own property, or that which he has received by consecration, as much as is sufficient for himself and family.

D&C 42:39-55 — Chiasmus 62, 42D

5] 39 For it shall come to pass, that which I spake by the mouths of my prophets shall be fulfilled; for *I will consecrate of the riches of those who embrace my gospel among the Gentiles unto the poor of my people who are of the house of Israel.*

4] 40 And again, thou shalt not be proud in thy heart; *let all thy garments be plain, and their beauty the beauty of the work of thine own hands*;

41 And let all things be done in cleanliness before me.

42 Thou shalt not be idle; for he that is idle shall not eat the bread nor wear the garments of the laborer.

3] 43 *And whosoever among you are sick, and have not faith to be healed, but believe, shall be nourished with all tenderness, with herbs and mild food, and that not by the hand of an enemy.*

44 And the elders of the church, two or more, shall be called, and shall pray for and lay their hands upon them in my name;

2] *and if they die they shall die unto me, and if they live they shall live unto me.*

1] 45 Thou shalt live together in love, insomuch that thou shalt weep for the loss of them that die, and more especially for those that have not hope of a glorious resurrection.

2] 46 And it shall come to pass that *those that die in me shall not taste of death, for it shall be sweet unto them;*

47 And they that die not in me, wo unto them, for their death is bitter.

3] 48 *And again, it shall come to pass that he that hath faith in me to be healed, and is not appointed unto death, shall be healed.*

49 He who hath faith to see shall see.

50 He who hath faith to hear shall hear.

51 The lame who hath faith to leap shall leap.

52 And they who have not faith to do these things, but believe in me, have power to become my sons; and inasmuch as they break not my laws thou shalt bear their infirmities.

53 Thou shalt stand in the place of thy stewardship.
4] 54 *Thou shalt not take thy brother's garment*; thou shalt pay for that which thou shalt receive of thy brother.
5] 55 *And if thou obtainest more than that which would be for thy support, thou shalt give it into my storehouse*, that all things may be done according to that which I have said.

D&C 42:39-55 **Analysis 42D**

5a/5b	General to specific:	**5a-** I will consecrate of the riches of those who embrace my gospel among the Gentiles unto the poor of my people who are of the house of Israel. **5b-** And if thou obtainest more than that which would be for thy support, thou shalt give it into my storehouse,
4a/4b	Parallel concepts:	**4a-** let all thy garments be plain, and their beauty the beauty of the work of thine own hands; **4b-** Thou shalt not take thy brother's garment;
3a/3b	Negative to positive:	**3a-** And whosoever among you are sick, and have not faith to be healed, but believe, shall be nourished with all tenderness, with herbs and mild food, and that not by the hand of an enemy. **3b-** And again, it shall come to pass that he that hath faith in me to be healed, and is not appointed unto death, shall be healed. He who hath faith to see shall see. He who hath faith to hear shall hear. The lame who hath faith to leap shall leap.
2a/2b	Parallel concepts:	**2a-** and if they die they shall die unto me, and if they live they shall live unto me. **2b-** those that die in me shall not taste of death, for it shall be sweet unto them; And they that die not in me, wo unto them, for their death is bitter.

1	Central theme:	**1-** Thou shalt live together in love, insomuch that thou shalt weep for the loss of them that die, and more especially for those that have not hope of a glorious resurrection.

D&C 70:7-11 **Chiasmus 102, 70B**

5] 7 Nevertheless, inasmuch as they receive more than is needful for their *necessities and their wants,*
4] *it shall be given into my storehouse;*
3] 8 And the benefits shall be consecrated unto the inhabitants of Zion, and unto their generations, *inasmuch as they become heirs*
2] *according to the laws of the kingdom.*
1] 9 Behold, *this is what the Lord requires of every man in his stewardship,*
1] even as *I, the Lord, have appointed or shall hereafter appoint unto any man.*
2] 10 And behold, *none are exempt from this law*
3] *who belong to the church of the living God;*
4] 11 *Yea, neither the bishop, neither the agent who keepeth the Lord's storehouse,*
5] neither he who is appointed in a stewardship over *temporal things.*

D&C 70:7-11 **Analysis 70B**

5a/5b	Parallel concepts:	**5a-** necessities and their wants, **5b-** temporal things.
4a/4b	Parallel concepts:	**4a-** it shall be given into my storehouse; **4b-** Yea, neither the bishop, neither the agent who keepeth the Lord's storehouse,
3a/3b	Parallel concepts:	**3a-** inasmuch as they become heirs **3b-** who belong to the church of the living God;
2a/2b	Parallel concepts:	**2a-** according to the laws of the kingdom. **2b-** none are exempt from this law
1a/1b	Parallel concepts:	**1a-** this is what the Lord requires of every man in his stewardship, **1b-** I, the Lord, have appointed or shall hereafter appoint unto any man.

D&C 82:1-7 **Chiasmus 122, 82A**

5] 1 *Verily, verily, I say unto you, my servants, that inasmuch as you have*
forgiven one another your trespasses, even so I, the Lord, forgive you.
4] 2 Nevertheless, *there are those among you who have sinned exceedingly;*
yea, even all of you have sinned;
3] *but verily I say unto you, beware from henceforth, and refrain from*
sin, lest sore judgments fall upon your heads.
2] 3 *For of him unto whom much is given much is required; and he*
who sins against the greater light shall receive the greater
condemnation.
1] 4 Ye call upon my name for revelations, and I give them
unto you;
2] *and inasmuch as ye keep not my sayings, which I give unto you,*
ye become transgressors; and justice and judgment are the penalty
which is affixed unto my law.
3] 5 *Therefore, what I say unto one I say unto all: Watch, for the*
adversary spreadeth his dominions, and darkness reigneth;
4] 6 And the anger of God kindleth against the inhabitants of the earth;
and none doeth good, for all have gone out of the way.
5] 7 *And now, verily I say unto you, I, the Lord, will not lay any sin to your*
charge; go your ways and sin no more; but unto that soul who sinneth
shall the former sins return, saith the Lord your God.

D&C 82:1-7 **Analysis 82A**

5a/5b	Parallel concepts:	**5a-** Verily, verily, I say unto you, my servants, that inasmuch as you have forgiven one another your trespasses, even so I, the Lord, forgive you. **5b-** And now, verily I say unto you, I, the Lord, will not lay any sin to your charge;
4a/4b	Parallel concepts:	**4a-** there are those among you who have sinned exceedingly; yea, even all of you have sinned; **4b-** and none doeth good, for all have gone out of the way.
3a/3b	Parallel concepts:	**3a-** but verily I say unto you, beware from henceforth, and refrain from sin, lest sore judgments fall upon your heads.

		3b- Therefore, what I say unto one I say unto all: Watch, for the adversary spreadeth his dominions, and darkness reigneth;
2a/2b	Parallel concepts:	**2a-** For of him unto whom much is given much is required; and he who sins against the greater light shall receive the greater condemnation. **2b-** and inasmuch as ye keep not my sayings, which I give unto you, ye become transgressors; and justice and judgment are the penalty which is affixed unto my law.
1	Central theme:	**1-** Ye call upon my name for revelations, and I give them unto you;

D&C 88:13-17 — Chiasmus 134, 88B

5] *who is in the bosom of eternity,*
4] *who is in the midst of all things.*
3] 14 Now, verily I say unto you, *that through the redemption which is made for you*
2] is brought to pass *the resurrection from the dead.*
1] 15 And the spirit and the body are the soul of man.
2] 16 And *the resurrection from the dead*
3] *is the redemption of the soul.*
4] 17 And the redemption of the soul is through him that quickeneth all things,
5] *in whose bosom it is decreed that the poor and the meek of the earth shall inherit it.*

D&C 88:13-17 — Analysis 88B

5a/5b	Parallel concepts:	**5a-** who is in the bosom of eternity, **5b-** in whose bosom it is decreed that the poor and the meek of the earth shall inherit it.
4a/4b	Parallel concepts:	**4a-** who is in the midst of all things. **4b-** through him that quickeneth all things,
3a/3b	Parallel concepts:	**3a-** that through the redemption which is made for you

		3b- is the redemption of the soul.
2a/2b	Identical words:	**2-** the resurrection from the dead
1a/1b	Central theme:	**1-** And the spirit and the body are the soul of man.

D&C 88:18-26 — Chiasmus 135, 88C

5] 18 *Therefore, it must needs be sanctified* from all unrighteousness,
4] *that it may be prepared for the celestial glory;*
19 *For after it hath filled the measure of its creation,* it shall be crowned with glory, even with the presence of God the Father;
3] 20 *That bodies who are of the celestial kingdom may possess it forever and ever;*
2] for, *for this intent was it made and created,*
1] *and for this intent are they sanctified.*
1] 21 *And they who are not sanctified* through the law which I have given unto you, even the law of Christ,
2] *must inherit another kingdom, even that of a terrestrial kingdom, or that of a telestial kingdom.*
3] 22 *For he who is not able to abide the law of a celestial kingdom cannot abide a celestial glory.*
23 And he who cannot abide the law of a terrestrial kingdom cannot abide a terrestrial glory.
24 And he who cannot abide the law of a telestial kingdom cannot abide a telestial glory; therefore he is not meet for a kingdom of glory. Therefore he must abide a kingdom which is not a kingdom of glory.
4] 25 And again, verily I say unto you, *the earth abideth the law of a celestial kingdom, for it filleth the measure of its creation,* and transgresseth not the law—
5] 26 *Wherefore, it shall be sanctified;* yea, notwithstanding it shall die, it shall be quickened again, and shall abide the power by which it is quickened, and the righteous shall inherit it.

D&C 88:18-26 — Analysis 88C

5a/5b	Parallel concepts:	**5a-** Therefore, it must needs be sanctified **5b-** Wherefore, it shall be sanctified;
4a/4b	Parallel concepts:	**4a-** that it may be prepared for the celestial glory; For after it hath filled the measure of its creation

3a/3b	Positive to negative:	**3a-** That bodies who are of the celestial kingdom may possess it forever and ever; **3b-** For he who is not able to abide the law of a celestial kingdom cannot abide a celestial glory.
2a/2b	Positive to negative:	**2a-** for this intent was it made and created, **2b-** must inherit another kingdom, even that of a terrestrial kingdom, or that of a telestial kingdom.
1a/1b	Positive to negative:	**1a-** and for this intent are they sanctified. **1a-** And they who are not sanctified

D&C 88:46-51 — Chiasmus 138, 88F

5] 46 *Unto what shall I liken these kingdoms, that ye may understand?*
47 Behold, all these are kingdoms, and any man who hath seen any or the least of these hath seen God moving in his majesty and power.
4] 48 I say unto you, *he hath seen him;*
3] nevertheless, he who came unto his own *was not comprehended.*
2] 49 *The light shineth*
1] in *darkness,*
1] and the *darkness*
2] *comprehendeth it not;*
3] nevertheless, the day shall come when *you shall comprehend* even God, being quickened in him and by him.
4] 50 Then shall ye know that *ye have seen me,* that I am, and that I am the true light that is in you, and that you are in me; otherwise ye could not abound.
5] 51 Behold, *I will liken these kingdoms unto a man having a field,* and he sent forth his servants into the field to dig in the field.

D&C 88:46-51 — Analysis 88F

5a/5b	Question-answer:	**5a-** Unto what shall I liken these kingdoms, **5b-** I will liken these kingdoms unto a man having a field,
4a/4b	Parallel concepts:	**4a-** he hath seen him; **4b-** ye have seen me,
3a/3b	Negative to positive:	**3a-** was not comprehended. **3b-** you shall comprehend

2a/2b Positive to negative: **2a-** The light shineth
2b- comprehendeth it not;
1a/1b Identical word: **1-** darkness

D&C 88:69-75 **Chiasmus 142, 88J**

5] 69 Remember *the great and last promise which I have made unto you;*
4] *cast away your idle thoughts and your excess of laughter far from you.*
3] 70 Tarry ye, tarry ye in this place, and *call a solemn assembly,*
2] even of those *who are the first laborers in this last kingdom.*
1] 71 And let those whom they have warned in their traveling call on the Lord, and ponder the warning in their hearts which they have received, for a little season.
72 Behold, and lo, I will take care of your flocks, and will raise up elders and send unto them.
73 Behold, I will hasten my work in its time.
2] 74 And I give unto you, *who are the first laborers in this last kingdom,*
3] a commandment that you *assemble yourselves together,*
4] and organize yourselves, and prepare yourselves, *and sanctify yourselves; yea, purify your hearts, and cleanse your hands and your feet before me,* that I may make you clean;
75 That I may testify unto your Father, and your God, and my God, that you are clean from the blood of this wicked generation;
5] that I may fulfill this promise, *this great and last promise, which I have made unto you,* when I will.

D&C 88:69-75 **Analysis 88J**

5a/5b	Identical words:	**5-** the/this great and last promise, which I have made unto you,
4a/4b	Parallel concepts:	**4a-** cast away your idle thoughts and your excess of laughter far from you. **4b-** and sanctify yourselves; yea, purify your hearts, and cleanse your hands and your feet before me,
3a/3b	Parallel concepts:	**3a-** call a solemn assembly, **3b-** assemble yourselves together,
2a2b	Identical words:	**2-** who are the first laborers in this last kingdom

1 Central theme: **1-** And let those whom they have warned in their traveling call on the Lord, and ponder the warning in their hearts which they have received, for a little season. Behold, and lo, I will take care of your flocks, and will raise up elders and send unto them.

D&C 88:94-98 Chiasmus 144, 88L

5] 94 *And another angel shall sound his trump, saying:* That great church, the
mother of abominations, that made all nations drink of the wine of the
wrath of her fornication, that persecuteth the saints of God, that shed
their blood—she who sitteth upon many waters, and upon the islands of
the sea—behold, she is the tares of the earth; she is bound in bundles; her
bands are made strong, no man can loose them; therefore, she is ready
to be burned. And he shall sound his trump both long and loud, and all
nations shall hear it.
95 And there shall be silence in heaven for the space of half an hour;
and immediately after shall the curtain of heaven be unfolded, as a scroll
is unfolded after it is rolled up, and the face of the Lord shall be
unveiled;

4] 96 And the saints that are upon the earth, who are alive, *shall be quickened and be caught up to meet him.*

3] 97 *And they who have slept in their graves* shall come forth, for their graves shall be opened;

2] *and they also shall be caught up to meet him* in the midst of the pillar of heaven—

1] 98 They are Christ's, the first fruits,

2] *they who shall descend with him first,*

3] and they who are on the earth and in their graves,

4] *who are first caught up to meet him;*

5] *and all this by the voice of the sounding of the trump of the angel of God.*

D&C 88:92-98 Analysis 88L

5a/5b Parallel concepts: **5a-** And another angel shall sound his trump, saying:

5b- and all this by the voice of the sounding of the trump of the angel of God.

4a/4b	Parallel concepts:	**4a-** shall be quickened and be caught up to meet him. **4b-** who are first caught up to meet him;
3a/3b	Parallel concepts:	**3a-** And they who have slept in their graves **3b-** and they who are on the earth and in their graves,
2a/2b	Parallel concepts:	**2a-** and they also shall be caught up to meet him **2b-** they who shall descend with him first,
1	Central theme:	**1-** They are Christ's, the first fruits,

D&C 91:3-6 — Chiasmus 147, 91A

5] 3 Verily, I say unto you, that *it is not needful that the Apocrypha should be translated.*
4] 4 Therefore, whoso readeth it, *let him understand,*
3] *for the Spirit*
2] *manifesteth truth;*
1] 5 And whoso is enlightened by the Spirit shall obtain benefit therefrom;
2] 6 *And whoso receiveth not*
3] *by the Spirit,*
4] *cannot be benefited.*
5] Therefore *it is not needful that it should be translated.* Amen.

D&C 91:3-6 — Analysis 91A

5a/5b	Parallel concepts:	**5a-** it is not needful that the Apocrypha should be translated. **5b-** it is not needful that it should be translated.
4a/4b	Positive to negative:	**4a-** let him understand, **4b-** cannot be benefited.
3a/3b	Identical words:	**3-** the spirit
2a/2b	Positive to negative:	**2a-** manifesteth truth; **2b-** receiveth not
1	Central theme:	**1-** And whoso is enlightened by the Spirit shall obtain benefit therefrom;

D&C 101:67-70 Chiasmus 174, 101F

5] 67 Therefore, a commandment I give unto all the churches, *that they shall continue to gather together*
4] unto *the places*
3] *which I have appointed.*
2] 68 *Nevertheless, as I have said unto you in a former commandment, let not your gathering be in haste, nor by flight;*
1] but let *all things be prepared before you.*
1] 69 And in order that *all things be prepared before you,*
2] *observe the commandment which I have given concerning these things—*
3] 70 Which saith, or teacheth, to purchase all the lands with money, which can be purchased for money, in the region round about the land *which I have appointed*
4] to be *the land of Zion,*
5] *for the beginning of the gathering of my saints;*

D&C 101:67-70 Analysis 101F

5a/5b	Parallel concepts:	**5a-** that they shall continue to gather together **5b-** for the beginning of the gathering of my saints;
4a/4b	Parallel concepts:	**4a-** the places **4b-** the land of Zion,
3a/3b	Identical words:	which I have appointed
2a/2b	Parallel concepts:	**2a-** Nevertheless, as I have said unto you in a former commandment, let not your gathering be in haste, nor by flight; **2b-** observe the commandment which I have given concerning these things—
1a/1b	Identical words:	**1-** all things be prepared before you.

D&C 103:15-18 Chiasmus 178, 103D

5] 15 Behold, I say unto you, *the redemption of Zion*
4] must needs come *by power;*
3] 16 *Therefore, I will raise up unto my people a man, who shall lead them*
2] *like as Moses*
1] led *the children of Israel.*

1] 17 For ye are *the children of Israel,*
2] *and of the seed of Abraham,*
3] *and ye must needs be led out of bondage*
4] *by power,* and with a stretched-out arm.
5] 18 And as your fathers were led at the first, even so shall *the redemption of Zion* be.

D&C 103:15-18 — Analysis 103D

5a/5b	Identical words:	**5-** the redemption of Zion
4a/4b	Identical words:	**4-** by power
3a/3b	Parallel concepts:	**3a-** Therefore, I will raise up unto my people a man, who shall lead them **3b-** and ye must needs be led out of bondage
2a/2b	Parallel concepts:	**2a-** like as Moses **2b-** and of the seed of Abraham,
1a/1b	Identical words:	**1-** the children of Israel

D&C 104:38-42 — Chiasmus 180, 104B

5] 38 *And inasmuch as he is faithful, I will multiply* a multiplicity of *blessings upon him.*
4] 39 And again, let my servant Newel K. Whitney have appointed unto him the houses and lot where he now resides, *and the lot and building on which the mercantile establishment stands,* and also the lot which is on the corner south of the mercantile establishment, and also the lot on which the ashery is situated.
3] 40 And all this *I have appointed unto my servant Newel K. Whitney*
2] *for his stewardship,*
1] for a blessing upon him and his seed after him, for the benefit of the mercantile establishment of my order which I have established for my stake in the land of Kirtland.
2] *41 Yea, verily, this is the stewardship*
3] which *I have appointed unto my servant N. K. Whitney,*
4] *even this whole mercantile establishment,* him and his agent, and his seed after him.
5] 42 *And inasmuch as he is faithful* in keeping my commandments, which I have given unto him, *I will multiply blessings upon him* and his seed after him, even a multiplicity of blessings.

D&C 104:38-42 **Analysis 104B**

5a/5b	Identical words:	**5-** And inasmuch as he is faithful, I will multiply . . . blessings upon him.
4a/4b	Parallel concepts:	**4a-** and the lot and building on which the mercantile establishment stands, **4b-** even this whole mercantile establishment,
3a/3b	Identical words:	**3-** I have appointed unto my servant Newel K. Whitney
2a/2b	Parallel concepts:	**2a-** for his stewardship, **2b-** this is the stewardship
1	Central theme:	**1-** for a blessing upon him and his seed after him, for the benefit of the mercantile establishment of my order which I have established for my stake in the land of Kirtland.

D&C 104:68,69 **Chiasmus 183, 104E**

68 And all moneys that you receive in your stewardships, by improving upon the properties which I have appointed unto you, in houses, or in lands, or in cattle, or in all things save it be the holy and sacred writings, which I have reserved unto myself for holy and sacred purposes, shall be cast into the treasury as fast as you receive moneys,

5] *by hundreds,*
4] *or by fifties,*
3] *or by twenties,*
2] *or by tens,*
1] *or by fives.*
69 *Or* in other words, if any man among you obtain
1] *five dollars* let him cast them into the treasury;
2] *or* if he obtain *ten*,
3] *or twenty*,
4] *or fifty*,
5] *or an hundred*, let him do likewise;

D&C 104:68,69 **Analysis 104E**

5a/5b	Parallel concepts:	**5a-** by hundreds, **5a-** an hundred,
4a/4b	Parallel concepts:	**4a-** or by fifties, **4b-** or fifty,

3a/3b	Parallel concepts:	**3a-** or by twenties, **3b-** or twenty,
2a/2b	Parallel concepts:	**2a-** or by tens, **2b-** or . . . ten,
1a/1b	Parallel concepts:	**1a-** or by fives, **1b-** or . . . five dollars

D&C 133:38-44 — Chiasmus 225, 133C

5] 38 *And the servants of God shall go forth, saying with a loud voice: Fear God and give glory to him, for the hour of his judgment is come;*
39 *And worship him that made heaven, and earth, and the sea, and the fountains of waters—*
40 *Calling upon the name of the Lord day and night, saying: O that thou wouldst rend the heavens, that thou wouldst come down,*
4] *That the mountains might flow down at thy presence.*
3] 41 *And it shall be answered upon their heads;*
2] *for the presence of the Lord shall be as the melting fire that burneth, and as the fire which causeth the waters to boil.*
1] 42 *O Lord, thou shalt come down to make thy name known to thine adversaries,*
1] *and all nations shall tremble at thy presence—*
2] 43 *When thou doest terrible things,*
3] *things they look not for;*
4] 44 Yea, when thou comest down, *and the mountains flow down at thy presence,*
5] *thou shalt meet him who rejoiceth and worketh righteousness, who remembereth thee in thy ways.*

D&C 133:38-44 — Analysis 133C

5a/5b	Parallel concepts:	**5a-** And the servants of God shall go forth, saying with a loud voice: Fear God and give glory to him, for the hour of his judgment is come; And worship him that made heaven, and earth, and the sea, and the fountains of waters—Calling upon the name of the Lord day and night, saying: O that thou wouldst rend the heavens, that thou wouldst come down,

		5b- thou shalt meet him who rejoiceth and worketh righteousness, who remembereth thee in thy ways.
4a/4b	Identical words:	**4-** the mountains (might) flow down at thy presence
3a/3b	Parallel concepts:	**3a-** And it shall be answered upon their heads;
		3b- things they look not for;
2a/2b	Parallel concepts:	**2a-** for the presence of the Lord shall be as the melting fire that burneth, and as the fire which causeth the waters to boil.
		2b- When thou doest terrible things,
1a/1b	Parallel concepts:	**1a-** O Lord, thou shalt come down to make thy name known to thine adversaries,
		1b- and all nations shall tremble at thy presence—

Six-Element Chiasma

D&C 1:2-10 Chiasmus 1, 1A

1 Hearken, O ye people of my church, saith the voice of him who dwells on high, and whose eyes are upon all men; yea, verily I say: Hearken ye people from afar; and ye that are upon the islands of the sea, listen together.

6] 2 For verily the voice of the Lord is unto all men, *and there is none to escape; and there is no eye that shall not see, neither ear that shall not hear, neither heart that shall not be penetrated.*

5] 3 *And the rebellious shall be pierced with much sorrow*; for their iniquities shall be spoken upon the housetops, and their secret acts shall be revealed.

4] 4 *And the voice of warning shall be unto all people,*

3] *by the mouths of my disciples, whom I have chosen in these last days.*

2] 5 And they shall go forth and none shall stay them, *for I the Lord have commanded them.*

1] 6 Behold, this is mine authority, and the authority of my servants, and my preface unto the book of my commandments, which I have given them to publish unto you, O inhabitants of the earth.

2] 7 Wherefore, fear and tremble, O ye people, *for what I the Lord have decreed in them shall be fulfilled.*

3] 8 And verily I say unto you, that *they who go forth,*

4] *bearing these tidings unto the inhabitants of the earth*, to them is power given to seal both on earth and in heaven, the unbelieving and rebellious;

5] 9 Yea, verily, to seal them up unto the day when *the wrath of God shall be poured out upon the wicked without measure—*

6] 10 Unto the day when the Lord shall come *to recompense unto every man according to his work, and measure to every man according to the measure which he has measured to his fellow man.*

D&C 1:2-10 Analysis 1A

6a/6b Negative to positive: **6a-** and there is none to escape; and there is no eye that shall not see, neither ear that shall not hear, neither heart that shall not be penetrated

6b- to recompense unto every man according to his work, and measure to every man according to the measure which he has measured to his fellow man

5a/5b Parallel concepts: **5a-** And the rebellious shall be pierced with much sorrow
5b- the wrath of God shall be poured out upon the wicked without measure

4a/4b Parallel concepts: **4a-** And the voice of warning shall be unto all people
4b- they who go forth, bearing these tidings unto the inhabitants of the earth

3a/3b Parallel concepts: **3a-** by the mouths of my disciples, whom I have chosen in these last days
3b- that they who go forth

2a/2b Parallel concepts: **2a-** for I the Lord have commanded them
2b- for what I the Lord have decreed in them shall be fulfilled

1 Central theme: **1-** Behold, this is mine authority, and the authority of my servants, and my preface unto the book of my commandments, which I have given them to publish unto you, O inhabitants of the earth.

D&C 18:6-9 — Chiasmus 26, 18B

6] 6 Behold, the world is ripening in iniquity; and *it must needs be that the*
children of men are stirred up unto repentance, both the Gentiles and also
the house of Israel.
5] 7 Wherefore, as thou hast been baptized by the hands of *my servant*
Joseph Smith, Jun., according to that which I have commanded him,
4] *he hath fulfilled the thing which I commanded him.*
3] 8 And now, marvel not that *I*
2] *have called* him
1] unto mine own *purpose*,
1] which *purpose*
2] *is known*
3] in *me*;
4] *wherefore, if he shall be diligent in keeping my commandments* he
shall be blessed unto eternal life;

5] *and his name is Joseph.*
6] 9 And now, Oliver Cowdery, I speak unto you, and also unto David Whitmer, by the way of commandment; *for, behold, I command all men everywhere to repent,*

D&C 18:6-9 — Analysis 18B

6a/6b	Parallel concepts:	**6a-** it must needs be that the children of men are stirred up unto repentance, **6b-** for, behold, I command all men everywhere to repent,
5a/5b	Parallel concepts:	**5a-** my servant Joseph Smith, Jun., **5b-** and his name is Joseph.
4a/4b	Past to future:	**4a-** he hath fulfilled the thing which I commanded him. **4b-** wherefore, if he shall be diligent in keeping my commandments
3a/3b	Parallel concepts:	**3a-** I **3b-** me;
2a/2b	Parallel concepts:	**2a-** have called **2a-** is known
1a/1b	Identical word:	**1-** purpose

D&C 19:28-38 — Chiasmus 37, 19B

6] 28 And again, *I command thee that thou shalt pray vocally as well as in thy heart; yea, before the world as well as in secret, in public as well as in private.*
5] 29 *And thou shalt declare glad tidings,*
4] *yea, publish it upon the mountains, and upon every high place, and among every people that thou shalt be permitted to see.*
3] 30 *And thou shalt do it with all humility, trusting in me*, reviling not against revilers.
2] 31 *And of tenets thou shalt not talk, but thou shalt declare repentance and faith on the Savior, and remission of sins by baptism, and by fire, yea, even the Holy Ghost.*
1] 32 Behold, this is a great and the last commandment which I shall give unto you concerning this matter; for this shall suffice for thy daily walk, even unto the end of thy life.

2] 33 *And misery thou shalt receive if thou wilt slight these counsels, yea, even the destruction of thyself and property.*

3] 34 *Impart a portion of thy property, yea, even part of thy lands, and all save the support of thy family.*
35 *Pay the debt thou hast contracted with the printer. Release thyself from bondage.*
36 *Leave thy house and home, except when thou shalt desire to see thy family;*

4] 37 *And speak freely to all;*

5] *yea, preach, exhort, declare the truth, even with a loud voice, with a sound of rejoicing, crying—Hosanna, hosanna, blessed be the name of the Lord God*!

6] 38 *Pray always*, and I will pour out my Spirit upon you, and great shall be your blessing—yea, even more than if you should obtain treasures of earth and corruptibleness to the extent thereof.

D&C 19:28-38 **Analysis 19B**

6a/6b	Specific to general:	**6a-** I command thee that thou shalt pray vocally as well as in thy heart; yea, before the world as well as in secret, in public as well as in private. **6b-** Pray always,
5a/5b	General to specific:	**5a-** And thou shalt declare glad tidings, **5b-** yea, preach, exhort, declare the truth, even with a loud voice, with a sound of rejoicing, crying—Hosanna, hosanna, blessed be the name of the Lord God!
4a/4b	Specific to general:	**4a-** yea, publish it upon the mountains, and upon every high place, and among every people that thou shalt be permitted to see. **4b-** And speak freely to all;
3a/3b	General to specific:	**3a-** And thou shalt do it with all humility, trusting in me, **3b-** Impart a portion of thy property, yea, even part of thy lands, and all save the support of thy family.
2a/2b	Instructions, consequence:	**2a-** And of tenets thou shalt not talk, but thou shalt declare repentance and faith on

		the Savior, and remission of sins by baptism, and by fire, yea, even the Holy Ghost. **2b-** And misery thou shalt receive if thou wilt slight these counsels, yea, even the destruction of thyself and property.
1	Central theme:	**1-** Behold, this is a great and the last commandment which I shall give unto you concerning this matter; for this shall suffice for thy daily walk, even unto the end of thy life.

D&C 38:9-15 — Chiasmus 53, 38A

6] 9 Wherefore, gird up your loins and be prepared. Behold, *the kingdom is yours,*

5] *and the enemy shall not overcome.*

4] 10 Verily I say unto you, *ye are clean, but not all;* and there is none else with whom I am well pleased;

3] 11 *For all flesh is corrupted before me; and the powers of darkness prevail upon the earth, among the children of men,*

2] *in the presence of all the hosts of heaven—*

1] 12 Which causeth silence to reign, and all eternity is pained, and the angels are waiting the great command to reap down the earth, to gather the tares that they may be burned; and, behold, the enemy is combined.

2] 13 And now I show unto you a mystery, *a thing which is had in secret chambers,*

3] *to bring to pass even your destruction in process of time, and ye knew it not;*

4] 14 But now I tell it unto you, and ye are blessed, not because of your iniquity, neither your hearts of unbelief; for verily *some of you are guilty before me,* but I will be merciful unto your weakness.

5] 15 Therefore, *be ye strong from henceforth; fear not,*

6] for *the kingdom is yours.*

D&C 38:9-15 — Analysis 38A

6a/6b	Identical words:	**6-** the kingdom is yours,
5a/5b	Relative strength:	**5a-** and the enemy shall not overcome. **5b-** be ye strong from henceforth; fear not,

4a/4b	Parallel concepts:	**4a-** ye are clean, but not all; **4b-** some of you are guilty before me,
3a/3b	General to specific:	**3a-** For all flesh is corrupted before me; and the powers of darkness prevail upon the earth, among the children of men, **3b-** to bring to pass even your destruction in process of time, and ye knew it not;
2a/2b	Public to private:	**2a-** in the presence of all the hosts of heaven— **2b-** a thing which is had in secret chambers,
1	Central theme:	**1-** Which causeth silence to reign, and all eternity is pained, and the angels are waiting the great command to reap down the earth, to gather the tares that they may be burned; and, behold, the enemy is combined.

D&C 45:39-52 — Chiasmus 70, 45D

6] 39 *And it shall come to pass that he that feareth me shall be looking forth for the great day of the Lord to come, even for the signs of the coming of the Son of Man.*

5] 40 *And they shall see signs and wonders, for they shall be shown forth in the heavens above, and in the earth beneath.*
41 And they shall behold blood, and fire, and vapors of smoke.
42 And before the day of the Lord shall come, the sun shall be darkened, and the moon be turned into blood, and the stars fall from heaven.
43 And the remnant shall be gathered unto this place;

4] 44 *And then they shall look for me, and, behold, I will come;* and they shall see me in the clouds of heaven, clothed with power and great glory; with all the holy angels; and he that watches not for me shall be cut off.

3] 45 *But before the arm of the Lord shall fall,* an angel shall sound his trump,

2] *and the saints that have slept shall come forth* to meet me in the cloud.

1] 46 Wherefore, if ye have slept in peace blessed are you; for as you now behold me and know that I am, even so

shall ye come unto me and your souls shall live, and
your redemption shall be perfected;
2] *and the saints shall come forth* from the four quarters of the
earth.
3] 47 *Then shall the arm of the Lord fall* upon the nations.
4] 48 *And then shall the Lord set his foot upon this mount,* and it shall
cleave in twain,
5] *and the earth shall tremble, and reel to and fro, and the heavens also
shall shake.*
*49 And the Lord shall utter his voice, and all the ends of the earth shall
hear it; and the nations of the earth shall mourn, and they that have
laughed shall see their folly.*
*50 And calamity shall cover the mocker, and the scorner shall be
consumed; and they that have watched for iniquity shall be hewn down
and cast into the fire.*
6] 51 *And then shall the Jews look upon me and say: What are these wounds
in thine hands and in thy feet?*
52 Then shall they know that I am the Lord; for I will say unto them:
These wounds are the wounds with which I was wounded in the house of
my friends. I am he who was lifted up. I am Jesus that was crucified.
I am the Son of God.

D&C 45:39-51 — Analysis 45D

6a/6b	Positive to negative:	**6a-** And it shall come to pass that he that feareth me shall be looking forth for the great day of the Lord to come, even for the signs of the coming of the Son of Man. **6b-** And then shall the Jews look upon me and say: What are these wounds in thine hands and in thy feet? Then shall they know that I am the Lord;
5a/5b	Parallel concepts:	**5a-** And they shall see signs and wonders, for they shall be shown forth in the heavens above, and in the earth beneath. And they shall behold blood, and fire, and vapors of smoke. And before the day of the Lord shall come, the sun shall be

		darkened, and the moon be turned into blood, and the stars fall from heaven.
		5b- and the earth shall tremble, and reel to and fro, and the heavens also shall shake. And the Lord shall utter his voice, and all the ends of the earth shall hear it; and the nations of the earth shall mourn, and they that have laughed shall see their folly. And calamity shall cover the mocker, and the scorner shall be consumed; and they that have watched for iniquity shall be hewn down and cast into the fire.
4a/4b	Parallel concepts:	**4a-** And then they shall look for me, and, behold, I will come;
		4b- And then shall the Lord set his foot upon this mount,
3a/3b	Parallel concepts:	**3a-** But before the arm of the Lord shall fall,
		3b- Then shall the arm of the Lord fall
2a/2b	Parallel concepts:	**2a-** and the saints that have slept shall come forth
		2b- and the saints shall come forth
1	Central theme:	**1-** Wherefore, if ye have slept in peace blessed are you; for as you now behold me and know that I am, even so shall ye come unto me and your souls shall live, and your redemption shall be perfected;

D&C 50:13-24 — Chiasmus 75, 50B

13 Wherefore, I the Lord ask you this question—unto what were ye ordained?

6] *To preach my gospel by the Spirit*, even the Comforter which was sent forth to teach the truth.

5] 15 *And then received ye spirits which ye could not understand, and received them to be of God*; and in this are ye justified?

4] 16 Behold ye shall answer this question yourselves; nevertheless, I will be merciful unto you; *he that is weak among you hereafter shall be made strong.*

3] 17 Verily I say unto you, *he that is ordained of me and sent forth to preach the word of truth by the Comforter, in the Spirit of truth, doth he preach it by the Spirit of truth* or some other way?

2] 18 And *if it be by some other way it is not of God.*

1] 19 And again, he that receiveth the word of truth, doth he receive it by the Spirit of truth or some other way?

2] 20 *If it be some other way it is not of God.*

3] 21 Therefore, why is it that ye cannot understand and know, *that he that receiveth the word by the Spirit of truth receiveth it as it is preached by the Spirit of truth*?

4] 22 Wherefore, he that preacheth and he that receiveth, understand one another, and *both are edified and rejoice together.*

5] 23 *And that which doth not edify is not of God, and is darkness.*

6] 24 *That which is of God is light*; and he that receiveth light, and continueth in God, receiveth more light; and that light groweth brighter and brighter until the perfect day.

D&C 50:13-24 — Analysis 50B

6a/6b	Parallel concepts:	**6a-** To preach my gospel by the Spirit, **6b-** That which is of God is light;
5a/5b	Parallel concepts:	**5a-** And then received ye spirits which ye could not understand, and received them to be of God; **5b-** And that which doth not edify is not of God, and is darkness.
4a/4b	Parallel concepts:	**4a-** he that is weak among you hereafter shall be made strong. **4b-** both are edified and rejoice together.
3a/3b	Parallel concepts:	**3a-** he that is ordained of me and sent forth to preach the word of truth by the Comforter, in the Spirit of truth, doth he preach it by the Spirit of truth **3b-** that he that receiveth the word by the Spirit of truth receiveth it as it is preached by the Spirit of truth?
2a/2b	Identical words:	**2-** if it be (by) some other way it is not of God.

1 Central theme: 1- And again, he that receiveth the word of truth, doth he receive it by the Spirit of truth or some other way?

D&C 60:6-17 — Chiasmus 86, 60B

6] 6 And from thence let *my servants, Sidney Rigdon, Joseph Smith, Jun., and Oliver Cowdery*, take their journey for Cincinnati;

5] *7 And in this place let them lift up their voice and declare my word with loud voices, without wrath or doubting, lifting up holy hands upon them.* For I am able to make you holy, and your sins are forgiven you.

4] 8 And let the residue take their journey from St. Louis, two by two, and preach the word, *not in haste,*

3] *among the congregations of the wicked,*

2] *until they return* to the churches from whence they came.

1] 9 And all this for the good of the churches; for this intent have I sent them.
10 And let my servant Edward Partridge impart of the money which I have given him, a portion unto mine elders who are commanded to return;
11 And he that is able, let him return it by the way of the agent; and he that is not, of him it is not required.
12 And now I speak of the residue who are to come unto this land.
13 Behold, they have been sent to preach my gospel among the congregations of the wicked; wherefore, *I give unto them a commandment, thus: Thou shalt not idle away thy time, neither shalt thou bury thy talent that it may not be known.*
14 And after thou hast come up unto the land of Zion, and hast proclaimed my word,

2] *thou shalt speedily return*, proclaiming my word

3] *among the congregations of the wicked,*

4] *not in haste*, neither in wrath nor with strife.

5] 15 *And shake off the dust of thy feet against those who receive thee not, not in their presence, lest thou provoke them, but in secret; and wash thy feet, as a testimony against them in the day of judgment.*
16 Behold, this is sufficient for you, and the will of him who hath sent you.

6] 17 And by the mouth of *my servant Joseph Smith, Jun.*, it shall be made known concerning *Sidney Rigdon and Oliver Cowdery.* The residue hereafter. Even so. Amen.

D&C 60:6-17 — Analysis 60B

6a/6b	Parallel concepts:	**6a-** my servants, Sidney Rigdon, Joseph Smith, Jun., and Oliver Cowdery, **6b-** my servant Joseph Smith, Jun . . . Sidney Rigdon and Oliver Cowdery.
5a/5b	Positive to negative:	**5a-** And in this place let them lift up their voice and declare my word with loud voices, without wrath or doubting, lifting up holy hands upon them. **5b-** And shake off the dust of thy feet against those who receive thee not, not in their presence, lest thou provoke them, but in secret; and wash thy feet, as a testimony against them in the day of judgment.
4a/4b	Identical words:	**4-** not is haste,
3a/3b	Identical words:	**3-** among the congregations of the wicked,
2a/2b	Parallel concepts:	**2a-** until they return **2b-** thou shalt speedily return,
1	Central theme:	**1-** I give unto them a commandment, thus: Thou shalt not idle away thy time, neither shalt thou bury thy talent that it may not be known.

D&C 88:51-61 — Chiasmus 139, 88G

6] *Behold, I will liken these kingdoms unto a man having a field,* and he sent forth his servants into the field to dig in the field.
52 And he said unto the first: Go ye and labor in the field, and in the first hour I will come unto you, and ye shall behold the joy of my countenance.
53 And he said unto the second: Go ye also into the field, and in the second hour I will visit you with the joy of my countenance.
54 And also unto the third, saying: I will visit you;
55 And unto the fourth, and so on unto the twelfth.
56 And the lord of the field went unto the first in the first hour, and tarried with him all that hour, and he was made glad with the light of the countenance of his lord.

57 And then he withdrew from the first that he might visit the second also, and the third, and the fourth, and so on unto the twelfth.

5] *And thus they all received the light*

4] of *the countenance of their lord,*

3] *every man in his hour, and in his time, and in his season—*

59 Beginning at the first, and so on unto the last,

2] *and from the last*

1] *unto the first,*

1] and *from the first*

2] *unto the last;*

3] 60 *Every man in his own order, until his hour was finished,* even according as his lord had commanded him,

4] *that his lord might be glorified in him, and he in his lord,*

5] *that they all might be glorified.*

6] 61 *Therefore, unto this parable I will liken all these kingdoms, and the inhabitants thereof*—every kingdom in its hour, and in its time, and in its season, even according to the decree which God hath made.

D&C 88:51-61 — Analysis 88G

6a/6b	Parallel concepts:	**6a-** Behold, I will liken these kingdoms unto a man having a field, **6b-** Therefore, unto this parable I will liken all these kingdoms, and the inhabitants thereof—
5a/5b	Parallel concepts:	**5a-** And thus they all received the light **5b-** that they all might be glorified.
4a/4b	Parallel concepts:	**4a-** the countenance of their lord, **4b-** that his lord might be glorified in him, and he in his lord,
3a/3b	Parallel concepts:	**3a-** every man in his hour, and in his time, and in his season— **3b-** Every man in his own order, until his hour was finished,
2a/2b	Parallel concepts:	**2a-** from the last **2b-** unto the last;
1a/1b	Parallel concepts:	**1a-** unto the first, **1b-** from the first

D&C 92:1,2 **Chiasmus 148, 92A**

6] Verily, thus saith the Lord, *I give unto the united order,*
5] organized agreeable to the *commandment*
4] *previously* given,
3] *a revelation and commandment*
2] concerning *my servant Frederick G. Williams,*
1] that ye shall receive him into the order. What I say unto one I say unto all.
2] 2 And again, I say unto you *my servant Frederick G. Williams,*
3] you shall be a lively member in this order; *and inasmuch as you are faithful*
4] in keeping all *former*
5] *commandments*
6] *you shall be blessed forever.* Amen.

D&C 92:1,2 **Analysis 92A**

6a/6b	Parallel concepts:	**6a-** I give unto the united order, **6b-** you shall be blessed forever.
5a/5b	Identical word:	**5-** commandment(s)
4a/4b	Parallel concepts:	**4a-** previously **4b-** former
3a/3b	Parallel concepts:	**3a-** a revelation and commandment **3b-** inasmuch as you are faithful
2a/2b	Identical words:	**2-** my servant Frederick G. Williams,
1	Central theme:	**1-** that ye shall receive him into the order. What I say unto one I say unto all.

D&C 107:8-18 **Chiasmus 188, 107B**

6] 8 *The Melchizedek Priesthood holds the right of presidency,*
5] and has *power and authority* over all the offices in the church in all ages of the world, to administer in spiritual things.
4] 9 *The Presidency of the High Priesthood, after the order of Melchizedek, have a right to officiate in all the offices in the church.*
3] 10 *High priests after the order of the Melchizedek Priesthood have a right* to officiate in their own standing, under the direction of the presidency, in administering spiritual things, and also in the office of an elder, priest (of the Levitical order), teacher, deacon, and member.

11 An elder has a right to officiate in his stead when the high priest is not present.

2] 12 *The high priest and elder are to administer in spiritual things*, agreeable to the covenants and commandments of the church; and they have a right to officiate in all these offices of the church when there are no higher authorities present.

1] 13 The second priesthood is called the Priesthood of Aaron, because it was conferred upon Aaron and his seed, throughout all their generations.

2] 14 Why it is called *the lesser priesthood* is because it is an appendage to the greater, or the Melchizedek Priesthood, and *has power in administering outward ordinances*.
15 The bishopric is the presidency of this priesthood, and holds the keys or authority of the same.

3] 16 *No man has a legal right* to this office, to hold the keys of this priesthood, except he be a literal descendant of Aaron.

4] 17 *But as a high priest of the Melchizedek Priesthood has authority to officiate in all the lesser offices*, he may officiate in the office of bishop when no literal descendant of Aaron can be found, provided he is called and set apart and ordained unto this power by the hands of the Presidency of the Melchizedek Priesthood.

5] 18 The *power and authority*
6] of *the higher, or Melchizedek Priesthood, is to hold the keys of all the spiritual blessings of the church—*

D&C 107:8-18 — Analysis 107B

6a/6b	Parallel concepts:	**6a-** The Melchizedek Priesthood holds the right of presidency, **6b-** the higher, or Melchizedek Priesthood, is to hold the keys of all the spiritual blessings of the church—
5a/5b	Identical words:	**5-** power and authority
4a/4b	Parallel concepts:	**4a-** The Presidency of the High Priesthood, after the order of Melchizedek, have a right to officiate in all the offices in the church.

		4b- But as a high priest of the Melchizedek Priesthood has authority to officiate in all the lesser offices,
3a3b	Positive to negative:	**3a-** High priests after the order of the Melchizedek Priesthood have a right to officiate in their own standing,
		3b- No man has a legal right to this office,
2a/2b	Parallel concepts:	**2a-** The high priest and elder are to administer in spiritual things,
		2b- the lesser priesthood . . . has power in administering outward ordinances.
1	Central theme:	**1-** the second priesthood is called the Priesthood of Aaron, because it was conferred upon Aaron and his seed, throughout all their generations.

D&C 124:56-60 **Chiasmus 216, 124E**

6] 56 And now I say unto you, *as pertaining to my boarding house which I have commanded you to build for the boarding of strangers,*
5] let it be built unto my name, *and let my name be named upon it,*
4] and *let my servant Joseph and his house have place therein, from generation to generation.*
3] 57 For this anointing have I put upon his head, *that his blessing*
2] *shall also be put upon the head of his posterity after him.*
1] 58 And as I said unto Abraham concerning the kindreds of the earth, even so I say unto my servant Joseph:
2] *In thee and in thy seed*
3] *shall the kindred of the earth be blessed.*
4] 59 Therefore, *let my servant Joseph and his seed after him have place in that house, from generation to generation, forever and ever,* saith the Lord.
5] 60 *And let the name of that house be called Nauvoo House;*
6] *and let it be a delightful habitation for man, and a resting-place for the weary traveler,* that he may contemplate the glory of Zion, and the glory of this, the corner-stone thereof;

D&C 124:56-60 **Analysis 124E**

6a/6b	Parallel concepts:	**6a-** as pertaining to my boarding house which I have commanded you to build for the boarding of strangers, **6b-** and let it be a delightful habitation for man, and a resting-place for the weary traveler,
5a/5b	Parallel concepts:	**5a-** and let my name be named upon it, **5b-** And let the name of that house be called Nauvoo House;
4a/4b	Parallel concepts:	**4a-** let my servant Joseph and his house have place therein, from generation to generation. **4b-** let my servant Joseph and his seed after him have place in that house, from generation to generation,
3a/3b	Specific to general:	**3a-** that his blessing **3b-** shall the kindred of the earth be blessed.
2a/2b	Parallel concepts:	**2a-** shall also be put upon the head of his posterity after him. **2b-** In thee and in thy seed
1	Central theme:	**1-** And as I said unto Abraham concerning the kindreds of the earth, even so I say unto my servant Joseph:

Seven-Element Chiasma

D&C 60:1-14 **Chiasmus 85, 60A**

7] 1 Behold, thus saith the Lord unto the elders of his church, who are to *return*

6] *speedily*

5] *to the land from whence they came*: Behold, it pleaseth me, that you have come up hither;

4] 2 But with some I am not well pleased, *for they will not open their mouths, but they hide the talent which I have given unto them*, because of the fear of man. Wo unto such, for mine anger is kindled against them.

3 And it shall come to pass, if they are not more faithful unto me, it shall be taken away, even that which they have.

4 For I, the Lord, rule in the heavens above, and among the armies of the earth; and in the day when I shall make up my jewels, all men shall know what it is that bespeaketh the power of God.

5 But, verily, I will speak unto you concerning your journey unto the land from whence you came. Let there be a craft made, or bought, as seemeth you good, it mattereth not unto me, and take your journey speedily for the place which is called St. Louis.

6 And from thence let my servants, Sidney Rigdon, Joseph Smith, Jun., and Oliver Cowdery, take their journey for Cincinnati;

7 And in this place let them lift up their voice and declare my word with loud voices, without wrath or doubting, lifting up holy hands upon them. For I am able to make you holy, and your sins are forgiven you.

8 And let the residue take their journey from St. Louis, two by two, and preach the word, not in haste,

3] *among the congregations of the wicked,*

2] *until they return to the churches from whence they came.*

9 And all this for the good of the churches; for this intent have I sent them.

1] 10 And let my servant Edward Partridge impart of the money which I have given him, a portion unto mine elders *who are commanded to return*;

1] 11 And he that is able, *let him return* it by the way of the agent; and he that is not, of him it is not required.
2] 12 And now I speak of the residue *who are to come unto this land.*
13 Behold, they have been sent to preach my gospel
3] *among the congregations of the wicked*; wherefore, I give unto them a commandment, thus: Thou shalt not idle away thy time,
4] *neither shalt thou bury thy talent that it may not be known.*
5] 14 And after thou hast come up *unto the land of Zion*, and hast proclaimed my word,
6] thou shalt *speedily*
7] *return*, proclaiming my word among the congregations of the wicked, not in haste, neither in wrath nor with strife.

D&C 60:1-14 — Analysis 60A

7a/7b	Identical word:	**7-** return
6a/6b	Identical word:	**6-** speedily
5a/5b	Parallel concepts:	**5a-** to the land from whence they came: **5b-** unto the land of Zion,
4a/4b	Parallel concepts:	**4a-** for they will not open their mouths, but they hide the talent which I have given unto them, **4b-** neither shalt thou bury thy talent that it may not be known.
3a/3b	Identical words:	**3-** among the congregations of the wicked
2a/2b	Parallel concepts:	**2a-** until they return to the churches from whence they came. **2b-** who are to come unto this land.
1a/1b	Parallel concepts:	**1a-** who are commanded to return; **1b-** let him return

D&C 75:3-12 — Chiasmus 106, 75A

7] 3 *Behold, I say unto you that it is my will that you should go forth* and not tarry, neither be idle but labor with your might—
6] 4 *Lifting up your voices as with the sound of a trump, proclaiming the truth according to the revelations and commandments which I have given you.*

5] 5 *And thus, if ye are faithful* ye shall be laden with many sheaves, and crowned with honor, and glory, and immortality, and eternal life.
4] 6 *Therefore, verily I say unto my servant William E. McLellin, I revoke the commission which I gave unto him*
3] *to go unto the eastern countries;*
2] 7 *And I give unto him a new commission and a new commandment,*
1] *in the which I, the Lord, chasten him for the murmurings of his heart;*
1] 8 *And he sinned;*
2] *nevertheless, I forgive him and say unto him again,*
3] *Go ye into the south countries.*
4] 9 *And let my servant Luke Johnson go with him, and proclaim the things which I have commanded them—*
5] 10 *Calling on the name of the Lord for the Comforter*, which shall teach them all things that are expedient for them—
6] 11 *Praying always that they faint not; and inasmuch as they do this, I will be with them even unto the end.*
7] 12 *Behold, this is the will of the Lord your God concerning you*. Even so. Amen.

D&C 75:3-12 — Analysis 75A

7a/7b	Parallel concepts:	**7a-** Behold, I say unto you that it is my will that you should go forth **7b-** Behold, this is the will of the Lord your God concerning you.
6a/6b	Parallel concepts:	**6a-** Lifting up your voices as with the sound of a trump, proclaiming the truth according to the revelations and commandments which I have given you. **6b-** Praying always that they faint not;
5a/5b	Parallel concepts:	**5a-** And thus, if ye are faithful **5b-** Calling on the name of the Lord for the Comforter,
4a/4b	Parallel instructions:	**4a-** Therefore, verily I say unto my servant William E. McLellin, I revoke the commission which I gave unto him

		4b- And let my servant Luke Johnson go with him, and proclaim the things which I have commanded them—
3a/3b	Parallel concepts:	**3a-** to go unto the eastern countries;
		3b- Go ye into the south countries.
2a/2b	Parallel concepts:	**2a-** And I give unto him a new commission and a new commandment,
		2b- nevertheless, I forgive him and say unto him again,
1a/1b	Parallel concepts:	**1a-** in the which I, the Lord, chasten him for the murmurings of his heart;
		1b- And he sinned;

D&C 76:36-44 — Chiasmus 114, 76G

7] 36 *These are they who shall go away into the lake of fire and brimstone, with the devil and his angels—*

6] 37 *And the only ones on whom the second death shall have any power;* 38 *Yea, verily, the only ones who shall not be redeemed in the due time of the Lord, after the sufferings of his wrath.*

5] 39 *For all the rest shall be brought forth by the resurrection of the dead,*

4] *through the triumph and the glory of the Lamb,*

3] *who was slain,*

2] *who was in the bosom of the Father before the worlds were made.*

1] 40 And this is the gospel, the glad tidings, which the voice out of the heavens bore record unto us—

2] 41 *That he came into the world, even Jesus,*

3] *to be crucified for the world,*

4] *and to bear the sins of the world, and to sanctify the world, and to cleanse it from all unrighteousness;*

5] 42 *That through him all might be saved whom the Father had put into his power and made by him;*

6] 43 Who glorifies the Father, *and saves all the works of his hands, except those sons of perdition who deny the Son after the Father has revealed him.*

7] 44 *Wherefore, he saves all except them—they shall go away into everlasting punishment, which is endless punishment, which is eternal punishment, to reign with the devil and his angels in eternity,* where their worm dieth not, and the fire is not quenched, which is their torment—

D&C 76:36-44 **Analysis 76G**

7a/7b	Parallel concepts:	**7a-** These are they who shall go away into the lake of fire and brimstone, with the devil and his angels— **7b-** they shall go away into everlasting punishment, which is endless punishment, which is eternal punishment, to reign with the devil and his angels in eternity
6a/6b	Parallel concepts:	**6a-** And the only ones on whom the second death shall have any power; Yea, verily, the only ones who shall not be redeemed in the due time of the Lord, after the sufferings of his wrath. **6b-** and saves all the works of his hands, except those sons of perdition who deny the Son after the Father has revealed him.
5a/5b	Parallel concepts:	**5a-** For all the rest shall be brought forth by the resurrection of the dead, **5b-** That through him all might be saved whom the Father had put into his power and made by him;
4a/4b	Parallel concepts:	**4a-** through the triumph and the glory of the Lamb, **4b-** and to bear the sins of the world, and to sanctify the world, and to cleanse it from all unrighteousness;
3a/3b	Parallel concepts:	**3a-** who was slain, **3b-** to be crucified for the world,
2a/2b	Parallel concepts:	**2a-** who was in the bosom of the Father before the worlds were made. **2b-** That he came into the world, even Jesus,
1	Central theme:	**1-** And this is the gospel, the glad tidings, which the voice out of the heavens bore record unto us—

D&C 93:37-39 Chiasmus 155, 93G

7] 37 *Light and truth*
6] *forsake*
5] *that evil one.*
4] 38 Every *spirit of man*
3] was *innocent*
2] *in the beginning;*
1] and God having redeemed man from the fall, men became again,
2] *in their infant state,*
3] *innocent*
4] before *God.*
5] 39 And *that wicked one*
6] *cometh and taketh away*
7] *light and truth,* through disobedience, from the children of men, and because of the tradition of their fathers.

D&C 93:37-39 Analysis 93G

7a/7b	Identical words:	**7-** Light and truth
6a/6b	Parallel concepts:	**6a-** forsake
		6b- cometh and taketh away
5a/5b	Parallel concepts:	**5a-** that evil one.
		5b- that wicked one
4a/4b	Temporal to spiritual:	**4a-** spirit of man
		4b- God
3a/3b	Identical word:	**3-** innocent
2a/2b	Parallel concepts:	**2a-** in the beginning;
		2b- in their infant state,
1	Central theme:	**1-** and God having redeemed man from the fall,

D&C 98:4-7 Chiasmus 165, 98A

7] 4 *And now, verily I say unto you concerning the laws of the land,* it is my will that my people should observe to do all things whatsoever I command them.
6] 5 And *that law of the land*
5] *which is constitutional,*
4] *supporting that principle of freedom* in maintaining rights and privileges,

3] belongs to *all mankind,*
2] and *is justifiable*
1] before *me.*
1] 6 Therefore, *I, the Lord,*
2] *justify you,*
3] and *your brethren of my church,*
4] *in befriending that law*
5] which is *the constitutional law*
6] *(law) of the land;*
7] 7 *And as pertaining to law of man,* whatsoever is more or less than this, cometh of evil.

D&C 98:4-7 — Analysis 98A

7a/7b	Parallel concepts:	**7a-** And now, verily I say unto you concerning the laws of the land, **7b-** And as pertaining to law of man,
6a/6b	Identical words:	**6-** law of the land
5a/5b	Identical words:	**5-** which is constitutional
4a/4b	Parallel concepts:	**4a-** supporting that principle of freedom **4b-** in befriending that law
3a/3b	Parallel concepts:	**3a-** all mankind, **3b-** your brethren of my church,
2a/2b	Parallel concepts:	**2a-** is justifiable **2b-** justify you,
1a/1b	Same person:	**1a-** me/I, the Lord

D&C 107:72-76 — Chiasmus 196, 107J

7] 72 And also *to be a judge in Israel,*
6] *to do the business of the church, to sit in judgment upon transgressors upon testimony as it shall be laid before him according to the laws,*
5] *by the assistance of his counselors,* whom he has chosen or will choose among the elders of the church.
4] 73 *This is the duty of a bishop*
3] *who is not a literal descendant of Aaron,* but has been ordained to the High Priesthood after the order of Melchizedek.
2] 74 *Thus shall he be a judge, even a common judge among the inhabitants of Zion,*

1] *or in a stake of Zion, or in any branch of the church*
where he shall be set apart unto this ministry,
1] *until the borders of Zion are enlarged*
2] *and it becomes necessary to have other bishops or judges*
in Zion or elsewhere.
75 And inasmuch as there are other bishops appointed
they shall act in the same office.
3] 76 *But a literal descendant of Aaron* has a legal right to the
presidency of this priesthood, to the keys of this ministry,
4] *to act in the office of bishop*
5] *independently, without counselors,*
6] *except in a case where a President of the High Priesthood, after the order*
of Melchizedek, is tried,
7] *to sit as a judge in Israel.*

D&C 107:72-76 **Analysis 107J**

7a/7b	Parallel concepts:	**7a-** to be a judge in Israel, **7b-** to sit as a judge in Israel.
6a/6b	Positive to negative:	**6a-** to do the business of the church, to sit in judgment upon transgressors upon testimony as it shall be laid before him according to the laws, **6b-** except in a case where a President of the High Priesthood, after the order of Melchizedek, is tried,
5a/5b	Positive to negative:	**5a-** by the assistance of his counselors, **5b-** independently, without counselors,
4a/4b	Parallel concepts:	**4a-** This is the duty of a bishop **4b-** to act in the office of bishop
3a/3b	Negative to positive:	**3a-** who is not a literal descendant of Aaron, **3b-** But a literal descendant of Aaron
2a/2b	Singular to plural:	**2a-** Thus shall he be a judge, even a common judge among the inhabitants of Zion, **2b-** and it becomes necessary to have other bishops or judges in Zion or elsewhere.
1a/1b	Parallel concepts:	**1a-** or in a stake of Zion, or in any branch of the church **1b-** until the borders of Zion are enlarged

Eleven-Element Chiasma

D&C 84:74-90 — Chiasmus 130, 84E

11] 74 *Verily, verily, I say unto you, they who believe not on your words, and are not baptized in water in my name, for the remission of their sins, that they may receive the Holy Ghost, shall be damned, and shall not come into my Father's kingdom where my Father and I am.*

10] 75 And this revelation unto you, and commandment, is in force from this very hour upon all the world, *and the gospel is unto all who have not received it.*

9] 76 But, verily I say unto all those to whom the kingdom has been given—*from you it must be preached unto them, that they shall repent of their former evil works; for they are to be upbraided for their evil hearts of unbelief,* and your brethren in Zion for their rebellion against you at the time I sent you.

8] 77 And again I say unto you, my friends, for from henceforth I shall call you friends, it is expedient that I give unto you this commandment, that ye become even as my friends *in days when I was with them, traveling to preach the gospel in my power;*

7] 78 *For I suffered them not to have purse or scrip,* neither two coats.

6] 79 *Behold, I send you out to prove the world,* and the laborer is worthy of his hire.

5] 80 *And any man that shall go and preach this gospel of the kingdom, and fail not to continue faithful in all things, shall not be weary in mind, neither darkened, neither in body, limb, nor joint; and a hair of his head shall not fall to the ground unnoticed. And they shall not go hungry, neither athirst.*

4] 81 Therefore, *take ye no thought*

3] for *the morrow,*

2] *for what ye shall eat, or what ye shall drink, or wherewithal ye shall be clothed.*

1] 82 For, consider the lilies of the field, how they grow, they toil not, neither do they spin; and the kingdoms of the world, in all their glory, are not arrayed like one of these.

2] 83 *For your Father, who is in heaven, knoweth that you have need of all these things.*

3] 84 Therefore, *let the morrow*

4] *take thought* for the things of itself.

5] 85 *Neither take ye thought beforehand what ye shall say; but treasure up in your minds continually the words of life, and it shall be given you in the very hour that portion that shall be meted unto every man.*

6] 86 Therefore, let no man among you, *for this commandment is unto all the faithful who are called of God in the church unto the ministry,*

7] *from this hour take purse or scrip,*

8] *that goeth forth to proclaim this gospel of the kingdom.*

9] 87 *Behold, I send you out to reprove the world of all their unrighteous deeds, and to teach them of a judgment which is to come.*

10] 88 *And whoso receiveth you, there I will be also, for I will go before your face. I will be on your right hand and on your left, and my Spirit shall be in your hearts, and mine angels round about you, to bear you up.*

11] 89 *Whoso receiveth you receiveth me; and the same will feed you, and clothe you, and give you money.*
90 And he who feeds you, or clothes you, or gives you money, shall in nowise lose his reward.

D&C 84:74-90 **Analysis 84E**

11a/11b Negative to positive: **11a-** Verily, verily, I say unto you, they who believe not on your words, and are not baptized in water in my name, for the remission of their sins, that they may receive the Holy Ghost, shall be damned, and shall not come into my Father's kingdom where my Father and I am.

		11b- Whoso receiveth you receiveth me; and the same will feed you, and clothe you, and give you money. And he who feeds you, or clothes you, or gives you money, shall in nowise lose his reward.
10a/10b	Parallel concepts:	**10a-** and the gospel is unto all who have not received it. **10b-** And whoso receiveth you, there I will be also, for I will go before your face. I will be on your right hand and on your left, and my Spirit shall be in your hearts, and mine angels round about you, to bear you up.
9a/9b	Parallel concepts:	**9a-** from you it must be preached unto them, that they shall repent of their former evil works; for they are to be upbraided for their evil hearts of unbelief, **9b-** Behold, I send you out to reprove the world of all their unrighteous deeds, and to teach them of a judgment which is to come.
8a/8b	Past to future:	**8a-** in days when I was with them, traveling to preach the gospel in my power; **8b-** that goeth forth to proclaim this gospel of the kingdom.
7a/7b	Past to future:	**7a-** For I suffered them not to have purse or scrip, **7b-** from this hour take purse or scrip,
6a/6b	Parallel concepts:	**6a-** Behold, I send you out to prove the world, **6b-** for this commandment is unto all the faithful who are called of God in the church unto the ministry,
5a/5b	Parallel concepts:	**5a-** And any man that shall go and preach this gospel of the kingdom, and fail not to continue faithful in all things, shall not be weary in mind, neither darkened, neither in body, limb, nor joint; and a hair of his head shall not fall to the ground unnotic-

		ed. And they shall not go hungry, neither athirst. **5b-** Neither take ye thought beforehand what ye shall say; but treasure up in your minds continually the words of life, and it shall be given you in the very hour that portion that shall be meted unto every man.
4a/4b	Negative to positive:	**4a-** take ye no thought **4b-** take thought
3a/3b	Identical words:	**3-** the morrow,
2a/2b	Parallel concepts:	**2a-** for what ye shall eat, or what ye shall drink, or wherewithal ye shall be clothed. **2b-** For your Father, who is in heaven, knoweth that you have need of all these things.
1	Central theme:	**1-** For, consider the lilies of the field, how they grow, they toil not, neither do they spin; and the kingdoms of the world, in all their glory, are not arrayed like one of these.

8

CHIASMA CONTAINING TWO-ELEMENT PARALLELISMS AS ONE OF THE CHIASTIC ELEMENTS

The parallelism is defined as a series of words, phrases or concepts that are repeated in the same order—as opposed to a chiasmus in which the series is repeated in inverse order. The parallel series is also a prominent element in ancient Hebrew religious writings. The following examples are a mixture of parallel and inverted parallel series. In each case, the repeated series of parallel elements as an entity are juxtaposed as mirror elements in the chiastic structure, thus identifying the series as a single chiastic element. We will proceed in the ensuing chapters from the simple to the more complex forms.

Two-Element Chiasma Containing Two-Element Parallelisms

D&C 4:2-4 — Chiasmus 4, 4A

2A] 2 Therefore, O ye that embark in the service of God, *see that ye serve him with all your heart,might, mind and strength,*
2B] *that ye may stand blameless before God* at the last day.
1] 3 Therefore, if ye have desires to serve God ye are called to the work;
2A] 4 For behold the field is white already to harvest; and lo, *he that thrusteth in his sickle with his might,*
2B] the same layeth up in store *that he perisheth not*, but bringeth salvation to his soul;

D&C 4:2-4 — Analysis 4A

2Aa/2Ab	Parallel concepts:	**2Aa-** see that ye serve him with all your heart, might, mind and strength, **2Ab-** he that thrusteth in his sickle with his might,
2Ba/2Bb	Parallel concepts:	**2Ba-** that ye may stand blameless before God **2Bb-** that he perisheth not
1	Central theme:	**1-** if ye have desires to serve God ye are called to the work

D&C 75:24-26 **Chiasmus 107, 75B**

2A] 24 Behold, I say unto you, that it is the duty of the church to assist in supporting the families of those, and also to *support the families of those who are called*

2B] *and must needs be sent unto the world* to proclaim the gospel unto the world.

1] 25 Wherefore, I, the Lord, give unto you this commandment, that ye *obtain places for your families,* inasmuch as your brethren are willing to open their hearts.

1] 26 And let all such as can *obtain places for their families,*

2A] *and support of the church for them,*

2B] *not fail to go into the world,* whether to the east or to the west, or to the north, or to the south.

D&C 75:24-26 **Analysis 75B**

2Aa/2Ab	Parallel concepts:	**2Aa-** support the families of those who are called **2Ab-** and support of the church for them,
2Ba/2Bb	Parallel concepts:	**2Ba-** and must needs be sent unto the world **2Bb-** not fail to go into the world,
1a/1b	Identical words:	**1-** obtain places for your/their families,

D&C 107:72-74 **Chiasmus 195, 107I**

2A] 72 *And also to be a judge in Israel*, to do the business of the church,

2B] *to sit in judgment upon transgressors* upon testimony as it shall be laid before him according to the laws, by the assistance of his counselors, whom he has chosen or will choose among the elders of the church.

1] 73 *This is the duty of a bishop who is not a literal descendant of Aaron,*

1] *but has been ordained to the High Priesthood after the order of Melchizedek.*

2A] 74 *Thus shall he be a judge,*

2B] *even a common judge among the inhabitants of Zion*, or in a stake of Zion, or in any branch of the church where he shall be set apart unto this ministry, until the borders of Zion are enlarged and it becomes necessary to have other bishops or judges in Zion or elsewhere.

D&C 107:72-74 — Analysis 107I

2Aa/2Ab	Parallel concepts:	**2Aa-** And also to be a judge in Israel, **2Ab-** Thus shall he be a judge,
2Ba/2Bb	Parallel concepts:	**2Ba-** to sit in judgment upon transgressors **2Bb-** even a common judge among the inhabitants of Zion,
1a/1b	Parallel concepts:	**1a-** This is the duty of a bishop who is not a literal descendant of Aaron, **1b-** but has been ordained to the High Priesthood after the order of Melchizedek

D&C 132:7-14 — Chiasmus 220, 132B

2A] 7 And verily I say unto you, that the conditions of this law are these: *All covenants, contracts, bonds, obligations, oaths, vows, performances, connections, associations, or expectations, that are not made and entered into and sealed by the Holy Spirit of promise, of him who is anointed, both as well for time and for all eternity*, and that too most holy, by revelation and commandment through the medium of mine anointed, whom I have appointed on the earth to hold this power (and I have appointed unto my servant Joseph to hold this power in the last days, and there is never but one on the earth at a time on whom this power and the keys of this priesthood are conferred), *are of no efficacy, virtue, or force in and after the resurrection from the dead*;

2B] *for all contracts that are not made unto this end have an end when men are dead.*

1] 8 *Behold, mine house is a house of order, saith the Lord God, and not a house of confusion.*

9 Will I accept of an offering, saith the Lord, that is not made in my name?

10 Or will I receive at your hands that which I have not appointed?

11 And will I appoint unto you, saith the Lord, except it be by law, even as I and my Father ordained unto you, before the world was?

12 I am the Lord thy God; and I give unto you this commandment—that no man shall come unto the Father but by me or by my word, which is my law, saith the Lord.

2A] 13 *And everything that is in the world, whether it be ordained of men, by thrones, or principalities, or powers, or things of name, whatsoever they may be, that are not by me or by my word, saith the Lord, shall be thrown down, and shall not remain after men are dead, neither in nor after the resurrection, saith the Lord your God.*

2B] 14 For whatsoever things remain are by me; *and whatsoever things are not by me shall be shaken and destroyed.*

D&C 132:7-14 **Analysis 132B**

2Aa/2Ab	Parallel concepts:	**2Aa-** All covenants, contracts, bonds, obligations, oaths, vows, performances, connections, associations, or expectations, that are not made and entered into and sealed by the Holy Spirit of promise, of him who is anointed, both as well for time and for all eternity...are of no efficacy, virtue, or force in and after the resurrection from the dead; **2Ab-** And everything that is in the world, whether it be ordained of men, by thrones, or principalities, or powers, or things of name, whatsoever they may be, that are not by me or by my word, saith the Lord, shall be thrown down, and shall not remain after men are dead, neither in nor after the resurrection, saith the Lord your God.
2Ba/2Bb	Parallel concepts:	**2Ba-** for all contracts that are not made unto this end have an end when men are dead. **2Bb-** and whatsoever things are not by me shall be shaken and destroyed.
1	Central theme:	**1-** *Behold, mine house is a house of order, saith the Lord God, and not a house of confusion.*

Three-Element Chiasma Containing Two-Element Parallelisms

D&C 5:24-28 — Chiasmus 6, 5B

3A] 24 Behold, I say unto him, he exalts himself and does not humble himself sufficiently before me; *but if he will bow down before me, and humble himself in mighty prayer and faith, in the sincerity of his heart,*

3B] *then will I grant unto him a view of the things which he desires to see.*

2] 25 And then he shall say unto the people of this generation: Behold, *I have seen the things which the Lord hath shown unto Joseph Smith, Jun.*, and I know of a surety that they are true, for I have seen them, *for they have been shown unto me by the power of God* and not of man.

1] 26 And I the Lord command him, my servant Martin Harris, that he shall say no more unto them concerning these things,

2] except he shall say: *I have seen them, and they have been shown unto me by the power of God*; and these are the words which he shall say.

27 But if he deny this he will break the covenant which he has before covenanted with me, and behold, he is condemned.

3A] 28 And now, *except he humble himself and acknowledge unto me the things that he has done which are wrong, and covenant with me that he will keep my commandments, and exercise faith in me,*

3B] *behold, I say unto him, he shall have no such views, for I will grant unto him no views of the things of which I have spoken.*

D&C 5:24-28 — Analysis 5B

3Aa/3Ab	Parallel admonitions:	**3Aa-** but if he will bow down before me, and humble himself in mighty prayer and faith, in the sincerity of his heart, **3Ab-** except he humble himself and acknowledge unto me the things that he has done which are wrong, and covenant with me that he will keep my commandments, and exercise faith in me,
3Ba/3Bb	Positive to negative:	**3Ba-** then will I grant unto him a view of the things which he desires to see. **3Bb-** for I will grant unto him no views of the things of which I have spoken.
2a/2b	Parallel concepts:	**2a-** I have seen the things which the Lord hath shown unto Joseph Smith, Jun. **2b-** I have seen them

	Identical words:	**2a/2b-** they have been shown unto me by the power of God
1	Central theme:	**1-** And I the Lord command him, my servant Martin Harris, that he shall say no more unto them concerning these things,

D&C 10:50-56 Chiasmus 18, 10H

3A] that *whosoever should believe in this gospel in this land might have eternal life;*
51 Yea, that it might be free unto all of whatsoever nation, kindred, tongue, or people they may be.

3B] 52 *And now, behold, according to their faith in their prayers will I bring this part of my gospel to the knowledge of my people.*

2] Behold, *I do not bring it to destroy that which they have received, but to build it up.*

1] 53 And for this cause have I said: If this generation harden not their hearts, I will establish my church among them.

2] 54 Now *I do not say this to destroy my church, but I say this to build up my church*;

3A] 55 Therefore, *whosoever belongeth to my church need not fear, for such shall inherit the kingdom of heaven.*

3B] 56 But it is they who do not fear me, neither keep my commandments but build up churches unto themselves to get gain, *yea, and all those that do wickedly and build up the kingdom of the devil—yea, verily, verily, I say unto you, that it is they that I will disturb, and cause to tremble and shake to the center.*

D&C 10:50-56 Analysis 10H

3Aa/3Ba	Parallel concepts:	**3Aa-** whosoever should believe in this gospel in this land might have eternal life; **3Ab-** whosoever belongeth to my church need not fear, for such shall inherit the kingdom of heaven.
3Ba/3Bb	Positive to negative:	**3Ba-** And now, behold, according to their faith in their prayers will I bring this part of my gospel to the knowledge of my people. **3Bb-** yea, and all those that do wickedly and build up the kingdom of the devil—yea, verily, verily, I say unto you, that it is

		they that I will disturb, and cause to tremble and shake to the center.
2a/2b	Parallel concepts:	**2a-** I do not bring it to destroy that which they have received, but to build it up. **2b-** I do not say this to destroy my church, but I say this to build up my church;
1	Central theme:	**1-** And for this cause have I said: If this generation harden not their hearts, I will establish my church among them.

D&C 18:2,3 — Chiasmus 25, 18A

3] *I give unto you these words*:
2A] 2 *Behold, I have manifested unto you, by my Spirit* in many instances,
2B] that *the things which you have written* are true;
1] wherefore *you know that they are true.*
1] 3 And if *you know that they are true,*
2A] *behold, I give unto you a commandment,*
2B] that you rely upon *the things which are written*;
3] 4 *For in them are all things written concerning the foundation of my church*, my gospel, and my rock.

D&C 18:2,3 — Analysis 18A

3a/3b	Parallel concepts:	**3a-** I give unto you these words **3b-** For in them are all things written concerning the foundation of my church
2Aa/2Ab	Parallel concepts:	**2Aa-** Behold, I have manifested unto you, by my Spirit **2Ab-** behold, I give unto you a commandment
2Ba/2Bb	Parallel concepts:	**2Ba-** the things which you have written **2Bb-** the things which are written
1a/1b	Identical words:	**1-** you know that they are true.

D&C 43:9-11 — Chiasmus 65, 43C

3] 9 And thus ye shall become instructed in the law of my church, and *be sanctified by that which ye have received,*
2] and *ye shall bind yourselves to act in all holiness before me—*
1A] 10 That *inasmuch as ye do this,*
1B] *glory shall be added to the kingdom which ye have received.*
1A] *Inasmuch as ye do it not,*

1B] *it shall be taken, even that which ye have received.*
2] 11 *Purge ye out the iniquity which is among you;*
3] *sanctify yourselves before me;*

D&C 43:9-11 **Analysis 43C**

3a/3b	Parallel concepts:	**3a-** be sanctified by that which ye have received, **3b-** sanctify yourselves before me;
2a/2b	Positive to negative:	**2a-** and ye shall bind yourselves to act in all holiness before me— **2b-** Purge ye out the iniquity which is among you;
1Aa/1Ab	Positive to negative:	**1Aa-** inasmuch as ye do this, **1Ab-** Inasmuch as ye do it not,
1Ba/1Bb	Positive to negative:	**1Ba-** glory shall be added to the kingdom which ye have received. **1Bb-** it shall be taken, even that which ye have received.

D&C 45:10-15 **Chiasmus 68, 45B**

3] Wherefore, come ye unto it, *and with him that cometh I will reason as with men in days of old*, and I will show unto you my strong reasoning.
2] 11 *Wherefore, hearken ye together and let me show unto you even my wisdom*—the wisdom of him whom ye say is the God of Enoch, and his brethren,
1A] 12 *Who were separated from the earth*, and were received unto myself—a city reserved until a day of righteousness shall come—
1B] a day which was sought for by all holy men, and *they found it not because of wickedness and abominations*;
1A] 13 *And confessed they were strangers and pilgrims on the earth*;
1B] 14 But obtained a promise that *they should find it and see it in their flesh.*
2] 15 *Wherefore, hearken and I will reason with you*, and
3] *I will speak unto you and prophesy, as unto men in days of old.*

D&C 45:10-15 **Analysis 45B**

3a/3b	Parallel concepts:	**3a-** and with him that cometh I will reason as with men in days of old, **3b-** I will speak unto you and prophesy, as unto men in days of old.

2a/2b	Parallel concepts:	**2a-** Wherefore, hearken ye together and let me show unto you even my wisdom— **2b-** Wherefore, hearken and I will reason with you,
1Aa/1Aa	Parallel concepts:	**1Aa-** Who were separated from the earth, **1Ab-** And confessed they were strangers and pilgrims on the earth;
1Ba/1Bb	Negative to positive:	**1Ba-** they found it not because of wickedness and abominations; **1Bb-** they should find it and see it in their flesh.

D&C 47:1-4 — Chiasmus 73, 47A

3] 1 *Behold, it is expedient in me that my servant John should write and keep a regular history,*

2A] *and assist you, my servant Joseph, in transcribing all things which shall be given you,*

2B] *until he is called to further duties.*

1] 2 Again, verily I say unto you that he can also lift up his voice in meetings, whenever it shall be expedient.

2A] 3 And again, I say unto you that *it shall be appointed unto him to keep the church record and history continually;*

2B] *for Oliver Cowdery I have appointed to another office.*

3] 4 *Wherefore, it shall be given him, inasmuch as he is faithful, by the Comforter, to write these things.* Even so. Amen.

D&C 47:1-4 — Analysis 47A

3a/3b	Parallel concepts:	**3a-** Behold, it is expedient in me that my servant John should write and keep a regular history, **3b-** Wherefore, it shall be given him, inasmuch as he is faithful, by the Comforter, to write these things.
2Aa/2Ab	Parallel concepts:	**2Aa-** and assist you, my servant Joseph, in transcribing all things which shall be given you, **2Ab-** it shall be appointed unto him to keep the church record and history continually;

2Ba/2Bb	Parallel concepts:	**2Ba-** until he is called to further duties. **2Bb-** For Oliver Cowdery I have appointed to another office.
1	Central theme:	**1-** Again, verily I say unto you that he can also lift up his voice in meetings, whenever it shall be expedient.

D&C 61:13-18 Chiasmus 88, 61B

3] *And now*, behold, for your good *I gave unto you a commandment* concerning these things; and I, the Lord, will reason with you as with men in days of old.

2A] 14 *Behold, I, the Lord, in the beginning blessed the waters;*

2B] *but in the last days*, by the mouth of my servant John, *I cursed the waters.*

1] 15 *Wherefore, the days will come that no flesh shall be safe upon the waters.*

1] 16 *And it shall be said in days to come that none is able to go up to the land of Zion upon the waters, but he that is upright in heart.*

2A] 17 *And, as I, the Lord, in the beginning cursed the land,*

2B] *even so in the last days have I blessed it*, in its time, for the use of my saints, that they may partake the fatness thereof.

3] 18 *And now I give unto you a commandment* that what I say unto one I say unto all, that you shall forewarn your brethren concerning these waters, that they come not in journeying upon them, lest their faith fail and they are caught in snares;

D&C 61:13-18 Analysis 61B

3a/3b	Identical words:	**3-** And now...I gave/give unto you a commandment
2Aa/2Ab	Positive to negative:	**2A3a-** Behold, I, the Lord, in the beginning blessed the waters; **2Ab-** And, as I, the Lord, in the beginning cursed the land,
2Ba/2Bb	Negative to positive:	**2Ba-** but in the last days...I cursed the waters. **2Bb-** even so in the last days have I blessed it,
1a/1b	Parallel concepts:	**1a-** Wherefore, the days will come that no flesh shall be safe upon the waters.

1b- And it shall be said in days to come that none is able to go up to the land of Zion upon the waters, but he that is upright in heart.

D&C 65:1-3 — Chiasmus 97, 65A

1 Hearken, and lo, a voice as of one sent down from on high, who is mighty and powerful, whose going forth is unto the ends of the earth, yea,

3A] *whose voice is unto men—*

3B] *Prepare ye the way of the Lord*, make his paths straight.

2] 2 *The keys of the kingdom of God are committed unto man on the earth,*

1] *and from thence shall the gospel roll forth unto the ends of the earth,*

1] *as the stone which is cut out of the mountain without hands shall roll forth,*

2] *until it has filled the whole earth.*

3A] 3 *Yea, a voice crying—*

3B] *Prepare ye the way of the Lord*, prepare ye the supper of the Lamb, make ready for the Bridegroom.

D&C 65:1-3 — Analysis 65A

3Aa/3Ab	Parallel concepts:	**3Aa-** whose voice is unto men— **3Ab-** Yea, a voice crying—
3Ba/3Bb	Identical words:	**3B-** prepare ye the way of the Lord,
2a/2b	Parallel concepts:	**2a-** The keys of the kingdom of God are committed unto man on the earth, **2b-** until it has filled the whole earth.
1a/1b	Parallel concepts:	**1a-** and from thence shall the gospel roll forth unto the ends of the earth, **1b-** as the stone which is cut out of the mountain without hands shall roll forth,

D&C 76:5-10 — Chiasmus 108, 76A

3] 5 *For thus saith the Lord—I, the Lord, am merciful and gracious unto those who fear me, and delight to honor those who serve me in righteousness and in truth unto the end.*

2] 6 *Great shall be their reward and eternal shall be their glory.*

1A] 7 *And to them will I reveal all mysteries,*

1B] *yea, all the hidden mysteries of my kingdom from days of old, and for ages to come, will I make known unto them the good pleasure of my will concerning all things pertaining to my kingdom.*
1A] 8 *Yea, even the wonders of eternity shall they know,*
1B] 9 *And things to come will I show them, even the things of many generations.*
2] *And their wisdom shall be great, and their understanding reach to heaven; and before them the wisdom of the wise shall perish, and the understanding of the prudent shall come to naught.*
3] 10 *For by my Spirit will I enlighten them, and by my power will I make known unto them the secrets of my will—yea, even those things which eye has not seen, nor ear heard, nor yet entered into the heart of man.*

D&C 76:5-10 **Analysis 76A**

3a/3b	Parallel concepts:	**3a-** For thus saith the Lord—I, the Lord, am merciful and gracious unto those who fear me, and delight to honor those who serve me in righteousness and in truth unto the end. **3b-** For by my Spirit will I enlighten them, and by my power will I make known unto them the secrets of my will—yea, even those things which eye has not seen, nor ear heard, nor yet entered into the heart of man.
2a/2b	Parallel concepts:	**2a-** Great shall be their reward and eternal shall be their glory. **2b-** And their wisdom shall be great, and their understanding reach to heaven; and before them the wisdom of the wise shall perish, and the understanding of the prudent shall come to naught.
1Aa/1Ab	Parallel concepts:	**1Aa-** And to them will I reveal all mysteries, **1Ab-** Yea, even the wonders of eternity shall they know,
1Ba/1Bb	Parallel concepts:	**1Ba-** yea, all the hidden mysteries of my kingdom from days of old, and for ages to come, will I make known unto them the

good pleasure of my will concerning all things pertaining to my kingdom.
1Bb- And things to come will I show them, even the things of many generations.

D&C 76:31-38 — Chiasmus 113, 76F

3A] 32 *They are they who are the sons of perdition,*
3B] *of whom I say that it had been better for them never to have been born;*
2] 33 *For they are vessels of wrath, doomed to suffer the wrath of God, with the devil and his angels in eternity;*
1] 34 *Concerning whom I have said there is no forgiveness in this world nor in the world to come—*
1] 35 *Having denied the Holy Spirit after having received it, and having denied the Only Begotten Son of the Father, having crucified him unto themselves and put him to an open shame.*
2] 36 *These are they who shall go away into the lake of fire and brimstone, with the devil and his angels—*
3A] 37 *And the only ones on whom the second death shall have any power;*
3B] 38 *Yea, verily, the only ones who shall not be redeemed in the due time of the Lord, after the sufferings of his wrath.*

D&C 76:31-38 — Analysis 76F

3Aa/3Ab	Parallel concepts:	**3Aa-** They are they who are the sons of perdition, **3Ab-** And the only ones on whom the second death shall have any power;
3Ba/3Bb	Parallel concepts:	**3Ba-** of whom I say that it had been better for them never to have been born; **3Bb-** Yea, verily, the only ones who shall not be redeemed in the due time of the Lord, after the sufferings of his wrath.
2a/2b	Parallel concepts:	**2a-** For they are vessels of wrath, doomed to suffer the wrath of God, with the devil and his angels in eternity; **2b-** These are they who shall go away into the lake of fire and brimstone, with the devil and his angels—

1a/1b	Parallel concepts:	**1a-** Concerning whom I have said there is no forgiveness in this world nor in the world to come— **1b-** Having denied the Holy Spirit after having received it, and having denied the Only Begotten Son of the Father, having crucified him unto themselves and put him to an open shame.

D&C 103:6-11 — Chiasmus 176, 103B

3A] 6 *Behold they shall, for I have decreed it, begin to prevail against mine enemies from this very hour.*
7 And by hearkening to observe all the words which I, the Lord their God, shall speak unto them,

3B] *they shall never cease to prevail until the kingdoms of the world are subdued under my feet, and the earth is given unto the saints, to possess it forever and ever.*

2] 8 *But inasmuch as they keep not my commandments, and hearken not to observe all my words, the kingdoms of the world shall prevail against them.*

1] 9 For they were set to be a light unto the world, and to be the saviors of men;

2] 10 *And inasmuch as they are not the saviors of men, they are as salt that has lost its savor, and is thenceforth good for nothing but to be cast out and trodden under foot of men.*

3A] 11 But verily I say unto you, *I have decreed that your brethren which have been scattered shall return to the lands of their inheritances,*

3B] *and shall build up the waste places of Zion.*

D&C 103:6-11 — Analysis 103B

3Aa/3Ab	Parallel concepts:	**3Aa-** Behold they shall, for I have decreed it, begin to prevail against mine enemies from this very hour. **3Ab-** I have decreed that your brethren which have been scattered shall return to the lands of their inheritances,
3Ba/3Bb	Parallel concepts:	**3Ba-** they shall never cease to prevail until the kingdoms of the world are subdued

		under my feet, and the earth is given unto the saints, to possess it forever and ever. **3Bb-** and shall build up the waste places of Zion.
2a/2b	Parallel concepts:	**2a-** But inasmuch as they keep not my commandments, and hearken not to observe all my words, the kingdoms of the world shall prevail against them. **2b-** And inasmuch as they are not the saviors of men, they are as salt that has lost its savor, and is thenceforth good for nothing but to be cast out and trodden under foot of men.
1	Central theme:	**1-** For they were set to be a light unto the world, and to be the saviors of men;

D&C 104:80-82 — Chiasmus 184, 104F

3] 80 *And inasmuch as you are diligent and humble, and exercise the prayer of faith,*
2A] Behold, *I will soften the hearts of those to whom you are in debt,*
2B] *until I shall send means unto you for your deliverance.*
1] 81 *Therefore write speedily to New York*
1] *and write according to that which shall be dictated by my Spirit;*
2A] *and I will soften the hearts of those to whom you are in debt,*
2B] *that it shall be taken away out of their minds to bring affliction upon you.*
3] 82 And *inasmuch as ye are humble and faithful and call upon my name,* behold, I will give you the victory.

D&C 104:80-82 — Analysis 104F

3a/3b	Parallel concepts:	**3a-** And inasmuch as you are diligent and humble, and exercise the prayer of faith, **3b-** And inasmuch as ye are humble and faithful and call upon my name,
2Aa/2Ab	Identical words:	**2A-** I will soften the hearts of those to whom you are in debt,
2Ba/2Bb	Parallel concepts:	**2Ba-** until I shall send means unto you for your deliverance. **2Bb-** that it shall be taken away out of their minds to bring affliction upon you.

1a/1b	Parallel concepts:	**1a-** Therefore write speedily to New York **1b-** and write according to that which shall be dictated by my Spirit;

D&C 121:1-4 **Chiasmus 210, 121A**

3A] 1 O God, where art thou? And where is the *pavilion*
3B] that covereth *thy hiding place*?
2] 2 *How long shall thy hand be stayed, and thine eye, yea thy pure eye, behold from the eternal heavens the wrongs of thy people and of thy servants,* and thine ear be penetrated with their cries?
1] 3 *Yea, O Lord, how long shall they suffer these wrongs and unlawful oppressions, before thine heart shall be softened toward them, and thy bowels be moved with compassion toward them?*
1] 4 *O Lord God Almighty, maker of heaven, earth, and seas, and of all things that in them are, and who controllest and subjectest the devil, and the dark and benighted dominion of Sheol—*
2] *stretch forth thy hand; let thine eye pierce;*
3A] let thy *pavilion* be taken up;
3B] let *thy hiding place* no longer be covered;

D&C 121:1-4 **Analysis 121A**

3Aa/3Ab	Identical word:	**3A-** pavilion
3Ba/3Bb	Identical words:	**3B-** thy hiding place
2a/2b	Parallel concepts:	**2a-** How long shall thy hand be stayed, and thine eye, yea thy pure eye, behold from the eternal heavens the wrongs of thy people and of thy servants, **2b-** stretch forth thy hand; let thine eye pierce;
1a/1b	Parallel concepts:	**1a-** Yea, O Lord, how long shall they suffer these wrongs and unlawful oppressions, before thine heart shall be softened toward them, and thy bowels be moved with compassion toward them? **1b-** O Lord God Almighty, maker of heaven, earth, and seas, and of all things that in them are, and who controllest and subjectest the devil, and the dark and benighted dominion of Sheol—

Four-Element Chiasma Containing Two-Element Parallelisms

D&C 6:10-25 — Chiasmus 7, 6A

4] 10 *Behold thou hast a gift,* and blessed art thou because of thy gift. Remember it is sacred and cometh from above—

11 And if thou wilt inquire, thou shalt know mysteries which are great and marvelous; therefore thou shalt exercise thy gift, that thou mayest find out mysteries, that thou mayest bring many to the knowledge of the truth, yea, convince them of the error of their ways.

12 Make not thy gift known unto any save it be those who are of thy faith. Trifle not with sacred things.

13 If thou wilt do good, yea, and hold out faithful to the end, thou shalt be saved in the kingdom of God, which is the greatest of all the gifts of God; for there is no gift greater than the gift of salvation.

14 Verily, verily, I say unto thee, blessed art thou for what thou hast done; for thou hast inquired of me, and behold, as often as thou hast inquired thou hast received instruction of my Spirit. If it had not been so, thou wouldst not have come to the place where thou art at this time.

15 Behold, thou knowest that thou hast inquired of me and I did enlighten thy mind; and now I tell thee these things that thou mayest know that thou hast been enlightened by the Spirit of truth;

3] 16 *Yea, I tell thee, that thou mayest know that there is none else save God that knowest thy thoughts and the intents of thy heart.*

2] 17 *I tell thee these things as a witness unto thee*—that the words or the work which thou hast been writing are true.

18 Therefore be diligent; stand by my servant Joseph, faithfully, in whatsoever difficult circumstances he may be for the word's sake.

19 Admonish him in his faults, and also receive admonition of him. Be patient; be sober; be temperate; have patience, faith, hope and charity.

1A] 20 *Behold, thou art Oliver,*

1B] *and I have spoken unto thee because of thy desires; therefore treasure up these words in thy heart. Be faithful and diligent in keeping the commandments of God, and I will encircle thee in the arms of my love.*

1A] 21 *Behold, I am Jesus Christ, the Son of God.*

1B] *I am the same that came unto mine own, and mine own received me not. I am the light which shineth in darkness, and the darkness comprehendeth it not.*

22 Verily, verily, I say unto you, if you desire a further witness, cast your mind upon the night that you cried unto me in your heart, that you might know concerning the truth of these things.
23 Did I not speak peace to your mind concerning the matter? What greater witness can you have than from God?
2] 24 *And now, behold, you have received a witness*;
3] *for if I have told you things which no man knoweth have you not received a witness?*
4] 25 *And, behold, I grant unto you a gift*, if you desire of me, to translate, even as my servant Joseph.

D&C 6:10-25 **Analysis 6A**

4a/4b	Parallel concepts:	**4a-** Behold thou hast a gift **4b-** And, behold, I grant unto you a gift
3a/3b	Cause to effect:	**3a-** Yea, I tell thee, that thou mayest know that there is none else save God that knowest thy thoughts and the intents of thy heart **3b-** for if I have told you things which no man knoweth have you not received a witness?
2a/2b	Parallel concepts:	**2a-** I tell thee these things as a witness unto thee **2b-** And now, behold, you have received a witness
1Aa/1Ab	Parallel concepts:	**1Aa-** Behold, thou art Oliver **1Ab-** Behold, I am Jesus Christ, the Son of God
1Ba/1Bb	Parallel concepts:	**1Ba-** and I have spoken unto thee because of thy desires; therefore treasure up these words in thy heart. Be faithful and diligent in keeping the commandments of God, and I will encircle thee in the arms of my love **1Bb-** I am the same that came unto mine own, and mine own received me not. I am the light which shineth in darkness, and the darkness comprehendeth it not.

D&C 10:27-33 Chiasmus 14, 10D

4] 27 *And thus he goeth up and down, to and fro in the earth, seeking to destroy the souls of men.*

3] 28 Verily, verily, I say unto you, *wo be unto him that lieth to deceive because he supposeth that another lieth to deceive*, for such are not exempt from the justice of God.

2A] 29 Now, behold, *they have altered these words,*

2B] because *Satan saith unto them: He hath deceived you—and thus he flattereth them away to do iniquity, to get thee to tempt the Lord thy God.*

1] 30 Behold, I say unto you, that you shall not translate again those words which have gone forth out of your hands;

2A] 31 For, behold, *they shall not accomplish their evil designs in lying against those words.*

2B] For, behold, *if you should bring forth the same words they will say that you have lied and that you have pretended to translate, but that you have contradicted yourself.*

3] 32 And, behold, they will publish this, and *Satan will harden the hearts of the people to stir them up to anger against you*, that they will not believe my words.

4] 33 *Thus Satan thinketh to overpower your testimony in this generation, that the work may not come forth in this generation.*

D&C 10:27-33 Analysis 10D

4a/4b	Parallel concepts:	**4a-** And thus he goeth up and down, to and fro in the earth, seeking to destroy the souls of men. **4b-** Thus Satan thinketh to overpower your testimony in this generation, that the work may not come forth in this generation.
3a/3b	Parallel concepts:	**3a-** wo be unto him that lieth to deceive because he supposeth that another lieth to deceive, **3b-** Satan will harden the hearts of the people to stir them up to anger against you,

2Aa/2Ab	Parallel concepts:	**2Aa-** they have altered these words, **2Ab-** they shall not accomplish their evil designs in lying against those words.
2Ba/2Bb	General to specific:	**2Ba-** Satan saith unto them: He hath deceived you—and thus he flattereth them away to do iniquity, to get thee to tempt the Lord thy God. **2Bb-** if you should bring forth the same words they will say that you have lied and that you have pretended to translate, but that you have contradicted yourself.
1a/1b	Specific to general:	**1a-** and thus he causeth them to catch themselves in their own snare. **1b-** And thus he goeth up and down, to and fro in the earth,

D&C 10:38-41 **Chiasmus 15, 10E**

4A] 38 And now, verily I say unto you, that *an account of those things that you have written,*
4B] *which have gone out of your hands,*
3] *is engraven upon the plates of Nephi;*
2] 39 Yea, and you remember it was said in those writings that *a more particular account*
1] *<account> was given of these things upon the plates of Nephi.*
1] 40 And now, because the *account which is engraven upon the plates of Nephi*
2] *is more particular* concerning the things which, in my wisdom, I would bring to the knowledge of the people *in this account—*
3] 41 Therefore, you shall translate *the engravings which are on the plates of Nephi,*
4A] *down even till you come to the reign of king Benjamin, or until you come to that which you have translated,*
4B] *which you have retained;*

D&C 10:38-41 **Analysis 10E**

4Aa/4Ab	Parallel concepts:	**4Aa-** an account of those things that you have written, **4Ab-** down even till you come to the reign of king Benjamin, or until you come to that which you have translated,
4Ba/4Bb	Negative to positive:	**4Ba-** which have gone out of your hands, **4Bb-** which you have retained;
3a/3b	Parallel concepts:	**3a-** is engraven upon the plates of Nephi; **3b-** the engravings which are on the plates of Nephi,
2a/2b	Parallel concepts:	**2a-** a more particular account **2b-** is more particular... in this account
1a/1b	Parallel concepts:	**1a-** <account> was given of these things upon the plates of Nephi. **1b-** account is engraven upon the plates of Nephi

NOTE: The word "account" in 2a and 1a is the same word; repeated in 1a to parallel the same word in 1b.

D&C 12:2-9 **Chiasmus 22, 12A**

4A] 2 Behold, *I am God*;
4B] *give heed to my word*, which is quick and powerful, sharper than a two-edged sword, to the dividing asunder of both joints and marrow; therefore, give heed unto my word.
3 Behold, the field is white already to harvest; therefore, whoso desireth to reap let him thrust in his sickle with his might, and reap while the day lasts, that he may treasure up for his soul everlasting salvation in the kingdom of God.
3] 4 Yea, *whosoever will thrust in his sickle and reap,*
2] *the same is called of God.*
1] 5 Therefore, *if you will ask of me you shall receive; if you will knock it shall be opened unto you.*
1] 6 Now, *as you have asked,*
2] behold, *I say unto you, keep my commandments, and seek to bring forth and establish the cause of Zion.*
3] *7 Behold, I speak unto you, and also to all those who have desires to bring forth and establish this work;*

8 And no one can assist in this work except he shall be humble and full of love, having faith, hope, and charity, being temperate in all things, whatsoever shall be entrusted to his care.

4A] 9 Behold, *I am the light and the life of the world*, that speak these words,

4B] therefore *give heed with your might*, and then you are called. Amen.

D&C 12:2-9 — Analysis 12A

4Aa/4Ab	Parallel concepts:	**4Aa-** I am God; **4Ab-** I am the light and the life of the world,
4Ba/4Bb	Parallel concepts:	**4Ba-** give heed to my word, **4Bb-** give heed with your might,
3a/3b	Parallel concepts:	**3a-** whosoever will thrust in his sickle and reap, **3b-** Behold, I speak unto you, and also to all those who have desires to bring forth and establish this work;
2a/2b	Parallel concepts:	**2a-** the same is called of God. **2b-** I say unto you, keep my commandments, and seek to bring forth and establish the cause of Zion.
1a/1b	Future to past:	**1a-** if you will ask of me you shall receive; if you will knock it shall be opened unto you. **1b-** as you have asked,

D&C 45:1-7 — Chiasmus 67, 45A

4] 1 Hearken, O ye people of my church, to whom the kingdom has been given; hearken ye and give ear to *him who laid the foundation of the earth, who made the heavens and all the hosts thereof, and by whom all things were made which live, and move, and have a being.*

3] 2 And again I say, *hearken unto my voice, lest death shall overtake you; in an hour when ye think not the summer shall be past, and the harvest ended, and your souls not saved.*

2] 3 *Listen to him who is the advocate with the Father, who is pleading your cause before him—*

1A] 4 Saying: Father, *behold the sufferings and death of him who did no sin,*

1B] *in whom thou wast well pleased;*
1A] *behold the blood of thy Son which was shed,*
1B] the blood of him *whom thou gavest that thyself might be glorified;*
2] 5 *Wherefore, Father, spare these my brethren that believe on my name, that they may come unto me and have everlasting life.*
3] 6 *Hearken, O ye people of my church, and ye elders listen together, and hear my voice while it is called today, and harden not your hearts;*
4] 7 For verily I say unto you that *I am Alpha and Omega, the beginning and the end, the light and the life of the world—a light that shineth in darkness and the darkness comprehendeth it not.*

D&C 45:1-7 **Analysis 45A**

4a/4b	Parallel concepts:	**4a-** him who laid the foundation of the earth, who made the heavens and all the hosts thereof, and by whom all things were made which live, and move, and have a being. **4b-** I am Alpha and Omega, the beginning and the end, the light and the life of the world—a light that shineth in darkness and the darkness comprehendeth it not.
3a/3b	Parallel concepts:	**3a-** hearken unto my voice, lest death shall overtake you; in an hour when ye think not the summer shall be past, and the harvest ended, and your souls not saved. **3b-** Hearken, O ye people of my church, and ye elders listen together, and hear my voice while it is called today, and harden not your hearts;
2a/2b	Declaration to Fulfillment:	**2a-** Listen to him who is the advocate with the Father, who is pleading your cause before him— **2b-** Wherefore, Father, spare these my brethren that believe on my name, that they may come unto me and have everlasting life.

1Aa/1Ab	Parallel concepts:	**1Aa-** behold the sufferings and death of him who did no sin, **1Ab-** behold the blood of thy Son which was shed,
1Ba/1Bb	Parallel concepts:	**1Ba-** in whom thou wast well pleased; **1Bb-** whom thou gavest that thyself might be glorified;

D&C 98:31 — Chiasmus 168, 98D

4A] Nevertheless, *thine enemy is in thine hands;* and if thou rewardest him according to his works
4B] *thou art justified;*
3] if *he*
2] *has sought*
1] *thy life,*
1] and *thy life*
2] *is endangered*
3] by *him,*
4A] *thine enemy is in thine hands*
4B] and *thou art justified.*

D&C 98:31 — Analysis 98D

4Aa/4Ab	Identical words:	**4A-** thine enemy is in thine hands
4Ba/4Bb	Identical words:	**4B-** thou art justified;
3a/3b	Parallel concepts:	**3a-** he **3b-** him
2a/2b	Parallel concepts:	**2a-** has sought **2b-** is endangered
1a/1b	Identical words:	**1-** thy life

D&C 103:1-10 — Chiasmus 175, 103A

4] 1 *Verily I say unto you, my friends, behold, I will give unto you a revelation and commandment,*
3] that you may know how to act in the discharge of your duties concerning the salvation and redemption of your brethren, who have been scattered on the land of Zion;
2 *Being driven and smitten by the hands of mine enemies, on whom I will pour out my wrath without measure in mine own time.*

3 For I have suffered them thus far, that they might fill up the measure of their iniquities, that their cup might be full;
4 And that those who call themselves after my name might be chastened for a little season with a sore and grievous chastisement,

2] *because they did not hearken altogether unto the precepts and commandments which I gave unto them.*

1A] 5 But verily I say unto you, *that I have decreed a decree* which my people shall realize,

1B] *inasmuch as they hearken from this very hour unto the counsel which I, the Lord their God, shall give unto them.*

1A] 6 Behold they shall, *for I have decreed it,*

1B] *begin to prevail against mine enemies from this very hour.*

2] 7 *And by hearkening to observe all the words which I, the Lord their God, shall speak unto them,*

3] *they shall never cease to prevail until the kingdoms of the world are subdued under my feet, and the earth is given unto the saints, to possess it forever and ever.*

4] 8 *But inasmuch as they keep not my commandments, and hearken not to observe all my words,* the kingdoms of the world shall prevail against them.

D&C 103:1-10 Analysis 103A

4a/4b	Positive to negative:	**4a-** Verily I say unto you, my friends, behold, I will give unto you a revelation and commandment, **4b-** But inasmuch as they keep not my commandments, and hearken not to observe all my words,
3a/3b	Negative to positive:	**3a-** Being driven and smitten by the hands of mine enemies, on whom I will pour out my wrath without measure in mine own time. **3b-** they shall never cease to prevail until the kingdoms of the world are subdued under my feet, and the earth is given unto the saints, to possess it forever and ever.
2a/2b	Negative to positive:	**2a-** because they did not hearken altogether unto the precepts and commandments which I gave unto them.

		2b- And by hearkening to observe all the words which I, the Lord their God, shall speak unto them,
1Aa/1Ab	Parallel concepts:	**1Aa-** that I have decreed a decree **1Ab-** for I have decreed it,
1Ba/1Bb	Parallel concepts:	**1Ba-** inasmuch as they hearken from this very hour **1Bb-** begin to prevail against mine enemies from this very hour.

D&C 103:10-14 — Chiasmus 177, 103C

4] 10 *And inasmuch as they are not the saviors of men, they are as salt that has lost its savor, and is thenceforth good for nothing but to be cast out and trodden under foot of men.*

3A] 11 *But verily I say unto you, I have decreed that your brethren which have been scattered shall return to the lands of their inheritances,*

3B] *and shall build up the waste places of Zion.*

2] 12 *For after much tribulation*, as I have said unto you in a former commandment,

1] *cometh the blessing.*

1] 13 *Behold, this is the blessing which I have promised*

2] *after your tribulations, and the tribulations of your brethren—*

3A] *your redemption, and the redemption of your brethren,*

3B] *even their restoration to the land of Zion*, to be established, no more to be thrown down.

4] 14 *Nevertheless, if they pollute their inheritances they shall be thrown down; for I will not spare them if they pollute their inheritances.*

D&C 103:10-14 — Analysis 103C

4a/4b	Parallel concepts:	**4a-** And inasmuch as they are not the saviors of men, they are as salt that has lost its savor, and is thenceforth good for nothing but to be cast out and trodden under foot of men. **4b-** Nevertheless, if they pollute their inheritances they shall be thrown down; for I will not spare them if they pollute their inheritances.

3Aa/3Ab	Parallel concepts:	**3Aa-** But verily I say unto you, I have decreed that your brethren which have been scattered shall return to the lands of their inheritances, **3Ab-** your redemption, and the redemption of your brethren,
3Ba/3Bb	Parallel concepts:	**3Ba-** and shall build up the waste places of Zion. **3Bb-** even their restoration to the land of Zion,
2a/2b	Parallel concepts:	**2a-** For after much tribulation, **2b-** after your tribulations, and the tribulations of your brethren—
1a/1b	Parallel concepts:	**1a-** cometh the blessing **1b-** Behold, this is the blessing which I have promised

Five-Element Chiasma Containing Two-Element Parallelisms

D&C 17:2-7 **Chiasmus 24, 17A**

5] 2 *And it is by your faith that you shall obtain a view of them*, even by that faith which was had by the prophets of old.
4] 3 *And after that you have obtained faith,*
3] *and have seen them with your eyes,*
2A] *you shall testify of them,*
2B] *by the power of God;*
1] 4 And this you shall do that my servant Joseph Smith, Jun., may not be destroyed, that I may bring about my righteous purposes unto the children of men in this work.
2A] 5 And *ye shall testify that you have seen them*, even as my servant Joseph Smith, Jun., has seen them;
2B] *for it is by my power*
3] *that he has seen them,*
4] *and it is because he had faith.*
6 And he has translated the book, even that part which I have commanded him, and as your Lord and your God liveth it is true.
5] 7 *Wherefore, you have received* the same power, and *the same faith*, and the same gift like unto him;

D&C 17:2-7 **Analysis 17A**

5a/5b	Parallel concepts:	**5a-** And it is by your faith that you shall obtain a view of them, **5b-** Wherefore, you have received . . . the same faith
4a/4b	Parallel concepts:	**4a-** And after that you have obtained faith **4b-** and it is because he had faith.
3a/3b	Parallel concepts:	**3a-** and have seen them with your eyes, **3b-** that he has seen them,
2Aa/2Ab	Parallel concepts:	**2Aa-** you shall testify of them, **2Ab-** ye shall testify that you have seen them,
2Ba/2Bb	Parallel concepts:	**2Ba-** by the power of God; **2Bb-** for it is by my power
1	Central theme:	**1-** And this you shall do that my servant Joseph Smith, Jun., may not be destroyed, that I may bring about my righteous purposes unto the children of men in this work.

D&C 42:4-10 — Chiasmus 59, 42A

4 Behold, verily I say unto you, I give unto you this first commandment,
5] that *ye shall go forth in my name, every one of you,*
4] excepting *my servants Joseph Smith, Jun., and Sidney Rigdon.*
5 And I give unto them a commandment that they shall go forth for
a little season,
3] *and it shall be given by the power of the Spirit when they shall return.*
2A] 6 *And ye shall go forth* in the power of my Spirit,
2B] *preaching my gospel, two by two, in my name, lifting up your*
voices as with the sound of a trump, declaring my word like unto
angels of God.
1] 7 And ye shall go forth baptizing with water, saying:
Repent ye, repent ye, for the kingdom of heaven is at hand.
2A] 8 *And* from this place *ye shall go forth* into the regions westward;
2B] *and inasmuch as ye shall find them that will receive you* ye shall
build up my church in every region--
3] 9 *Until the time shall come when it shall be revealed unto you from*
on high, when the city of the New Jerusalem shall be prepared,
that ye may be gathered in one, that ye may be my people and I will
be your God.
4] 10 And again, I say unto you, that *my servant Edward Partridge*
5] *shall stand in the office whereunto I have appointed him.* And it shall come
to pass, that if he transgress another shall be appointed in his stead.
Even so. Amen.

D&C 42:4-10 — Analysis 42A

5a/5b	Parallel concepts:	**5a-** ye shall go forth in my name, every one of you, **5b-** shall stand in the office whereunto I have appointed him.
4a/4b	Parallel concepts:	**4a-** my servants Joseph Smith, Jun., and Sidney Rigdon. **4b-** my servant Edward Partridge
3a/3b	Parallel concepts:	**3a-** and it shall be given by the power of the Spirit when they shall return. **3b-** Until the time shall come when it shall be revealed unto you from on high . . . that ye may be gathered in one,

2Aa/2Ab	Identical words:	**2A-** And ye shall go forth
2Ba/2Bb	Parallel concepts:	**2Ba-** preaching my gospel, two by two, in my name, lifting up your voices as with the sound of a trump, declaring my word like unto angels of God. **2Bb-** and inasmuch as ye shall find them that will receive you
1	Central Theme:	**1-** And ye shall go forth baptizing with water, saying: Repent ye, repent ye, for the kingdom of heaven is at hand.

D&C 68:14-19 — Chiasmus 99, 68A

5] 14 *There remain hereafter, in the due time of the Lord, other bishops to be set apart unto the church, to minister even according to the first;*

4A] 15 *Wherefore they shall be high priests who are worthy, and they shall be appointed by the First Presidency of the Melchizedek Priesthood,*

4B] *except they be literal descendants of Aaron.*

3] 16 *And if they be literal descendants of Aaron*

2] *they have a legal right to the bishopric,* if they are the firstborn among the sons of Aaron;

1] 17 For the firstborn holds the right of the presidency over this priesthood, and the keys or authority of the same.

2] 18 *No man has a legal right to this office, to hold the keys of this priesthood,*

3] *except he be a literal descendant and the firstborn of Aaron.*

4A] 19 *But, as a high priest of the Melchizedek Priesthood has authority to officiate in all the lesser offices*

4B] he may officiate in the office of bishop *when no literal descendant of Aaron can be found,*

5] *provided he is called and set apart and ordained unto this power, under the hands of the First Presidency of the Melchizedek Priesthood.*

D&C 68:14-19 — Analysis 68A

5a/5b	Parallel concepts:	**5a-** There remain hereafter, in the due time of the Lord, other bishops to be set apart unto the church, to minister even according to the first; **5b-** provided he is called and set apart and ordained unto this power, under the hands of the First Presidency of the Melchizedek Priesthood.

4Aa/4Ab	Parallel concepts:	**4Aa-** Wherefore they shall be high priests who are worthy, and they shall be appointed by the First Presidency of the Melchizedek Priesthood, **4Ab-** But, as a high priest of the Melchizedek Priesthood has authority to officiate in all the lesser offices
4Ba/4Bb	Positive to negative:	**4Ba-** except they be literal descendants of Aaron. **4Bb-** when no literal descendant of Aaron can be found,
3a/3b	Parallel concepts:	**3a-** And if they be literal descendants of Aaron **3b-** except he be a literal descendant and the firstborn of Aaron.
2a/2b	Positive to negative:	**2a-** they have a legal right to the bishopric, **2b-** No man has a legal right to this office, to hold the keys of this priesthood,
1	Central theme:	**1-** For the firstborn holds the right of the presidency over this priesthood, and the keys or authority of the same.

D&C 70:2-6 — Chiasmus 101, 50A

5] 2 For *I give unto them*
4] *a commandment;*
3] *wherefore* hearken and hear, for thus saith the Lord unto them--
2A] 3 *I, the Lord, have appointed them,*
2B] *and ordained them to be stewards over the revelations and commandments which I have given unto them, and which I shall hereafter give unto them;*
1] 4 And an account of this stewardship will I require of them in the day of judgment.
2A] 5 Wherefore, *I have appointed unto them,*
2B] and this is their business in the church of God, to manage them and the concerns thereof, yea, the benefits thereof.
3] 6 *Wherefore,*
4] *a commandment*
5] *I give unto them,*
that they shall not give these things unto the church, neither unto the world;

D&C 70:2-6 **Analysis 70A**

5a/5b	Identical words:	**5-** I give unto them
4a/4b	Identical words:	**4-** a commandment
3a/3b	Identical words:	**3-** wherefore
2Aa/2Ba	Parallel concepts:	**2Aa-** I, the Lord, have appointed them, **2Ab-** I have appointed unto them,
2Ba/2Bb	Parallel concepts:	**2Ba-** and ordained them to be stewards over the revelations and commandments which I have given unto them, and which I shall hereafter give unto them; **2Bb-** and this is their business in the church of God, to manage them and the concerns thereof, yea, the benefits thereof.
1	Central theme:	**1-** And an account of this stewardship will I require of them in the day of judgment.

D&C 97:15-17 **Chiasmus 162, 97C**

5] 15 And inasmuch as my people build a house unto me in the name of the Lord, and do not suffer *any unclean thing*
4] *to come into it,*
3A] *that it be not defiled,*
3B] *my glory shall rest upon it;*
2] 16 Yea, and *my presence shall be there,*
1] *for I will come into it,*
1] *and all the pure in heart that shall come into it*
2] *shall see God.*
3A] 17 *But if it be defiled* I will not come into it,
3B] and *my glory shall not be there;*
4] for *I will not come into*
5] *unholy temples.*

D&C 97:15-17 **Analysis 97C**

5a/5b	General to specific:	**5a-** any unclean thing **5b-** unholy temples.
4a/4b	Positive to negative:	**4a-** to come into **4b-** I will not come into
3Aa/3Ab	Negative to positive:	**3Aa-** that it be not defiled, **3Ab-** But if it be defiled
3Ba/3Bb	Positive to negative:	**3Ba-** my glory shall rest upon it; **3Bb-** my glory shall not be there;

2a/2b	Parallel concepts:	**2a-** my presence shall be there, **2b-** shall see God.
1a/1b	Parallel concepts:	**1a-** for I will come into it, **1b-** and all the pure in heart that shall come into it

D&C 130:6-9 — Chiasmus 218, 130A

5A] *The angels do not reside on a planet like this earth;*
5B] 7 But they reside *in the presence of God, on a globe like a sea of glass and fire,*
4] *where all things for their glory are manifest, past, present, and future, and are continually before the Lord.*
3] 8 *The place where God resides*
2] is a great *Urim and Thummim.*
1] 9 This earth, in its sanctified and immortal state, will be made like unto crystal
[illegible] and will be a *Urim and Thummim*
[illegible] to *the inhabitants who dwell thereon,*
4] *whereby all things pertaining to an inferior kingdom, or all kingdoms of a lower order, will be manifest*
5A] *to those who dwell on it;*
5B] and *this earth will be Christ's.*

D&C 130:6-9 — Analysis 130A

5Aa/5Ab	Negative to positive:	**5Aa-** The angels do not reside on a planet like this earth; **5Ab-** to those who dwell on it;
5Ba/5Bb	Parallel concepts:	**5Ba-** in the presence of God, on a globe like a sea of glass and fire, **5Bb-** this earth will be Christ's.
4a/4b	Parallel concepts:	**4a-** where all things for their glory are manifest, past, present, and future, and are continually before the Lord. **4b-** whereby all things pertaining to an inferior kingdom, or all kingdoms of a lower order, will be manifest
3a/3b	Parallel concepts:	**3a-** The place where God resides **3b-** the inhabitants who dwell thereon,
2a/2b	Identical words:	**2-** Urim and Thummim
1	Central theme:	**1-** This earth, in its sanctified and immortal state, will be made like unto crystal

Six-Element Chiasma Containing Two-Element Parallelisms

D&C 9:1-14 — Chiasmus 10, 9A

6] 1 Behold, I say unto you, my son, that because you did not translate according to that which you desired of me, and did commence again to write for my servant, Joseph Smith, Jun., even so *I would that ye should continue until you have finished this record*, which I have entrusted unto him.

5A] 2 And then, behold, *other records have I, that I will give unto you power that you may assist to translate.*

5B] 3 *Be patient, my son, for it is wisdom in me,*

4] and *it is not expedient that you should translate at this present time.*

3] 4 Behold, *the work which you are called to do is to write for my servant Joseph.*

2] 5 And, behold, it is because that *you did not continue as you commenced*, when you began to translate, that I have taken away this privilege from you.

1] 6 Do not murmur, my son, for it is wisdom in me that I have dealt with you after this manner.
7 Behold, you have not understood; you have supposed that I would give it unto you, when you took no thought save it was to ask me.

2] 8 But, behold, I say unto you, *that you must study it out in your mind; then you must ask me if it be right, and if it is right I will cause that your bosom shall burn within you; therefore, you shall feel that it is right.*
9 But if it be not right you shall have no such feelings, but you shall have a stupor of thought that shall cause you to forget the thing which is wrong;

3] therefore, *you cannot write that which is sacred save it be given you from me.*

4] 10 Now, if you had known this you could have translated; nevertheless, *it is not expedient that you should translate now.*
11 Behold, it was expedient when you commenced; but you feared, and the time is past, and it is not expedient now;
12 For, do you not behold that I have given unto my servant Joseph sufficient strength, whereby it is made up? And neither of you have I condemned.

5A] 13 *Do this thing which I have commanded you*, and you shall prosper.

5B] *Be faithful, and yield to no temptation.*

6] 14 *Stand fast in the work wherewith I have called you*, and a hair of your head shall not be lost, and you shall be lifted up at the last day. Amen.

D&C 9:1-14 **Analysis 9A**

6a/6b	Parallel concepts:	**6a-** I would that ye should continue until you have finished this record, **6b-** Stand fast in the work wherewith I have called you,
5Aa/5Ab	Parallel commandments:	**5Aa-** other records have I, that I will give unto you power that you may assist to translate. **5Ab-** Do this thing which I have commanded you,
5Ba/5Bb	Parallel commandments:	**5Ba-** Be patient, my son, for it is wisdom in me, **5Bb-** Be faithful, and yield to no temptation.
4a/4b	Parallel concepts:	**4a-** it is not expedient that you should translate at this present time. **4b-** it is not expedient that you should translate now.
3a/3b	Positive to negative:	**3a-** the work which you are called to do is to write for my servant Joseph. **3b-** you cannot write that which is sacred save it be given you from me.
2a/2b	Negative to positive:	**2a-** you did not continue as you commenced, **2b-** you must study it out in your mind; then you must ask me if it be right, and if it is right I will cause that your bosom shall burn within you; therefore, you shall feel that it is right.
1	Central theme:	**1-** Do not murmur, my son, for it is wisdom in me that I have dealt with you after this manner. Behold, you have not understood; you have supposed that I would give it unto you, when you took no thought save it was to ask me.

Seven-Element Chiasma Containing Two-Element Parallelisms

D&C 95:1-12 — Chiasmus 159, 95A

1 Verily, thus saith the Lord unto you whom I love, and whom I love I also chasten that their sins may be forgiven, for with the chastisement I prepare a way for their deliverance in all things out of temptation,

7] *and I have loved you—*

6] 2 *Wherefore, ye must needs be chastened and stand rebuked before my face;*

5] 3 *For ye have sinned against me a very grievous sin,*

4A] in that *ye have not considered the great commandment in all things, that I have given unto you concerning the building of mine house;*

4B] 4 For the preparation wherewith I design to prepare *mine apostles* to prune my vineyard for the last time,

3] *that I may bring to pass my strange act, that I may pour out my Spirit upon all flesh—*

2] 5 But behold, verily I say unto you, *that there are many who have been ordained among you, whom I have called*

1] but *few of them are chosen.*

1] 6 *They who are not chosen*

2] *have sinned a very grievous sin, in that they are walking in darkness at noon-day.*

3] 7 And for this cause I gave unto you a commandment *that you should call your solemn assembly, that your fastings and your mourning might come up into the ears of the Lord of Sabaoth,* which is by interpretation, the creator of the first day, the beginning and the end.

4A] 8 Yea, verily I say unto you, *I gave unto you a commandment that you should build a house,* in the which house I design to endow those whom I have chosen with power from on high;

4B] 9 For this is the promise of the Father unto you; therefore I command you to tarry, *even as mine apostles at Jerusalem.*

5] 10 *Nevertheless, my servants sinned a very grievous sin;* and contentions arose in the school of the prophets; which was very grievous unto me, saith your Lord;

6] *therefore I sent them forth to be chastened.*

7] 11 Verily I say unto you, it is my will that you should build a house. If you keep my commandments you shall have power to build it.

12 *If you keep not my commandments, the love of the Father shall not continue with you*, therefore you shall walk in darkness.

D&C 95:1-12 **Analysis 95A**

7a/7b	Positive to negative:	**7a-** and I have loved you— **7a-** If you keep not my commandments, the love of the Father shall not continue with you,
6a/6b	Parallel concepts:	**6a-** Wherefore, ye must needs be chastened and stand rebuked before my face; **6b-** therefore I sent them forth to be chastened.
5a/5b	Parallel concepts:	**5a-** For ye have sinned against me a very grievous sin, **5b-** Nevertheless, my servants sinned a very grievous sin;
4Aa/4Ab	Negative to positive:	**4Aa-** ye have not considered the great commandment in all things, that I have given unto you concerning the building of mine house; **4Ab-** I gave unto you a commandment that you should build a house,
4Ba/4Bb	Parallel concepts:	**4Ba-** mine apostles **4Bb-** even as mine apostles at Jerusalem.
3a/3b	The Lord's action vs the Saints' action:	**3a-** that I may bring to pass my strange act, that I may pour out my Spirit upon all flesh— **3b-** that you should call your solemn assembly, that your fastings and your mourning might come up into the ears of the Lord of Sabaoth,
2a/2b	Positive to negative:	**2a-** that there are many who have been ordained among you, whom I have called **2b-** have sinned a very grievous sin, in that they are walking in darkness at noon--day.
1a/1b	Positive to negative:	**1a-** few of them are chosen. **1b-** They who are not chosen

D&C 98:23-44 **Chiasmus 167, 98E**

7] 23 *Now, I speak unto you concerning your families—if men will smite you, or your families, once, and ye bear it patiently and revile not against them, neither seek revenge, ye shall be rewarded;*
24 But if ye bear it not patiently, it shall be accounted unto you as being meted out as a just measure unto you.
25 And again, if your enemy shall smite you the second time, and you revile not against your enemy, and bear it patiently, your reward shall be an hundred fold.
26 And again, if he shall smite you the third time, and ye bear it patiently, your reward shall be doubled unto you four-fold;
27 And these three testimonies shall stand against your enemy if he repent not, and shall not be blotted out.

6A] 33 And again, this is the law that I gave unto mine ancients, *that they should not go out unto battle*
6B] *against any nation, kindred, tongue, or people,*
5] *save I, the Lord, commanded them.*
4] 34 And if any *nation, tongue,*
3] or *people*
2] *should proclaim war*
1] against *them,*
1] *they*
2] *should first lift a standard of peace*
3] unto that *people,*
4] *nation*, or *tongue*;
35 And if that people did not accept the offering of peace, neither the second nor the third time, they should bring these testimonies before the Lord;
5] 36 *Then I, the Lord, would give unto them a commandment,*
6A] *and justify them in going out to battle*
6B] *against that nation, tongue, or people.*

7] 39 *And again, verily I say unto you, if after thine enemy has come upon thee the first time, he repent and come unto thee praying thy forgiveness, thou shalt forgive him, and shalt hold it no more as a testimony against thine enemy—*
40 And so on unto the second and third time; and as oft as thine enemy repenteth of the trespass wherewith he has trespassed against thee, thou shalt forgive him, until seventy times seven.

41 And if he trespass against thee and repent not the first time, nevertheless thou shalt forgive him.
42 And if he trespass against thee the second time, and repent not, nevertheless thou shalt forgive him.
43 And if he trespass against thee the third time, and repent not, thou shalt also forgive him.
44 But if he trespass against thee the fourth time thou shalt not forgive him, but shalt bring these testimonies before the Lord; and they shall not be blotted out until he repent and reward thee four-fold in all things wherewith he has trespassed against thee.

D&C 98:23-44

Analysis 98E

7a/7b Parallel concepts:

7a- Now, I speak unto you concerning your families—if men will smite you, or your families, once, and ye bear it patiently and revile not against them, neither seek revenge, ye shall be rewarded; But if ye bear it not patiently, it shall be accounted unto you as being meted out as a just measure unto you. And again, if your enemy shall smite you the second time, and you revile not against your enemy, and bear it patiently, your reward shall be an hundred fold. And again, if he shall smite you the third time, and ye bear it patiently, your reward shall be doubled unto you four-fold; And these three testimonies shall stand against your enemy if he repent not, and shall not be blotted out

7b- And again, verily I say unto you, if after thine enemy has come upon thee the first time, he repent and come unto thee praying thy forgiveness, thou shalt forgive him, and shalt hold it no more as a testimony against thine enemy—And so on unto the second and third time; and as oft as thine enemy repenteth of the trespass wherewith he has trespassed against thee,

		thou shalt forgive him, until seventy times seven. And if he trespass against thee and repent not the first time, nevertheless thou shalt forgive him. And if he trespass against thee the second time, and repent not, nevertheless thou shalt forgive him. And if he trespass against thee the third time, and repent not, thou shalt also forgive him. But if he trespass against thee the fourth time thou shalt not forgive him, but shalt bring these testimonies before the Lord; and they shall not be blotted out until he repent and reward thee four-fold in all things wherewith he has trespassed against thee.
6Aa/6Ab	Negative to positive:	**6Aa-** that they should not go out unto battle **6Ab-** and justify them in going out to battle
6Ba/6Bb	Parallel concepts:	**6Ba-** against any nation, kindred, tongue, or people, **6Bb-** against that nation, tongue, or people.
5a/5b	Parallel concepts:	**5a-** save I, the Lord, commanded them. **5b-** Then I, the Lord, would give unto them a commandment,
4a/4b	Identical words:	**4-** nation, tongue
3a/3b	Identical words:	**3-** people
2a/2b	Negative to positive:	**2a-** should proclaim war **2b-** should first lift a standard of peace
1a/1b	Parallel concepts:	**1a-** them **1b-** they

D&C 61:23-30 — Chiasmus 89, 61C

7A] 23 And now, concerning *my servants, Sidney Rigdon, Joseph Smith, Jun., and Oliver Cowdery,*

7B] *let them come not again upon the waters, save it be upon the canal, while journeying unto their homes; or in other words they shall not come upon the waters to journey, save upon the canal.*

6] 24 Behold, I, the Lord, have appointed a way *for the journeying*
5] *of my saints;*
4] *and behold, this is the way—that after they leave the canal they shall journey by land, inasmuch as they are commanded to journey and go up unto the land of Zion;*
3] 25 *And they shall do like unto the children of Israel,* pitching their tents by the way.
2] 26 And, behold, *this commandment*
1] *you shall give* unto all your brethren.
1] 27 Nevertheless, *unto whom is given* power
2] *to command* the waters, unto him it is given by the Spirit to know all his ways;
3] 28 *Wherefore, let him do as the Spirit of the living God commandeth him,* whether upon the land or upon the waters, as it remaineth with me to do hereafter.
4] 29 *And unto you is given the course for the saints, or the way*
5] *for the saints* of the camp of the Lord,
6] *to journey.*
7A] 30 And again, verily I say unto you, *my servants, Sidney Rigdon, Joseph Smith, Jun., and Oliver Cowdery,*
7B] *shall not open their mouths in the congregations of the wicked until they arrive at Cincinnati;*

D&C 61:23-30 — Analysis 61C

7Aa/7Ab	Identical words:	**7A-** my servants, Sidney Rigdon, Joseph Smith, Jun., and Oliver Cowdery,
7Ba/7Bb	Parallel concepts:	**7Ba-** let them come not again upon the waters, save it be upon the canal, while journeying unto their homes; or in other words they shall not come upon the waters to journey, save upon the canal. **7Bb-** shall not open their mouths in the congregations of the wicked until they arrive at Cincinnati;
6a/6b	Parallel concepts:	**6a-** for the journeying **6b-** to journey.
5a/5b	Identical word:	**5-** (of my/for the) saints;

4a/4b	Parallel concepts:	**4a-** and behold, this is the way—that after they leave the canal they shall journey by land, inasmuch as they are commanded to journey and go up unto the land of Zion; **4b-** And unto you is given the course for the saints, or the way
3a/3b	Parallel concepts:	**3a-** And they shall do like unto the children of Israel, **3b-** Wherefore, let him do as the Spirit of the living God commandeth him,
2a/2b	Parallel concepts:	**2a-** this commandment **2b-** to command
1a/1b	Parallel concepts:	**1a-** you shall give **1b-** unto whom is given

Nine-Element Chiasma Containing Two-Element Parallelisms

D&C 1:11-24 **Chiasmus 2, 1B**

9] 11 Wherefore *the voice*

8] of *the Lord*

7] is *unto the ends of the earth*, that all that will hear may hear:
12 Prepare ye, prepare ye for that which is to come, for the Lord
is nigh;
13 And the anger of the Lord is kindled, and his sword is bathed
in heaven, and it shall fall upon the inhabitants of the earth.

6] 14 And the arm of the Lord shall be revealed; *and the day*
cometh that they who will not hear the voice of the Lord, neither
the voice of his servants, neither give heed to the words of the
prophets and apostles, shall be cut off from among the people;

5] 15 For *they have strayed* from mine ordinances, *and have*
broken

4] *mine everlasting covenant*;

3] 16 *They seek not the Lord to establish his righteous-*
ness,

2A] *but every man walketh in his own way, and*
after the image of his own God,

2B] *whose image is in the likeness of the world*, and
whose substance is that of an idol, which
waxeth old and shall perish in Babylon, even
Babylon the great, which shall fall.

1] 17 Wherefore, I the Lord, knowing the
calamity which should come upon the
inhabitants of the earth, called upon my
servant Joseph Smith, Jun., and spake
unto him from heaven, and gave him
commandments;
18 And also gave commandments to
others, that they should proclaim these
things unto the world; and all this that
it might be fulfilled, which was written
by the prophets—
19 The weak things of the world shall
come forth and break down the mighty
and strong ones, that man should not

counsel his fellow man, neither trust in the arm of flesh—

2A] 20 *But that every man might speak in the name of God the Lord,*

2B] *even the Savior of the world;*

3] 21 *That faith also might increase in the earth;*

4] 22 That *mine everlasting covenant*

5] *might be established;*

6] 23 *That the fulness of my gospel might be proclaimed by the weak and the simple*

7] *unto the ends of the world,* and before kings and rulers.

8] 24 Behold, *I am God*

9] and *have spoken* it; these commandments are of me, and were given unto my servants in their weakness, after the manner of their language, that they might come to understanding.

D&C 1:1-24 **Analysis 1B**

9a/9b	Parallel concepts:	**9a-** the voice (noun), **9b-** have spoken (verb)
8a/8b	Parallel concepts:	**8a-** the Lord, **8b-** God
7a/7b	Parallel concepts:	**7a-** unto the ends of the earth **7b-** unto the ends of the world
6a/6b	Negative to positive:	**6a-** that they who will not hear the voice . . . shall be cut off **6b-** that the . . . gospel might be proclaimed . . . unto the ends of the world
5a/5b	Negative to positive:	**5a-** they have strayed . . . and have broken **5b-** might be established
4a/4b	Identical words:	**4-** mine everlasting covenant
3a/3b	Negative to positive:	**3a-** They seek not the Lord to establish his righteousness, **3b-** That faith also might increase in the earth;
2Aa/2Ab	Worldly to spiritual:	**2Aa-** but every man walketh in his own way, and after the image of his own God, **2Ab-** But that every man might speak in the name of God the Lord,

2Ba/2Bb	Worldly to spiritual:	**2Ba-** whose image is in the likeness of the world **2Bb-** even the Savior of the world
1	Central theme:	**1-** Joseph Smith and others are called to proclaim the gospel to the world.

D&C 5:1-23 — Chiasmus 5, 5A

9] 1 *Behold, I say unto you, that as my servant Martin Harris has desired a
witness at my hand, that you, my servant Joseph Smith, Jun., have got the
plates of which you have testified and borne record that you have
received of me;
2 And now, behold, this shall you say unto him—he who spake unto you,
said unto you: I, the Lord, am God, and have given these things unto
you, my servant Joseph Smith, Jun.,
8] *and have commanded you that you should stand as a witness of these
things*;
7] 3 And I have caused you that you should enter into a covenant
with me, *that you should not show them*
6] *except to those persons to whom I commanded you*; and you
have no power over them except I grant it unto you.
4 And you have a gift to translate the plates; and this is the
first gift that I bestowed upon you; and I have commanded that
you should pretend to no other gift until my purpose is
fulfilled in this; for I will grant unto you no other gift until it
is finished.
5] 5 Verily, I say unto you, that *woe shall come unto the
inhabitants of the earth if they will not hearken unto my
words*;
4] 6 *For hereafter you shall be ordained* and go forth and
deliver my words unto the children of men.
3] 7 *Behold, if they will not believe my words, they would
not believe you, my servant Joseph, if it were possible
that you should show them all these things which I
have committed unto you.*
8 Oh, this unbelieving and stiffnecked generation—
mine anger is kindled against them.
9 Behold, verily I say unto you, I have reserved those
things which I have entrusted unto you, my servant

Joseph, for a wise purpose in me, and it shall be
made known unto future generations;
10 But this generation shall have my word through
you;
2A] 11 And in addition to your testimony, *the testi-*
mony of three of my servants, whom I shall call
and ordain, unto whom I will show these things,
2B] *and they shall go forth with my words that are*
given through you.
12 Yea, they shall know of a surety that these
things are true, for from heaven will I declare it
unto them.
1] 13 *I will give them power that they may behold*
and view these things as they are;
1] 14 *And to none else will I grant this power, to*
receive this same testimony among this genera-
tion, in this the beginning of the rising up and
the coming forth of my church out of the wilderness—clear as the moon, and fair as the
sun, and terrible as an army with banners.
2A] 15 *And the testimony of three witnesses*
2B] *will I send forth of my word.*
3] 16 *And behold, whosoever believeth on my words,*
them will I visit with the manifestation of my Spirit;
and they shall be born of me, even of water and of
the Spirit—
4] 17 *And you must wait yet a little while, for ye are not yet*
ordained—
5] 18 *And their testimony shall also go forth unto the condem-*
nation of this generation if they harden their hearts against
them;
19 For a desolating scourge shall go forth among the
inhabitants of the earth, and shall continue to be poured
out from time to time, if they repent not, until the earth is
empty, and the inhabitants thereof are consumed away and
utterly destroyed by the brightness of my coming.
20 Behold, I tell you these things, even as I also told the
people of the destruction of Jerusalem; and my word shall
be verified at this time as it hath hitherto been verified.

6] 21 *And now I command you*, my servant Joseph, to repent and walk more uprightly before me,
7] *and to yield to the persuasions of men no more*;
8] 22 *And that you be firm in keeping the commandments wherewith I have commanded you*; and if you do this, behold I grant unto you eternal life, even if you should be slain.
9] 23 *And now, again, I speak unto you, my servant Joseph, concerning the man that desires the witness—*

D&C 3:4-9 **Analysis 5A**

9a/9b	Parallel concepts:	**9a-** Behold, I say unto you, that as my servant Martin Harris has desired a witness at my hand, **9b-** And now, again, I speak unto you, my servant Joseph, concerning the man that desires the witness—
8a/8b	Parallel concepts:	**8a-** and have commanded you that you should stand as a witness of these things; **8b-** And that you be firm in keeping the commandments wherewith I have commanded you;
7a/7b	Specific to general:	**7a-** that you should not show them **7b-** and to yield to the persuasions of men no more;
6a/6b	Past to present:	**6a-** except to those persons to whom I commanded you; **6b-** And now I command you,
5a/5b	Parallel concepts:	**5a-** woe shall come unto the inhabitants of the earth if they will not hearken unto my words; **5b-** And their testimony shall also go forth unto the condemnation of this generation if they harden their hearts against them;
4a/4b	Parallel concepts:	**4a-** For hereafter you shall be ordained **4b-** And you must wait yet a little while, for ye are not yet ordained—
3a/3b	Negative to positive:	**3a-** Behold, if they will not believe my words, they would not believe you, my servant Joseph, if it were possible that you

		should show them all these things which I have committed unto you.
		3b- And behold, whosoever believeth on my words, them will I visit with the manifestation of my Spirit;
2Aa/2Ab	Parallel concepts:	**2Aa-** the testimony of three of my servants,
		2Ab- And the testimony of three witnesses
2Ba/2Bb	Parallel concepts:	**2Ba-** and they shall go forth with my words that are given through you.
		2Bb- will I send forth of my word.
1a/1b	Positive to negative:	**1a-** I will give them power that they may behold and view these things as they are;
		1b- And to none else will I grant this power, to receive this same testimony among this generation,

9

CHIASMA CONTAINING THREE-TO-SIX-ELEMENT PARALLELISMS AS ONE OF THE CHIASTIC ELEMENTS

Three-Element Parallelisms

D&C 3:4-9 **Chiasmus 3, 3A**

4A] 4 *For although a man may have many revelations, and have power to do many mighty works,*
4B] *yet if he boasts in his own strength, and sets at naught the counsels of God, and follows after the dictates of his own will and carnal desires,*
4C] *he must fall* and incur the vengeance of a just God upon him.
3] 5 *Behold, you have been entrusted with these things, but how strict were your commandments; and remember also the promises which were made to you, if you did not transgress them.*
2] 6 *And behold, how oft you have transgressed the commandments and the laws of God, and have gone on in the persuasions of men.*
1] 7 For, behold, you should not have feared man more than God.
2] *Although men set at naught the counsels of God, and despise his words—*
3] 8 *Yet you should have been faithful; and he would have extended his arm and supported you against all the fiery darts of the adversary; and he would have been with you in every time of trouble.*
4A] 9 *Behold, thou art Joseph, and thou wast chosen to do the work of the Lord,*
4B] *but because of transgression,*
4C] if thou art not aware *thou wilt fall.*

D&C 3:4-9 **Analysis 3A**

4Aa/4Ab	General to specific:	**4Aa-** For although a man may have many revelations, and have power to do many mighty works
		4Ab- Behold, thou are Joseph, and was chosen to do the work of the Lord,
4Ba/4Bb	Specific to general:	**4Ba-** yet if he boasts in his own strength, and sets at naught the counsels of God, and follows after the dictates of his own will and carnal desires,
		4Bb- but because of transgression
4Ca/4Cb	General to specific:	**4Ca-** he must fall,
		4Cb- thou wilt fall
3a/3b	Parallel admonitions:	**3a-** Behold, you have been entrusted with these things, but how strict were your commandments; and remember also the promises which were made to you, if you did not transgress them.
		3b- Yet you should have been faithful; and he would have extended his arm and supported you against all the fiery darts of the adversary; and he would have been with you in every time of trouble.
2a/2b	Specific to general:	**2a-** And behold, how oft you have transgressed the commandments and the laws of God, and have gone on in the persuasions of men.
		2b- Although men set at naught the counsels of God, and despise his words—
1	Central theme:	**1-** For, behold, you should not have feared man more than God.

D&C 18:9-14 **Chiasmus 27, 18C**

3] and I speak unto you, even as unto Paul mine apostle, *for you are called even with that same calling with which he was called.*

2] 10 *Remember the worth of souls is great in the sight of God;*

1A] 11 *For, behold, the Lord your Redeemer suffered death in the flesh*; wherefore he suffered the pain of all men,

1B] *that all men might repent*

1C] *and come unto him.*
1A] 12 *And he hath risen again from the dead,*
1C] *that he might bring all men unto him,*
1B] *on conditions of repentance.*
2] 13 *And how great is his joy in the soul that repenteth!*
3] 14 *Wherefore, you are called to cry repentance unto this people.*

D&C 18:9-14 — Analysis 18C

3a/3b Parallel concepts: **3a-** for you are called even with that same calling with which he was called.
3b- Wherefore, you are called to cry repentance unto this people.

2a/2b Parallel concepts: **2a-** Remember the worth of souls is great in the sight of God;
2b- And how great is his joy in the soul that repenteth!

1Aa/1Ab Completed concept: **1Aa-** For, behold, the Lord your Redeemer suffered death in the flesh;
1Ab- And he hath risen again from the dead,

1Ba/1Bb Parallel concepts: **1Ba-** that all men might repent
1Bb- on conditions of repentance.

1Ca/1Cb Parallel concepts: **1Ca-** and come unto him.
1Cb- that he might bring all men unto him,

NOTE: Elements 1A and 1B,1C form a two-element series, the second element, 1B,1C, being chiastically arranged.

D&C 19:2-19 — Chiasmus 35, 19A

6] 2 *I, having accomplished and finished the will of him whose I am, even the Father, concerning me—having done this that I might subdue all things unto myself—*
3 Retaining all power, even to the destroying of Satan and his works at the end of the world, and the last great day of judgment, which I shall pass upon the inhabitants thereof, judging every man according to his works and the deeds which he hath done.
5A] 4 *And surely every man must repent or suffer*, for I, God, am endless.
5B] 5 *Wherefore, I revoke not the judgments which I shall pass,*

5C] *but woes shall go forth, weeping, wailing and gnashing of teeth, yea, to those who are found on my left hand.*

4] 6 Nevertheless, it is not written that there shall be no end to this torment, *but it is written endless torment.*

3] 7 Again, it is written *eternal damnation*; wherefore it is more express than other scriptures, that it might work upon the hearts of the children of men, altogether for my name's glory.

2] 8 *Wherefore, I will explain unto you this mystery*, for it is meet unto you to know even as mine apostles.

1] 9 I speak unto you that are chosen in this thing, even as one, that you may enter into my rest.

2] 10 *For, behold, the mystery of godliness, how great is it*! For, behold, I am endless, and the punishment which is given from my hand is endless punishment, for Endless is my name. Wherefore—

3] 11 *Eternal punishment* is God's punishment.

4] 12 *Endless punishment is God's punishment.*

5A] 13 *Wherefore, I command you to repent*, and keep the commandments which you have received by the hand of my servant Joseph Smith, Jun., in my name;

5B] 14 *And it is by my almighty power that you have received them*;
15 Therefore I command you to repent—repent, lest I smite you by the rod of my mouth, and by my wrath, and by my anger,

5C] *and your sufferings be sore—how sore you know not, how exquisite you know not, yea, how hard to bear you know not.*

6] 16 *For behold, I, God, have suffered these things for all, that they might not suffer if they would repent*;
17 But if they would not repent they must suffer even as I;
18 *Which suffering caused myself, even God, the greatest of all, to tremble because of pain, and to bleed at every pore, and to suffer both body and spirit—and would that I might not drink the bitter cup, and shrink—*
19 *Nevertheless, glory be to the Father, and I partook and finished my preparations unto the children of men.*

D&C 19:2-19 **Analysis 19A**

6a/6b	Parallel concepts:	**6a-** I, having accomplished and finished the will of him whose I am, even the Father, concerning me—having done this that I might subdue all things unto myself— **6b-** For behold, I, God, have suffered these things for all, that they might not suffer if they would repent; Which suffering caused myself, even God, the greatest of all, to tremble because of pain, and to bleed at every pore, and to suffer both body and spirit—and would that I might not drink the bitter cup, and shrink— Nevertheless, glory be to the Father, and I partook and finished my preparations unto the children of men.
5Aa/5Ab	General to specific:	**5Aa-** And surely every man must repent or suffer, **5Ab-** Wherefore, I command you to repent,
5Ba/5Bb	Parallel actions:	**5Ba-** Wherefore, I revoke not the judgments which I shall pass, **5Bb-** And it is by my almighty power that you have received them;
5Ca/5Cb	General to specific:	**5Ca-** but woes shall go forth, weeping, wailing and gnashing of teeth, yea, to those who are found on my left hand. **5Cb-** and your sufferings be sore—how sore you know not, how exquisite you know not, yea, how hard to bear you know not.
4a/4b	Parallel concepts:	**4a-** but it is written endless torment. **4b-** Endless punishment is God's punishment.
3a/3b	Parallel concepts:	**3a-** eternal damnation; **3b-** eternal punishment
2a/2b	Parallel concepts:	**2a-** Wherefore, I will explain unto you this mystery,

		2b- For, behold, the mystery of godliness, how great is it!
1	Central theme:	**1-** I speak unto you that are chosen in this thing, even as one, that you may enter into my rest.

D&C 27:15-17 **Chiasmus 44, 27B**

15 Wherefore, lift up your hearts and rejoice,
2A] and *gird up*
2B] *your loins,*
2C] *and take upon you my whole armor,*
1] that ye may be able to withstand the evil day, having done all, *that ye may be able to stand.*
1] 16 *Stand, therefore,*
2B] having *your loins*
2A] *girt about* with truth,
2C] *having on the breastplate of righteousness, and your feet shod with the preparation of the gospel of peace*, which I have sent mine angels to commit unto you;
17 *Taking the shield of faith* wherewith ye shall be able to quench all the fiery darts of the wicked;

D&C 27:15-17 **Analysis 27B**

2Aa/2Ab	Parallel concepts:	**2Aa-** gird up **2Ab-** girt about
2Ba/2Bb	Identical words:	**2B-** your loins
2Ca/2Cb	Parallel concepts:	**2Ca-** and take upon you my whole armor, **2Cb-** having on the breastplate of righteousness, and your feet shod with the preparation of the gospel of peace,
1a/1b	Parallel concepts:	**1a-** that ye may be able to stand. **1b-** Stand, therefore,

NOTE: The elements 2A2B and 2C form a two-element parallelism, with the first element chiastically arraigned.

D&C 61:6-11 — Chiasmus 87, 61A

5] 6 Nevertheless, *all flesh is in mine hand,*
4] *and he that is faithful among you shall not perish by the waters.*
3A] *Wherefore, it is expedient that my servant Sidney Gilbert and my servant William W. Phelps*
3B] *be in haste*
3C] *upon their errand and mission.*
2] 8 *Nevertheless, I would not suffer that ye should part*
1] until you were chastened for all your sins, that you might be one, that you might not perish in wickedness;
2] 9 *But now, verily I say, it behooveth me that ye should part.*
3A] *Wherefore let my servants Sidney Gilbert and William W. Phelps* take their former company,
3C] *and let them take their journey*
3B] *in haste* that they may fill their mission, and through faith they shall overcome;
4] 10 *And inasmuch as they are faithful they shall be preserved,*
5] *and I, the Lord, will be with them.*

D&C 61:6-11 — Analysis 61A

5a/5b	General to specific:	**5a-** all flesh is in mine hand, **5b-** I, the Lord, will be with them.
4a/4b	Parallel concepts:	**4a-** and he that is faithful among you shall not perish by the waters. **4b-** And inasmuch as they are faithful they shall be preserved,
3Aa/3Ab	Parallel concepts:	**3Aa-** Wherefore, it is expedient that my servant Sidney Gilbert and my servant William W. Phelps **3Ab-** Wherefore let my servants Sidney Gilbert and William W. Phelps
3Ba/3Bb	Identical words:	**3b-** in haste
3Ca/3Cb	Parallel concepts:	**3Ca-** upon their errand and mission. **3Cb-** and let them take their journey
2a/2b	Negative to positive:	**2a-** Nevertheless, I would not suffer that ye should part **2b-** But now, verily I say, it behooveth me that ye should part.

1 Central theme: 1- until you were chastened for all your sins, that you might be one, that you might not perish in wickedness;

D&C 63:5-13 **Chiasmus 89, 91, 63AB**

6] 5 *Behold, I, the Lord, utter my voice, and it shall be obeyed.*

5A] 6 *Wherefore, verily I say, let the wicked take heed, and let the rebellious fear and tremble; and let the unbelieving hold their lips, for the day of wrath shall come upon them as a whirlwind, and all flesh shall know that I am God.*

5B] 7 *And he that seeketh signs shall see signs, but not unto salvation.*

5C] 8 *Verily, I say unto you, there are those among you who seek signs, and there have been such even from the beginning;*

4] 3) 9 But, behold, *faith*

3] 2) *cometh*

2] 1) not by *signs*, (See Chapter 6, p. 90.)

1] 1) but *signs*

2) *follow* those

3) that *believe.*

1] 10 Yea, *signs* come by faith, not by the will of men, nor as they please, but by the will of God.

2] 11 Yea, *signs*

3] *come* by

4] *faith*, unto mighty works, for without faith no man pleaseth God;

5A] *and with whom God is angry he is not well pleased;*

5B] *wherefore, unto such he showeth no signs, only in wrath unto their condemnation.*

5C] 12 *Wherefore, I, the Lord, am not pleased with those among you who have sought after signs and wonders for faith, and not for the good of men unto my glory.*

6] 13 *Nevertheless, I give commandments, and many have turned away from my commandments and have not kept them.*

D&C 63:5-13

Analysis 63A

6a/6b	Positive to negative:	**6a-** Behold, I, the Lord, utter my voice, and it shall be obeyed. **6b-** Nevertheless, I give commandments, and many have turned away from my commandments and have not kept them.
5Aa/5Ab	Parallel concepts:	**5Aa-** Wherefore, verily I say, let the wicked take heed, and let the rebellious fear and tremble; and let the unbelieving hold their lips, for the day of wrath shall come upon them as a whirlwind, and all flesh shall know that I am God. **5Ab-** and with whom God is angry he is not well pleased;
5Ba/5Bb	Parallel concepts:	**5Ba-** And he that seeketh signs shall see signs, but not unto salvation. **5Bb-** wherefore, unto such he showeth no signs, only in wrath unto their condemnation.
5Ca/5Cb	Parallel concepts:	**5Ca-** Verily, I say unto you, there are those among you who seek signs, and there have been such even from the beginning; **5Cb-** Wherefore, I, the Lord, am not pleased with those among you who have sought after signs and wonders for faith, and not for the good of men unto my glory.
4a/4b	Identical word:	**4-** faith
3a/3b	Identical word:	**3a-** cometh 3b. come
2a/2b	Identical word:	**2-** signs
1a/1b	Identical word:	**1-** signs

NOTE: A second chiasmus is found in verse 9, which is represented by elements 1] to 4] in the first half of the principle chiasmus. It is analyzed as follows:

D&C 76:50-65 **Chiasmus 116, 76I**

4] 50 And again we bear record—for we saw and heard, and this is the testimony of the gospel of Christ *concerning them who shall come forth in the resurrection of the just—*

3] 51 *They are they who received the testimony of Jesus, and believed on his name and were baptized after the manner of his burial*, being buried in the water in his name, and this according to the commandment which he has given—

52 That by keeping the commandments they might be washed and cleansed from all their sins, and receive the Holy Spirit by the laying on of the hands of him who is ordained and sealed unto this power;

2] 53 *And who overcome by faith, and are sealed by the Holy Spirit of promise*, which the Father sheds forth upon all those who are just and true.

1A] 54 *They are they who are the church of the Firstborn.*

1B] 55 *They are they into whose hands the Father has given all things—*

1C] 56 *They are they who are priests and kings, who have received of his fulness, and of his glory;*

57 *And are priests of the Most High, after the order of Melchizedek, which was after the order of Enoch, which was after the order of the Only Begotten Son.*

1A] 58 *Wherefore, as it is written, they are gods, even the sons of God—*

1B] 59 *Wherefore, all things are theirs, whether life or death, or things present, or things to come, all are theirs*

1C] *and they are Christ's, and Christ is God's.*

2] 60 *And they shall overcome all things.*

3] 61 Wherefore, let no man glory in man, but rather let him glory in God, who shall subdue all enemies under his feet.

62 *These shall dwell in the presence of God and his Christ forever and ever.*

63 These are they whom he shall bring with him, when he shall come in the clouds of heaven to reign on the earth over his people.

64 These are they who shall have part in the first resurrection.

4] 65 *These are they who shall come forth in the resurrection of the just.*

D&C 76:50-65 — Analysis 76I

4a/4b	Identical words:	**4a-** concerning them who shall come forth in the resurrection of the just **4b-** These are they who shall come forth in the resurrection of the just.
3a/3b	Parallel concepts:	**3a-** They are they who received the testimony of Jesus, and believed on his name and were baptized after the manner of his burial, **3b-** These shall dwell in the presence of God and his Christ forever and ever.
2a/2b	Parallel concepts:	**2a-** And who overcome by faith, and are sealed by the Holy Spirit of promise, **2b-** And they shall overcome all things.
1Aa/1Ab	Parallel concepts:	**1Aa-** They are they who are the church of the Firstborn. **1Ab-** Wherefore, as it is written, they are gods, even the sons of God—
1Ba/1Bb	Parallel concepts:	**1Ba-** They are they into whose hands the Father has given all things— **1Bb-** Wherefore, all things are theirs, whether life or death, or things present, or things to come, all are theirs
1Ca/1Cb	Parallel concepts:	**1Ca-** They are they who are priests and kings, who have received of his fulness, and of his glory; And are priests of the Most High, after the order of Melchizedek, which was after the order of Enoch, which was after the order of the Only Begotten Son. **1Cb-** and they are Christ's, and Christ is God's.

D&C 84:49-53 — Chiasmus 127, 84B

4A] 49 *And the whole world* lieth in sin, and *groaneth*
4B] *under darkness*
  4C] and *under the bondage of sin.*
3]   50 *And by this you may know*
2]   they are *under the bondage of sin,*

1] because they *come not unto me.*
1] 51 For whoso *cometh not unto me*
2] is *under the bondage of sin.*
52 And whoso receiveth not my voice is not acquainted with my voice, and is not of me.
3] 53 *And by this you may know* the righteous from the wicked,
4A] *and that the whole world groaneth*
4C] *under sin*
4B] *and darkness* even now.

D&C 84:49-53 — Analysis 84B

4Aa/4Ab	Identical words:	**4Aa-** And the whole world...groaneth **4Ab-** and...the whole world groaneth
4Ba/4Bb	Identical word:	darkness
4Ca/4Cb	Identical words:	**4C-** under (the bondage of) sin
3a/3b	Identical words:	**3-** and by this you may know
2a/2b	Identical words:	**2-** under the bondage of sin
1a/1b	Identical words:	**1a-** come not unto me. **1b-** cometh not unto me

NOTE: Elements 4A and 4B4C form a two-element parallelism, with the second element chiastically arranged.

D&C 104:29-35 — Chiasmus 179, 104A

3A] 29 *And let my servants Frederick G. Williams and Oliver Cowdery have the printing office*
3B] *and all things that pertain unto it.*
30 And this shall be their stewardship which shall be appointed unto them.
3C] 31 *And inasmuch as they are faithful, behold I will bless, and multiply blessings upon them.*
2] «31 *And inasmuch as they are faithful, behold I will bless, and multiply blessings upon them.*»
1] 32 And this is the beginning of the stewardship which I have appointed them, for them and their seed after them.
2] 33 *And, inasmuch as they are faithful, I will multiply blessings upon them* and their seed after them, even a multiplicity of blessings.
3A] 34 *And again, let my servant John Johnson have the house in which he lives, and the inheritance,*

3B] *all save the ground which has been reserved for the building of my houses, which pertains to that inheritance, and those lots which have been named for my servant Oliver Cowdery.*
3C] 35 *And inasmuch as he is faithful, I will multiply blessings upon him.*

D&C 104:29-35 — Analysis 104A

3Aa/3Ab	Parallel concepts:	**3Aa-** And let my servants Frederick G. Williams and Oliver Cowdery have the printing office **3Ab-** And again, let my servant John Johnson have the house in which he lives, and the inheritance,
3Ba/3Bb	Parallel concepts:	**3Ba-** and all things that pertain unto it. **3Bb-** all save the ground which has been reserved for the building of my houses,
3Ca/3Cb	Identical words:	**3C-** And inasmuch as (they are/he is) faithful, behold I will bless, and multiply blessings upon (them/him).
2a/2b	Identical words:	**2-** And inasmuch as they are faithful, behold I will (bless, and) multiply blessings upon them.
1	Central theme:	**1-** And this is the beginning of the stewardship which I have appointed them, for them and their seed after them.

D&C 107:23-34 — Chiasmus 189, 107C

2A] 23 *The twelve traveling councilors are called to be the Twelve Apostles,*
2B] *or special witnesses of the name of Christ in all the world*—thus differing from other officers in the church in the duties of their calling.
24 And they form a quorum, equal in authority and power to the three presidents previously mentioned.
2C] 25 *The Seventy are also called to preach the gospel*, and to be especial witnesses unto the Gentiles and in all the world—thus differing from other officers in the church in the duties of their calling.
26 And they form a quorum, equal in authority to that of the Twelve special witnesses or Apostles just named.
1] 27 *And every decision made by either of these quorums must be by the unanimous voice of the same; that is, every member in each*

quorum must be agreed to its decisions, in order to make their
decisions of the same power or validity one with the other—
28 A majority may form a quorum when circumstances render it
impossible to be otherwise—
29 Unless this is the case, their decisions are not entitled to the
same blessings which the decisions of a quorum of three presidents were anciently, who were ordained after the order of
Melchizedek, and were righteous and holy men.
1] 30 *The decisions of these quorums, or either of them, are to be made
in all righteousness, in holiness, and lowliness of heart, meekness and
long suffering, and in faith, and virtue, and knowledge, temperance,
patience, godliness, brotherly kindness and charity;*
31 Because the promise is, if these things abound in them they
shall not be unfruitful in the knowledge of the Lord.
32 And in case that any decision of these quorums is made in
unrighteousness, it may be brought before a general assembly of
the several quorums, which constitute the spiritual authorities of
the church; otherwise there can be no appeal from their decision.
2A] 33 *The Twelve are a Traveling Presiding High Council,*
2B] *to officiate in the name of the Lord*, under the direction of the
Presidency of the Church, agreeable to the institution of heaven; to
build up the church, and regulate all the affairs of the same in all
nations, first unto the Gentiles and secondly unto the Jews.
2C] 34 *The Seventy are to act in the name of the Lord,*

D&C 107:23-34 — Analysis 107C

2Aa/2Ab	Parallel concepts:	**2Aa-** The twelve traveling councilors are called to be the Twelve Apostles, **2Ab-** The Twelve are a Traveling Presiding High Council,
2Ba/2Bb	Parallel concepts:	**2Ba-** or special witnesses of the name of Christ in all the world— **2Bb-** to officiate in the name of the Lord,
2Ca/2Cb	Parallel concepts:	**2Ca-** The Seventy are also called to preach the gospel, **2Cb-** The Seventy are to act in the name of the Lord,

1a/1b	Parallel concepts:	**1a-** And every decision made by either of these quorums must be by the unanimous voice of the same; that is, every member in each quorum must be agreed to its decisions, **1b-** The decisions of these quorums, or either of them, are to be made in all righteousness, in holiness, and lowliness of heart, meekness and long suffering, and in faith, and virtue, and knowledge, temperance, patience, godliness, brotherly kindness and charity;

Four-Element Parallelisms

D&C 63:17-49 **Chiasmus 93, 63C**

10] 17 *Wherefore, I, the Lord, have said that the fearful, and the unbelieving, and all liars, and whosoever loveth and maketh a lie, and the whoremonger, and the sorcerer, shall have their part in that lake which burneth with fire and brimstone, which is the second death.*
18 *Verily I say, that they shall not have part in the first resurrection.*
19 And now behold, I, the Lord, say unto you that ye are not justified, because these things are among you.

9A] 20 Nevertheless,he that *endureth*
9B] *in faith* and doeth my will,
9C] the same *shall overcome*,
9D] *and shall receive an inheritance upon the earth when the day of transfiguration shall come*;
21 When the earth shall be transfigured, even according to the pattern which was shown unto mine apostles upon the mount; of which account the fulness ye have not yet received.

8] 22 *And now, verily I say unto you, that as I said that I would make known my will unto you, behold I will make it known unto you*, not by the way of commandment, for there are many who observe not to keep my commandments.
23 But unto him that keepeth my commandments I will give the mysteries of my kingdom, and the same shall be in him a well of living water, springing up unto everlasting life.
24 *And now, behold, this is the will of the Lord your God concerning his saints, that they should assemble themselves together unto the land of Zion*, not in haste, lest there should be confusion, which bringeth pestilence.

7] 25 *Behold, the land of Zion*—I, the Lord, hold it in mine own hands;

6] 26 *Nevertheless, I, the Lord, render unto Caesar the things which are Caesar's.*

5] 27 *Wherefore, I the Lord will that you should purchase the lands, that you may have advantage of the world, that you may have claim on the world, that they may not be stirred up unto anger.*

4] 28 *For Satan putteth it into their hearts to*
anger against you, and to the shedding of blood.
3] 29 *Wherefore, the land of Zion shall not be*
obtained but by purchase or by blood, other-
wise there is none inheritance for you.
30 And if by purchase, behold you are
blessed;
31 And if by blood, as you are forbidden to
shed blood, lo, your enemies are upon you,
and ye shall be scourged from city to city,
and from synagogue to synagogue, and but
few shall stand to receive an inheritance.
2] 32 *I, the Lord, am angry with the wick-*
ed; I am holding my Spirit from the
inhabitants of the earth.
33 I have sworn in my wrath, and de-
creed wars upon the face of the earth,
and the wicked shall slay the wicked,
and fear shall come upon every man;
1] 34 And the saints also shall hardly
escape;
2] nevertheless, *I, the Lord, am with them,*
and will come down in heaven from the
presence of my Father and consume the
wicked with unquenchable fire.
35 And behold, this is not yet, but by
and by.
3] 36 *Wherefore, seeing that I, the Lord, have*
decreed all these things upon the face of the
earth, I will that my saints should be as-
sembled upon the land of Zion;
4] 37 *And that every man should take righteous-*
ness in his hands and faithfulness upon his
loins, and lift a warning voice unto the inhabi-
tants of the earth; and declare both by word
and by flight that desolation shall come upon
the wicked.
38 Wherefore, let my disciples in Kirtland
arrange their temporal concerns, who dwell
upon this farm.

5] 39 *Let my servant Titus Billings, who has the care*
thereof, dispose of the land, that he may be pre-
pared in the coming spring to take his journey up
unto the land of Zion, with those that dwell upon
the face thereof, excepting those whom I shall
reserve unto myself, that shall not go until I shall
command them.

6] 40 *And let all the moneys which can be spared, it*
mattereth not unto me whether it be little or much,

7] *be sent up unto the land of Zion*, unto them whom I
have appointed to receive.

8] 41 *Behold, I, the Lord, will give unto my servant Joseph*
Smith, Jun., power that he shall be enabled to discern by the
Spirit those who shall go up unto the land of Zion, and those
of my disciples who shall tarry.

42 Let my servant Newel K. Whitney retain his store, or in
other words, the store, yet for a little season.

43 Nevertheless, let him impart all the money which he can
impart, to be sent up unto the land of Zion.

44 Behold, these things are in his own hands, let him do
according to wisdom.

45 Verily I say, let him be ordained as an agent unto the
disciples that shall tarry, and let him be ordained unto this
power;

46 And now speedily visit the churches, expounding these
things unto them, with my servant Oliver Cowdery.
Behold, this is my will, obtaining moneys even as I have
directed.

9B] 47 *He that is faithful*

9A] and *endureth*

9C] *shall overcome* the world.

9D] 48 He that sendeth up treasures unto the land of Zion *shall*
receive an inheritance in this world, and his works shall follow him,
and also a reward in the world to come.

10] 49 *Yea, and blessed are the dead that die in the Lord, from henceforth,*
when the Lord shall come, and old things shall pass away, and all things
become new, they shall rise from the dead and shall not die after, and
shall receive an inheritance before the Lord, in the holy city.

D&C 63:17-49 — Analysis 63C

10a/10b	Negative to positive:	**10a-** Wherefore, I, the Lord, have said that the fearful, and the unbelieving, and all liars, and whosoever loveth and maketh a lie, and the whoremonger, and the sorcerer, shall have their part in that lake which burneth with fire and brimstone, which is the second death. Verily I say, that they shall not have part in the first resurrection. **10b-** Yea, and blessed are the dead that die in the Lord, from henceforth, when the Lord shall come, and old things shall pass away, and all things become new, they shall rise from the dead and shall not die after, and shall receive an inheritance before the Lord, in the holy city.
9Aa/9Ab	Identical word:	**9A-** endureth
9Ba/9Bb	Parallel concepts:	**9Ba-** in faith **9Bb-** He that is faithful
9Ca/9Cb	Identical words:	**9C-** shall overcome
9Da/9Db	Parallel concepts:	**9Da-** shall receive an inheritance upon the earth when the day of transfiguration shall come; **9Db-** shall receive an inheritance in this world, and his works shall follow him, and also a reward in the world to come.
8a/8b	Parallel concepts:	**8a-** And now, verily I say unto you, that as I said that I would make known my will unto you, behold I will make it known unto you...And now, behold, this is the will of the Lord your God concerning his saints, that they should assemble themselves together unto the land of Zion, **8b-** Behold, I, the Lord, will give unto my servant Joseph Smith, Jun., power that he shall be enabled to discern by the Spirit those who shall go up unto the land of Zion, and those of my disciples who shall tarry.

7a/7b	Identical words:	**7-** the land of Zion
6a/6b	Parallel concepts:	**6a-** Nevertheless, I, the Lord, render unto Caesar the things which are Caesar's. **6b-** And let all the moneys which can be spared, it mattereth not unto me whether it be little or much,
5a/5b	Positive to negative:	**5a-** Wherefore, I the Lord will that you should purchase the lands, that you may have advantage of the world, that you may have claim on the world, that they may not be stirred up unto anger. **5b-** Let my servant Titus Billings, who has the care thereof, dispose of the land, that he may be prepared in the coming spring to take his journey up unto the land of Zion, with those that dwell upon the face thereof, excepting those whom I shall reserve unto myself, that shall not go until I shall command them.
4a/4b	Parallel concepts:	**4a-** For Satan putteth it into their hearts to anger against you, and to the shedding of blood. **4b-** And that every man should take righteousness in his hands and faithfulness upon his loins, and lift a warning voice unto the inhabitants of the earth; and declare both by word and by flight that desolation shall come upon the wicked.
3a/3b	Parallel concepts:	**3a-** Wherefore, the land of Zion shall not be obtained but by purchase or by blood, otherwise there is none inheritance for you. And if by purchase, behold you are blessed; And if by blood, as you are forbidden to shed blood, lo, your enemies are upon you, and ye shall be scourged from city to city, and from synagogue to synagogue, and but few shall stand to receive an inheritance.

		3b- Wherefore, seeing that I, the Lord, have decreed all these things upon the face of the earth, I will that my saints should be assembled upon the land of Zion;
2a/2b	Parallel concepts:	**2a-** I, the Lord, am angry with the wicked; I am holding my Spirit from the inhabitants of the earth. 33 I have sworn in my wrath, and decreed wars upon the face of the earth, and the wicked shall slay the wicked, and fear shall come upon every man; **2b-** I, the Lord, am with them, and will come down in heaven from the presence of my Father and consume the wicked with unquenchable fire.
1	Central theme:	And the saints also shall hardly escape;

NOTE: Elements 9A to 9D form a three-element series, with the first element chiastically arranged.

D&C 87:1-8 — Chiasmus 132, 87A

6] 1 *Verily, thus saith the Lord concerning the wars that will shortly come to pass, beginning at the rebellion of South Carolina,*
5] *which will eventually terminate in the death and misery of many souls;*
4] 2 *And the time will come that war will be poured out upon all nations, beginning at this place.*
3] 3 *For behold, the Southern States shall be divided against the Northern States, and the Southern States will call on other nations, even the nation of Great Britain, as it is called, and they shall also call upon other nations, in order to defend themselves against other nations;*
2] *and then war shall be poured out upon all nations.*
1A] 4 *And it shall come to pass,* after many days,
1B] *slaves shall rise up against their masters,*
1C] *who shall be marshaled*
1D] *and disciplined for war.*
1A] 5 *And it shall come to pass* also
1B] *that the remnants who are left of the land*
1C] *will marshal themselves,*

1D] *and shall become exceedingly angry, and shall vex the Gentiles with a sore vexation.*

2] 6 *And thus, with the sword and by bloodshed the inhabitants of the earth shall mourn;*

3] *and with famine, and plague, and earthquake, and the thunder of heaven, and the fierce and vivid lightning also, shall the inhabitants of the earth be made to feel the wrath, and indignation, and chastening hand of an Almighty God,*

4] *until the consumption decreed hath made a full end of all nations;*

5] 7 *That the cry of the saints, and of the blood of the saints, shall cease to come up into the ears of the Lord of Sabaoth, from the earth, to be avenged of their enemies.*

6] 8 *Wherefore, stand ye in holy places, and be not moved, until the day of the Lord come;* for behold, it cometh quickly, saith the Lord. Amen.

D&C 87:1-8 **Analysis 87A**

6a/6b	Negative to positive:	**6a-** Verily, thus saith the Lord concerning the wars that will shortly come to pass, beginning at the rebellion of South Carolina, **6b-** Wherefore, stand ye in holy places, and be not moved, until the day of the Lord come;
5a/5b	Parallel concepts:	**5a-** which will eventually terminate in the death and misery of many souls; **5b-** That the cry of the saints, and of the blood of the saints, shall cease to come up into the ears of the Lord of Sabaoth, from the earth, to be avenged of their enemies.
4a/4B	Parallel concepts:	**4a-** And the time will come that war will be poured out upon all nations, beginning at this place. **4b-** until the consumption decreed hath made a full end of all nations;
3a/3b	Mortal conflict vs Divine displeasure:	**3a-** For behold, the Southern States shall be divided against the Northern States, and the Southern States will call on other nations, even the nation of Great Britain,

		as it is called, and they shall also call upon other nations, in order to defend themselves against other nations;
		3b- and with famine, and plague, and earthquake, and the thunder of heaven, and the fierce and vivid lightning also, shall the inhabitants of the earth be made to feel the wrath, and indignation, and chastening hand of an Almighty God,
2a/2b	Parallel concepts:	**2a-** and then war shall be poured out upon all nations.
		2b- And thus, with the sword and by bloodshed the inhabitants of the earth shall mourn;
1Aa/1Ab	Identical words:	**1a-** And it shall come to pass,
1Ba/1Bb	Parallel concepts:	**1Ba-** slaves shall rise up against their masters,
		1Bb- that the remnants who are left of the land
1Ca/1Cb	Parallel concepts:	**1Ca-** who shall be marshaled
		1Cb- will marshal themselves,
1Da/1Db	Parallel concepts:	**1Da-** and disciplined for war.
		1Db- and shall become exceedingly angry, and shall vex the Gentiles with a sore vexation.

D&C 101:44-53 — Chiasmus 173, 101E

7A] 44 A certain nobleman had a spot of land, very choice; *and he said unto his servants: Go ye unto my vineyard, even upon this very choice piece of land,*

7B] *and plant twelve olive-trees*;

7C] 45 *And set watchmen round about them, and build a tower*, that one may overlook the land round about,

7D] *to be a watchman upon the tower,*

6] that *mine olive-trees*

5] *may not be broken down*

4] *when the enemy shall come to spoil* and take upon themselves the fruit of my vineyard.

3] 46 *Now, the servants of the nobleman went and did as
their lord commanded them, and planted the olive-trees,
and built a hedge round about, and set watchmen, and
began to build a tower*

2] 47 And while they were yet laying the foundation
thereof, they began to say among themselves: *And
what need hath my lord of this tower*?

1] 48 And consulted for a long time, saying among
themselves:

2] *What need hath my lord of this tower*, seeing this is a
time of peace?

49 Might not this money be given to the exchangers?
For there is no need of these things.

3] 50 *And while they were at variance one with another they
became very slothful, and they hearkened not unto the
commandments of their lord.*

4] 51 *And the enemy came by night, and broke down the hedge*;
and the servants of the nobleman arose and were affrighted,
and fled; and the enemy destroyed their works,

5] *and broke down*

6] *the olive-trees.*

52 Now, behold, the nobleman, the lord of the vineyard, called
upon his servants, and said unto them, Why! what is the cause of
this great evil?

7A] 53 *Ought ye not to have done even as I commanded you*, and—

7B] *after ye had planted the vineyard*, and built the hedge round about,

7C] *and set watchmen upon the walls thereof—built the tower also*,

7D] *and set a watchman upon the tower*, and watched for my vineyard, and
not have fallen asleep, lest the enemy should come upon you?

D&C 101:44-53 **Analysis 101E**

7Aa/7Ab	Positive to negative:	**6Aa-** and he said unto his servants: Go ye unto my vineyard, even upon this very choice piece of land, **6Ab-** Ought ye not to have done even as I commanded you,
7Ba/7Bb	Parallel concepts:	**6Ba-** and plant twelve olive-trees; **6Bb-** after ye had planted the vineyard.

7Ca/7Cb	Parallel concepts:	**6Ca-** And set watchmen round about them, and build a tower, **6Cb-** and set watchmen upon the walls thereof—built the tower also,
7Da/7Db	Identical words:	**7-** a watchman upon the tower,
6a/6b	Parallel concepts:	**6a-** mine olive-trees **6b-** the olive-trees.
5a/5b	Parallel concepts:	**5a-** may not be broken down **5b-** and broke down
4a/4b	Future to past:	**4a-** when the enemy shall come to spoil **4b-** And the enemy came by night, and broke down the hedge;
3a/3b	Positive to negative:	**3a-** Now, the servants of the nobleman went and did as their lord commanded them, and planted the olive-trees, and built a hedge round about, and set watchmen, and began to build a tower **3b-** And while they were at variance one with another they became very slothful, and they hearkened not unto the commandments of their lord.
2a/2b	Identical words:	**2-** What need hath my lord of this tower
1	Central theme:	**1-** and consulted for a long time, saying among themselves:

Five-Element Parallelisms

D&C 14:2-11 — Chiasmus 23, 14A

4A] 2 *Behold, I am God*; give heed to my word, which is quick and powerful, sharper than a two-edged sword, to the dividing asunder of both joints and marrow; therefore give heed unto my word.

4B] 3 *Behold, the field is white already to harvest*;

4C] therefore, *whoso desireth to reap let him thrust in his sickle with his might,*

4D] *and reap while the day lasts,*

4E] *that he may treasure up for his soul everlasting salvation in the kingdom of God.*

3] 4 Yea, whosoever will thrust in his sickle and reap, *the same is called of God.*

2] 5 Therefore, *if you will ask of me you shall receive*; if you will knock it shall be opened unto you.

1] 6 Seek to bring forth and establish my Zion. *Keep my commandments in all things.*

1] 7 And, *if you keep my commandments and endure to the end* you shall have eternal life, which gift is the greatest of all the gifts of God.

2] 8 And it shall come to pass, that *if you shall ask the Father in my name, in faith believing, you shall receive the Holy Ghost,*

3] which giveth utterance, *that you may stand as a witness of the things of which you shall both hear and see, and also that you may declare repentance unto this generation.*

4A] 9 *Behold, I am Jesus Christ*, the Son of the living God, who created the heavens and the earth, a light which cannot be hid in darkness;

4B] 10 *Wherefore, I must bring forth the fulness of my gospel from the Gentiles unto the house of Israel.*

4C] 11 And behold, *thou art David, and thou art called to assist;*

4D] *which thing if ye do, and are faithful,*

4E] *ye shall be blessed both spiritually and temporally, and great shall be your reward.* Amen.

D&C 14:2-11 Analysis 14A

4Aa/4Ab	Parallel concepts:	**4Aa-** Behold, I am God; **4Ab-** Behold, I am Jesus Christ,
4Ba/4Bb	General to specific:	**4Ba-** Behold, the field is white already to harvest; **4Bb-** Wherefore, I must bring forth the fulness of my gospel from the Gentiles unto the house of Israel.
4Ca/4Cb	General to specific:	**4Ca-** whoso desireth to reap let him thrust in his sickle with his might, **4Cb-** thou art David, and thou art called to assist;
4Da/4Db	Parallel concepts:	**4Da-** and reap while the day lasts, **4Db-** which thing if ye do, and are faithful,
4Ea/4Eb	Parallel concepts:	**4Ea-** that he may treasure up for his soul everlasting salvation in the kingdom of God. **4Eb-** ye shall be blessed both spiritually and temporally, and great shall be your reward.
3a/3b	General to specific:	**3a-** the same is called of God. **3b-** that you may stand as a witness of the things of which you shall both hear and see, and also that you may declare repentance unto this generation.
2a/2b	Parallel concepts:	**2a-** if you will ask of me you shall receive; **2b-** if you shall ask the Father in my name, in faith believing, you shall receive the Holy Ghost,
1a/1b	Parallel concepts:	**1a-** Keep my commandments in all things. **1b-** if you keep my commandments and endure to the end

D&C 45:19-33 Chiasmus 69, 45C

6A] 19 *But, verily I say unto you,*
6B] *that desolation shall come upon this generation* as a thief in the night,
6C] *and this people shall be destroyed and scattered among all nations.*
6D] 20 *And this temple which ye now see shall be thrown down that there shall not be left one stone upon another.*

6E] 21 And it shall come to pass, that this generation of Jews shall not
pass away until *every desolation which I have told you concerning them*
shall come to pass.

5] 23 *And in this ye say truly, for so it is; but these things which I have*
told you shall not pass away until all shall be fulfilled.
24 And this I have told you concerning Jerusalem; and when that
day shall come, shall a remnant be scattered among all nations;

4] 25 But they shall be gathered again; *but they shall remain until*
the times of the Gentiles be fulfilled.
26 And in that day shall be heard of wars and rumors of wars,
and the whole earth shall be in commotion,

3] *and men's hearts shall fail them, and they shall say that*
Christ delayeth his coming until the end of the earth.

2] 27 And the love of men shall wax cold, *and iniquity shall*
abound.

1] 28 And when the times of the Gentiles is come in,
a light shall break forth among them that sit in
darkness, and it shall be the fulness of my gospel;

2] 29 But they receive it not; *for they perceive not the light,*

3] *and they turn their hearts from me because of the precepts of*
men.

4] 30 *And in that generation shall the times of the Gentiles be*
fulfilled.

5] 31 *And there shall be men standing in that generation, that shall not*
pass until they shall see an overflowing scourge;

6A] 22 *Ye say that ye know*

6B] *that the end of the world cometh*; ye say also that ye know that the
heavens and the earth shall pass away; *for a desolating sickness shall*
cover the land.

6C] 32 *But my disciples shall stand in holy places, and shall not be moved;*

6D] *but among the wicked, men shall lift up their voices and curse God and*
die.

6E] 33 *And there shall be earthquakes also in divers places, and many*
desolations; yet men will harden their hearts against me, and they will
take up the sword, one against another, and they will kill one another.

D&C 45:19-33 **Analysis 45C**

6Aa/6Ab	Parallel concepts:	**6Aa-** But, verily I say unto you, **6Ab-** Ye say that ye know
6Ba/6Bb	Parallel concepts:	**6Ba-** that desolation shall come upon this generation **6Bb-** that the end of the world cometh... for a desolating sickness shall cover the land.
6Ca/6Cb	Negative to positive:	**6Ca-** and this people shall be destroyed and scattered among all nations. **6Cb-** But my disciples shall stand in holy places, and shall not be moved;
6Da/6Db	Parallel concepts:	**6Da-** And this temple which ye now see shall be thrown down that there shall not be left one stone upon another. **6Db-** but among the wicked, men shall lift up their voices and curse God and die.
6Ea/6Eb	General to specific:	**6Ea-** every desolation which I have told you concerning them shall come to pass. **6Eb-** And there shall be earthquakes also in divers places, and many desolations; yet men will harden their hearts against me, and they will take up the sword, one against another, and they will kill one another.
5a/5b	Parallel concepts:	**5a-** but these things which I have told you shall not pass away until all shall be fulfilled. **5b-** And there shall be men standing in that generation, that shall not pass until they shall see an overflowing scourge;
4a/4b	Parallel concepts:	**4a-** (but they shall remain until) the times of the Gentiles be fulfilled. **4b-** (And in that generation shall) the times of the Gentiles be fulfilled.
3a/3b	Parallel concepts:	**3a-** and men's hearts shall fail them, and they shall say that Christ delayeth his coming until the end of the earth.

		3b- and they turn their hearts from me because of the precepts of men.
2a/2b	Parallel concepts:	**2a-** and iniquity shall abound.
		2b- for they perceive not the light,
1	Central theme:	**1-** And when the times of the Gentiles is come in, a light shall break forth among them that sit in darkness, and it shall be the fulness of my gospel;

Six-Element Parallelisms

D&C 10:58-61 — Chiasmus 19, 10I

2] 58 *I am the light which shineth in darkness*, and the darkness comprehendeth it not.

1A] 59 *I am he who said—*

1B] *Other sheep*

1C] *have*

1D] *I*

1E] *which*

1F] *are not of this fold*—unto my disciples, and many there were that understood me not.

1A] 60 And *I will show unto this people*

1E] *that*

1D] *I*

1C] *had*

1B] *other sheep,*

1F] and that they *were a branch of the house of Jacob*;

2] 61 And *I will bring to light their marvelous works*, which they did in my name;

D&C 10:58-61 — Analysis 10I

2a/2b	Parallel concepts:	**2a-** I am the light which shineth in darkness, **2b-** I will bring to light their marvelous works,
1Aa/1Ab	Parallel concepts:	**1Aa-** I am he who said— **1Ab-** I will show unto this people
1Ba/1Bb	Identical words:	**1b-** other sheep
1Ca/1Cb	present to past:	**1Ca-** have **1Cb-** had
1Da/1Db	Identical word:	**1D-** I
1Ea/1Eb	Similar parts of speech:	**1Ea-** which **1Eb-** that
1Fa/1Fb	Negative to positive:	**1Fa-** are not of this fold— **1Fb-** were a branch of the house of Jacob;

NOTE: The six parts (1A . . . 1E) of the central pair of chiastic elements form a three-part series; the second element of which is comprised of a four-part chiasmus—1B,1C,1D,1E.

D&C 109:7-19 **Chiasmus 198, 109B**

4A] 7 And as all have not faith, seek ye diligently and *teach one another words of wisdom;*

4B] yea, seek ye *out of the best books* words of wisdom,

4C] *seek learning even by study and also by faith;*

4D] 8 *Organize yourselves; prepare every needful thing,*

4E] *and establish a house, even a house of prayer, a house of fasting, a house of faith, a house of learning, a house of glory, a house of order, a house of God;*

4F] 9 *That your incomings may be in the name of the Lord, that your outgoings may be in the name of the Lord, that all your salutations may be in the name of the Lord, with uplifted hands unto the Most High—*

3] 10 *And now, Holy Father, we ask thee to assist us, thy people, with thy grace, in calling our solemn assembly, that it may be done to thine honor and to thy divine acceptance;*
11 *And in a manner that we may be found worthy, in thy sight, to secure a fulfilment of the promises which thou hast made unto us, thy people, in the revelations given unto us;*

2] 12 *That thy glory may rest down* upon thy people, and *upon this thy house,*

1] which we now dedicate to thee, that it may be sanctified and consecrated to be holy,

2] and *that thy holy presence may be continually in this house;*

3] 13 *And that all people who shall enter upon the threshold of the Lord's house may feel thy power, and feel constrained to acknowledge that thou hast sanctified it, and that it is thy house, a place of thy holiness.*

4A] 14 And do thou grant, Holy Father, that all those who shall worship in this house *may be taught words of wisdom*

4B] *out of the best books,*

4C] and that they may *seek learning even by study, and also by faith,* as thou hast said;

4D] 15 And that they may grow up in thee, and receive a fulness of the Holy Ghost, *and be organized according to thy laws, and be prepared to obtain every needful thing;*

4E] 16 *And that this house may be a house of prayer, a house of fasting, a house of faith, a house of glory and of God,* even thy house;

4F] 17 *That all the incomings of thy people, into this house, may be in the name of the Lord;*
18 That all their outgoings from this house may be in the name of the Lord;
19 And that all their salutations may be in the name of the Lord, with holy hands, uplifted to the Most High;

D&C 109:7-19 **Analysis 109B**

4Aa/4Ab	Parallel concepts:	**4Aa-** teach one another words of wisdom; **4Ab-** may be taught words of wisdom
4Ba/4Bb	Identical words:	**4B-** out of the best books
4Ca/4Cb	Identical words:	**4C-** seek learning even by study and also by faith;
4Da/4Db	Parallel concepts:	**4Da-** Organize yourselves; prepare every needful thing, **4Db-** and be organized according to thy laws, and be prepared to obtain every needful thing;
4Ea/4Eb	Parallel concepts:	**4Ea-** and establish a house, even a house of prayer, a house of fasting, a house of faith, a house of learning, a house of glory, a house of order, a house of God; **4Eb-** And that this house may be a house of prayer, a house of fasting, a house of faith, a house of glory and of God,
4Fa/4Fb	Parallel concepts:	**4Fa-** That your incomings may be in the name of the Lord, that your outgoings may be in the name of the Lord, that all your salutations may be in the name of the Lord, with uplifted hands unto the Most High— **4Fb-** That all the incomings of thy people, into this house, may be in the name of the Lord; That all their outgoings from this house may be in the name of the Lord; And that all their salutations may be in the name of the Lord, with holy hands, uplifted to the Most High;

3a/3b	Similar appeals to the Lord:	**3a-** And now, Holy Father, we ask thee to assist us, thy people, with thy grace, in calling our solemn assembly, that it may be done to thine honor and to thy divine acceptance; And in a manner that we may be found worthy, in thy sight, to secure a fulfilment of the promises which thou hast made unto us, thy people, in the revelations given unto us; **3b-** And that all people who shall enter upon the threshold of the Lord's house may feel thy power, and feel constrained to acknowledge that thou hast sanctified it, and that it is thy house, a place of thy holiness.
2a/2b	Parallel concepts:	**2a-** That thy glory may rest down...upon this thy house, **2b-** that thy holy presence may be continually in this house;
1	Central theme:	**1-** which we now dedicate to thee, that it may be sanctified and consecrated to be holy,

D&C 132:15-18 — Chiasmus 221, 132C

2A] 15 Therefore, *if a man marry him a wife* in the world,
2B] *and he marry her not by me nor by my word,*
2C] *and he covenant with her so long as he is in the world and she with him,*
2D] *their covenant and marriage are not of force when they are dead,*
2E] and *when they are out of the world;*
2F] therefore, *they are not bound by any law when they are out of the world.*
1] 16 *Therefore, when they are out of the world they neither marry nor are given in marriage; but are appointed angels in heaven, which angels are ministering servants, to minister for those who are worthy of a far more, and an exceeding, and an eternal weight of glory.*

1] 17 For these angels did not abide my law; *therefore, they cannot be enlarged, but remain separately and singly, without exaltation, in their saved condition, to all eternity; and from henceforth are not gods, but are angels of God forever and ever.*

2A] 18 And again, verily I say unto you, *if a man marry a wife,*

2C] *and make a covenant with her for time and for all eternity,*

2B] *if that covenant is not by me or by my word,* which is my law, and is not sealed by the Holy Spirit of promise, through him whom I have anointed and appointed unto this power, then it is not valid neither of force when they are out of the world, because they are not joined by me, saith the Lord, neither by my word;

2E] *when they are out of the world*

2D] *it cannot be received there,*

2F] because the angels and the gods are appointed there, by whom they cannot pass; *they cannot, therefore, inherit my glory*; for my house is a house of order, saith the Lord God.

DC 132:15-18 — Analysis 132C

2Aa/2Ab	Identical words:	**2a-** if a man marry (him) a wife
2Ba/2Bb	Parallel concepts:	**2Ba-** and he marry her not by me nor by my word, **2Bb-** if that covenant is not by me or by my word,
2Ca/2Cb	Negative to positive:	**2Ca-** and he covenant with her so long as he is in the world and she with him, **2Cb-** and make a covenant with her for time and for all eternity,
2Da/2Db	Parallel concepts:	**2Da-** their covenant and marriage are not of force when they are dead, **2Db-** it cannot be received there,
2Ea/2Eb	Identical words:	**2E-** when they are out of the world
2Fa/2Fb	Parallel concepts:	**2Fa-** they are not bound by any law when they are out of the world. **2Fb-** they cannot, therefore, inherit my glory;

1a/1b Parallel concepts: **1a-** Therefore, when they are out of the world they neither marry nor are given in marriage; but are appointed angels in heaven, which angels are ministering servants, to minister for those who are worthy of a far more, and an exceeding, and an eternal weight of glory.

1b- therefore, they cannot be enlarged, but remain separately and singly, without exaltation, in their saved condition, to all eternity; and from henceforth are not gods, but are angels of God forever and ever.

NOTE: Elements 2A to 2F form a four-element series, with the elements 2B2C and 2D2E, respectively, being chiastically arranged.

10

CHIASMA CONTAINING PARALLELISMS IN TWO OR MORE MIRROR ELEMENTS

Chiasma Containing Double Parallelisms

D&C 8:1-12 Chiasmus 9, 8A

10] 1 Oliver Cowdery, verily, verily, *I say unto you*,
9] that assuredly as the Lord liveth, *who is your God and your Redeemer*,
8] even so surely *shall you receive a knowledge of whatsoever things you shall ask in faith*, with an honest heart, believing
7A] *that you shall receive a knowledge*
7B] concerning *the engravings of old records*,
7C] *which are ancient*,
6] which contain those parts of my scripture of which has been spoken by *the manifestation of my Spirit*.
5] 2 Yea, behold, *I will tell you in your mind and in your heart*, by the Holy Ghost, which shall come upon you and which shall dwell in your heart.
3 Now, behold, this is the spirit of revelation; behold, this is the spirit by which Moses brought the children of Israel through the Red Sea on dry ground.
4A] 4 Therefore *this is thy gift*; apply unto it, and blessed art thou,
4B] for *it shall deliver you out of the hands of your enemies*, when,
4C] *if it were not so, they would slay you and bring your soul to destruction.*
3] 5 Oh, remember these words, and keep my commandments. Remember, *this is your gift.*
2] 6 Now *this is not all thy gift*;
1] for you have another gift,

2] *which is the gift of Aaron*; behold, it has
told you many things;
3] 7 Behold, there is no other power, save the
power of God, that can cause *this gift of*
Aaron to be with you.
4A] 8 Therefore, doubt not, for *it is the gift of God*;
4B] and *you shall hold it in your hands*, and do marvelous works;
4C] and *no power shall be able to take it away out of*
your hands, for it is the work of God.
5] 9 And, therefore, *whatsoever you shall ask me to tell*
you by that means, that will I grant unto you, and you
shall have knowledge concerning it.
10 Remember that without faith you can do nothing;
therefore ask in faith. Trifle not with these things;
do not ask for that which you ought not.
6] 11 Ask that you may know *the mysteries of God*,
7A] and *that you may* translate and *receive knowledge*
7C] from *all those ancient records*
7B] *which have been hid up*, that are sacred;
8] and *according to your faith shall it be done unto you.*
9] 12 Behold, *it is I* that have spoken it;
10] and *I am the same that spake unto you* from the beginning. Amen.

D&C 8:1-12 — Analysis 8A

10a/10b	Parallel concepts:	**10a-** I say unto you, **10b-** I am the same that spake unto you
9a/9b	Parallel concepts:	**9a-** who is your God and your Redeemer, **9b-** it is I
8a/8b	Parallel concepts:	**8a-** shall you receive a knowledge of whatsoever things you shall ask in faith **8b-** according to your faith shall it be done unto you.
7Aa/7Ab	Parallel concepts:	**7Aa-** that you shall receive a knowledge **7Ab-** that you may . . . receive knowledge
7Ba/7Bb	Completed action:	**7Ba-** the engravings of old records, **7Bb-** which have been hid up
7Ca/7Cb	Parallel concepts:	**7Ca-** which are ancient, **7Cb-** all those ancient records

6Aa/6Ab	Parallel concepts:	**6Aa-** The manifestation of my Spirit. **6Ab-** the mysteries of God,
5a/5b	Parallel concepts:	**5a-** I will tell you in your mind and in your heart, **5b-** whatsoever you shall ask me to tell you by that means, that will I grant unto you,
4Aa/4Ab	Clarification:	**4Aa-** this is thy gift; **4Ab-** it is the gift of God;
4Ba/4Bb	Parallel action:	**4Ba-** it shall deliver you out of the hands of your enemies **4Bb-** you shall hold it in your hands,
4Ca/4Cb	Negative to positive:	**4Ca-** if it were not so, they would slay you and bring your soul to destruction. **4Cb-** no power shall be able to take it away out of your hands,
3a/3b	Clarification:	**3a-** this is your gift. **3b-** this gift of Aaron
2a/2b	Clarification:	**2a-** this is not all thy gift; **2b-** which is the gift of Aaron;
1	Central theme:	**1-** you have another gift

Note: 7Aa and 7Ba,7Ca form a parallelism with 7Ab and 7Bb,7C-b, the second elements being chiastically arranged.

D&C 10:10-25 — Chiasmus 12, 10B

6A] 10 And, behold, *Satan hath put it into their hearts to alter the words which you have caused to be written*, or which you have translated, which have gone out of your hands.

6B] 11 *And behold, I say unto you, that because they have altered the words, they read contrary from that which you translated and caused to be written;*

5] 12 *And, on this wise, the devil has sought to lay a cunning plan, that he may destroy this work;*

4A] 13 *For he hath put into their hearts to do this, that by lying they may say they have caught you in the words which you have pretended to translate.*

4B] 14 *Verily, I say unto you, that I will not suffer that Satan shall accomplish his evil design in this thing.*

3] 15 *For behold, he has put it into their hearts to get thee to tempt the Lord thy God, in asking to translate it over again.*

2] 16 And then, behold, they say and think in their hearts—
We will see if God has given him power to translate;

1] *if so, he will also give him power again;*

1] 17 *And if God giveth him power again*, or if he translates again, or, in other words, if he bringeth forth the same words, behold, we have the same with us, and we have altered them; 18 Therefore they will not agree, and we will say that he has lied in his words, and that he has no gift, and that he has no power;

2] 19 *Therefore we will destroy him, and also the work*; and we will do this that we may not be ashamed in the end, and that we may get glory of the world.

3] 20 *Verily, verily, I say unto you, that Satan has great hold upon their hearts; he stirreth them up to iniquity against that which is good*;

4A] 21 *And their hearts are corrupt, and full of wickedness and abominations; and they love darkness rather than light, because their deeds are evil*; therefore they will not ask of me.

4B] 22 *Satan stirreth them up, that he may lead their souls to destruction.*

5] 23 *And thus he has laid a cunning plan, thinking to destroy the work of God*; but I will require this at their hands, and it shall turn to their shame and condemnation in the day of judgment.

6A] 24 *Yea, he stirreth up their hearts to anger against this work.*

6B] 25 *Yea, he saith unto them: Deceive and lie in wait to catch, that ye may destroy*; behold, this is no harm. And thus he flattereth them, and telleth them that it is no sin to lie that they may catch a man in a lie, that they may destroy him.

D&C 10:10-25 **Analysis 10B**

6Aa/6Ab Specific to general: **6Aa-** Satan hath put it into their hearts to alter the words which you have caused to be written,
6Ab- Yea, he stirreth up their hearts to anger against this work.

6Ba/6Bb	Specific to general:	**6Ba-** And behold, I say unto you, that because they have altered the words, they read contrary from that which you translated and caused to be written; Yea, he saith unto them: Deceive and lie in wait to catch, that ye may destroy;
5a/5b	Parallel concepts:	**5a-** And, on this wise, the devil has sought to lay a cunning plan, that he may destroy this work; **5b-** And thus he has laid a cunning plan, thinking to destroy the work of God;
4Aa/4Ab	Specific to general:	**4Aa-** For he hath put into their hearts to do this, that by lying they may say they have caught you in the words which you have pretended to translate. **4Ab-** And their hearts are corrupt, and full of wickedness and abominations; and they love darkness rather than light, because their deeds are evil;
4Ba/4Bb	Specific to general:	**4Ba-** Verily, I say unto you, that I will not suffer that Satan shall accomplish his evil design in this thing. **4Bb-** Satan stirreth them up, that he may lead their souls to destruction.
3a/3b	Specific to general:	**3a-** For behold, he has put it into their hearts to get thee to tempt the Lord thy God, in asking to translate it over again. **3b-** Verily, verily, I say unto you, that Satan has great hold upon their hearts; he stirreth them up to iniquity against that which is good;
2a/2b	Parallel concepts:	**2a-** We will see if God has given him power to translate; **2b-** Therefore we will destroy him, and also the work;
1a/1b	Parallel concepts:	**1a-** if so, he will also give him power again **1b-** And if God giveth him power again

D&C 50:4-9 — Chiasmus 74, 50A

3] 4 *Behold, I, the Lord, have looked upon you, and have seen abominations in the church that profess my name.*
2A] 5 *But blessed are they who are faithful and endure,*
2B] whether *in life or in death,*
2C] *for they shall inherit eternal life.*
1A] 6 *But wo unto them that are deceivers*
1B] *and hypocrites,*
1C] for, thus saith the Lord, *I will bring them to judgment.*
1B] 7 Behold, verily I say unto you, *there are hypocrites among you,*
1A] *who have deceived some,* which has given the adversary power;
1C] but behold *such shall be reclaimed;*
2A] 8 *But the hypocrites shall be detected and shall be cut off,*
2B] either *in life or in death,* even as I will;
2C] and wo unto them who are cut off from my church, *for the same are overcome of the world.*
3] 9 *Wherefore, let every man beware lest he do that which is not in truth and righteousness before me.*

D&C 50:4-9 — Analysis 50A

3a/3b	General to specific:	**3a-** Behold, I, the Lord, have looked upon you, and have seen abominations in the church that profess my name. **3b-** Wherefore, let every man beware lest he do that which is not in truth and righteousness before me.
2Aa/2Ab	Positive to negative:	**2Aa-** But blessed are they who are faithful and endure, **2Ab-** But the hypocrites shall be detected and shall be cut off,
2Ba/2Bb	Identical words:	**2b-** in life or in death,
2Ca/2Cb	Positive to negative:	**2Ca-** for they shall inherit eternal life. **2Cb-** for the same are overcome of the world.
1Aa/1Ab	Parallel concepts:	**1Aa-** But wo unto them that are deceivers **1Ab-** who have deceived some,
1Ba/1Bb	Parallel concepts:	**1Ba-** and hypocrites, **1Bb-** there are hypocrites among you,
1Ca/1Cb	Negative to positive:	**1Ca-** I will bring them to judgment. **1Cb-** such shall be reclaimed;

NOTE: The elements 1A1B and 1C form a two-element parallelism, with the first element chiastically arranged.

D&C 57:1-15 **Chiasmus 84, 57A**

6A] 1 *Hearken, O ye elders of my church, saith the Lord your God, who have assembled yourselves together,*
6B] *according to my commandments,*
6C] *in this land*, which is the land of Missouri,
5] *which is the land which I have appointed and consecrated for the gathering of the saints.*
4] 2 Wherefore, this is the land of promise, and *the place for the city of Zion.*
3] 3 And thus saith the Lord your God, *if you will receive wisdom here is wisdom.* Behold, the place which is now called Independence is the center place; and a spot for the temple is lying westward, upon a lot which is not far from the court-house.
4 Wherefore, it is wisdom that the land should be purchased by the saints, and also every tract lying westward, even unto the line running directly between Jew and Gentile;
5 And also every tract bordering by the prairies, inasmuch as my disciples are enabled to buy lands. Behold, this is wisdom, that they may obtain it for an everlasting inheritance.
2A] 6 *And let my servant Sidney Gilbert stand in the office to which I have appointed him*, to receive moneys, to be an agent unto the church, to buy land in all the regions round about, inasmuch as can be done in righteousness, and as wisdom shall direct.
2B] 7 *And let my servant Edward Partridge stand in the office to which I have appointed him*, and divide unto the saints their inheritance, even as I have commanded; and also those whom he has appointed to assist him.
1] 8 And again, verily I say unto you, let my servant Sidney Gilbert plant himself in this place, and establish a store, that he may sell goods without fraud, that he may obtain money to buy lands for the good of the saints, and that he may obtain whatsoever things the disciples may need to plant them in their inheritance.

2A] 9 *And also let my servant Sidney Gilbert obtain a license—*
behold here is wisdom, and whoso readeth let him
understand—that he may send goods also unto the
people, even by whom he will as clerks employed in his
service;
10 And thus provide for my saints, that my gospel may
be preached unto those who sit in darkness and in the
region and shadow of death.
2B] 11 *And again, verily I say unto you, let my servant William*
W. Phelps be planted in this place, and be established as
a printer unto the church.
3] 12 And lo, *if the world receive his writings—behold here is*
wisdom—let him obtain whatsoever he can obtain in
righteousness, for the good of the saints.
13 And let my servant Oliver Cowdery assist him, even as
I have commanded, in whatsoever place I shall appoint
unto him, to copy, and to correct, and select, that all things
may be right before me, as it shall be proved by the Spirit
through him.
4] 14 And thus let those of whom I have spoken be planted *in the*
land of Zion, as speedily as can be, with their families, to do
those things even as I have spoken.
5] 15 *And now concerning the gathering—*
6A] *Let the bishop and the agent make preparations for those families*
6B] *which have been commanded to come*
6C] *to this land*, as soon as possible, and plant them in their inheritance.

D&C 57:1-15 — Analysis 57A

6Aa/6Ab	Parallel concepts:	**6Aa-** Hearken, O ye elders of my church, saith the Lord your God, who have assembled yourselves together, **6Ab-** Let the bishop and the agent make preparations for those families
6Ba/6Bb	Parallel concepts:	**6Ba-** according to my commandments, which have been commanded to come
6Ca/6Cb	Identical word:	**6C-** to/in this land,
5a/5b	Parallel concepts:	**5a-** which is the land which I have appointed and consecrated for the gathering of the saints. **5b-** And now concerning the gathering—

4a/4b	Parallel concepts:	**4a-** the place for the city of Zion. **4b-** in the land of Zion,
3a/3b	Parallel concepts:	**3a-** if you will receive wisdom here is wisdom. **3b-** if the world receive his writings—behold here is wisdom—
2Aa/2Ab	Parallel concepts:	**2Aa-** And let my servant Sidney Gilbert stand in the office to which I have appointed him, **2Ab-** And also let my servant Sidney Gilbert obtain a license—
2Ba/2Bb	Parallel concepts:	2Ba. And let my servant Edward Partridge stand in the office to which I have appointed him, **2Bb-** And again, verily I say unto you, let my servant William W. Phelps be planted in this place,
1	Central theme:	**1-** And again, verily I say unto you, let my servant Sidney Gilbert plant himself in this place, and establish a store, that he may sell goods without fraud, that he may obtain money to buy lands for the good of the saints, and that he may obtain whatsoever things the disciples may need to plant them in their inheritance.

D&C 66:1-13 — Chiasmus 98, 66A

1 Behold, thus saith the Lord unto my servant William E. McLellin—Blessed are you, inasmuch as you have turned away from your iniquities, and have received my truths,

6] *saith the Lord your Redeemer, the Savior of the world, even of as many as believe on my name.*

5A] 2 Verily I say unto you, *blessed are you for receiving mine everlasting covenant*, even the fulness of my gospel, sent forth unto the children of men,

5B] *that they might have life and be made partakers of the glories which are to be revealed in the last days,*

5C] *as it was written by the prophets and apostles in days of old.*

4A] 3 Verily I say unto you, my servant William, that *you are clean, but not all*;

4B] *repent, therefore, of those things which are not pleasing in my sight, saith the Lord, for the Lord will show them unto you.*

3] 4 *And now, verily, I, the Lord, will show unto you what I will concerning you, or what is my will concerning you.*

2] 5 *Behold, verily I say unto you, that it is my will that you should proclaim my gospel from land to land, and from city to city, yea, in those regions round about where it has not been proclaimed.*

1] 6 Tarry not many days in this place; go not up unto the land of Zion as yet; but inasmuch as you can send, send; otherwise, think not of thy property.

2] 7 *Go unto the eastern lands, bear testimony in every place, unto every people and in their synagogues, reasoning with the people.*

3] 8 *Let my servant Samuel H. Smith go with you, and forsake him not, and give him thine instructions; and he that is faithful shall be made strong in every place; and I, the Lord, will go with you.*
9 *Lay your hands upon the sick, and they shall recover. Return not till I, the Lord, shall send you. Be patient in affliction. Ask, and ye shall receive; knock, and it shall be opened unto you.*

4A] 10 Seek not to be cumbered. *Forsake all unrighteousness.*

4B] *Commit not adultery—a temptation with which thou hast been troubled.*

5A] 11 *Keep these sayings, for they are true and faithful*; and thou shalt magnify thine office,

5B] *and push many people to Zion with songs of everlasting joy upon their heads.*

5C] 12 *Continue in these things even unto the end*, and you shall have a crown of eternal life at the right hand of my Father, who is full of grace and truth.

6] 13 *Verily, thus saith the Lord your God, your Redeemer, even Jesus Christ.* Amen.

D&C 66:1-13 Analysis 66A

6a/6b Parallel concepts:

6a- saith the Lord your Redeemer, the Savior of the world, even of as many as believe on my name.

6b- Verily, thus saith the Lord your God, your Redeemer, even Jesus Christ.

5Aa/5Ab	Parallel concepts:	**5Aa-** blessed are you for receiving mine everlasting covenant, **5Ab-** Keep these sayings, for they are true and faithful;
5Ba/5Bb	General to specific:	**5Ba-** that they might have life and be made partakers of the glories which are to be revealed in the last days, **5Bb-** and push many people to Zion with songs of everlasting joy upon their heads.
5Ca/5Cb	Past to future:	**5Ca-** as it was written by the prophets and apostles in days of old. **5Cb-** Continue in these things even unto the end,
4Aa/4Ab	Parallel concepts:	**4Aa-** you are clean, but not all; **4Ab-** Forsake all unrighteousness.
4Ba/4Bb	General to specific:	**4Ba-** repent, therefore, of those things which are not pleasing in my sight, saith the Lord, **4Bb-** Commit not adultery—
3a/3b	Promise to fulfillment:	**3a-** And now, verily, I, the Lord, will show unto you what I will concerning you, or what is my will concerning you. **3b-** Let my servant Samuel H. Smith go with you, and forsake him not, and give him thine instructions; and he that is faithful shall be made strong in every place; and I, the Lord, will go with you. Lay your hands upon the sick, and they shall recover. Return not till I, the Lord, shall send you. Be patient in affliction. Ask, and ye shall receive; knock, and it shall be opened unto you.
2a/2b	Parallel concepts:	**2a-** Behold, verily I say unto you, that it is my will that you should proclaim my gospel from land to land, and from city to city, yea, in those regions round about where it has not been proclaimed.

2b- Go unto the eastern lands, bear testimony in every place, unto every people and in their synagogues, reasoning with the people.

1 Central theme: **1-** Tarry not many days in this place; go not up unto the land of Zion as yet; but inasmuch as you can send, send; otherwise, think not of thy property.

D&C 76:63-106 — Chiasmus 115, 76J

4] **D&C 76:63-70** — **Parallelism 76A**

1) 63 These are they whom he shall bring with him, when he shall come in the clouds of heaven to reign on the earth over his people.
2) 64 These are they who shall have part in the first resurrection.
3) 65 These are they who shall come forth in the resurrection of the just.
4) 66 These are they who are come unto Mount Zion, and unto the city of the living God, the heavenly place, the holiest of all.
5) 67 These are they who have come to an innumerable company of angels, to the general assembly and church of Enoch, and of the Firstborn.
6) 68 These are they whose names are written in heaven, where God and Christ are the judge of all.
7) 69 These are they who are just men made perfect through Jesus the mediator of the new covenant, who wrought out this perfect atonement through the shedding of his own blood.
8) 70 These are they whose bodies are celestial, whose glory is that of the sun, even the glory of God, the highest of all, whose glory the sun of the firmament is written of as being typical.

3] 71 And again, we saw the terrestrial world, and behold and lo, these are they who are of the terrestrial, whose glory differs from that of the church of the Firstborn who have received the fulness of the Father, even as that of the moon differs from the sun in the firmament.

2] **D&C 76:72-79** — **Parallelism 76B**

1) 72 Behold, these are they who died without law;
2) 73 And also they who are the spirits of men kept in prison, whom the Son visited, and preached the gospel unto them, that they might be judged according to men in the flesh;

74 Who received not the testimony of Jesus in the flesh, but afterwards received it.

3) 75 These are they who are honorable men of the earth, who were blinded by the craftiness of men.

4) 76 These are they who receive of his glory, but not of his fulness.

5) 77 These are they who receive of the presence of the Son, but not of the fulness of the Father.

78 Wherefore, they are bodies terrestrial, and not bodies celestial, and differ in glory as the moon differs from the sun.

6) 79 These are they who are not valiant in the testimony of Jesus; wherefore, they obtain not the crown over the kingdom of our God.

1] 80 *And now this is the end of the vision which we saw of the terrestrial*, that the Lord commanded us to write while we were yet in the Spirit.

1] 81 *And again, we saw the glory of the telestial*, which glory is that of the lesser, even as the glory of the stars differs from that of the glory of the moon in the firmament.

2] **D&C 76:82-88** **Parallelism 76C**

1) 82 These are they who received not the gospel of Christ, neither the testimony of Jesus.

2) 83 These are they who deny not the Holy Spirit.

3) 84 These are they who are thrust down to hell.

4) 85 These are they who shall not be redeemed from the devil until the last resurrection, until the Lord, even Christ the Lamb, shall have finished his work.

5) 86 These are they who receive not of his fulness in the eternal world, but of the Holy Spirit through the ministration of the terrestrial;

87 And the terrestrial through the ministration of the celestial.

88 And also the telestial receive it of the administering of angels who are appointed to minister for them, or who are appointed to be ministering spirits for them; for they shall be heirs of salvation.

3] **D&C 76:89-98** **Chiasmus 118, 76K**

3) 89 And thus we saw, in the heavenly vision, *the glory of the telestial*, which surpasses all understanding;
90 And no man knows it except him to whom God has revealed it.

2) 91 And thus we saw *the glory of the terrestrial* which excels in all things the glory of the telestial, even in glory, and in power, and in might, and in dominion.

1) 92 And thus we saw *the glory of the celestial*, which excels in all things—where God, even the Father, reigns upon his throne forever and ever;
93 Before whose throne all things bow in humble reverence, and give him glory forever and ever.
94 They who dwell in his presence are the church of the Firstborn; and they see as they are seen, and know as they are known, having received of his fulness and of his grace;
95 And he makes them equal in power, and in might, and in dominion.

1) 96 And *the glory of the celestial* is one, even as the glory of the sun is one.

2) 97 And *the glory of the terrestrial* is one, even as the glory of the moon is one.

3) 98 And *the glory of the telestial* is one, even as the glory of the stars is one; for as one star differs from another star in glory, even so differs one from another in glory in the telestial world;

4] **D&C 76:99-107** **Parallelism 76D**

1) 99 For these are they who are of Paul, and of Apollos, and of Cephas.
2) 100 These are they who say they are some of one and some of another—some of Christ and some of John, and some of Moses, and some of Elias, and some of Esaias, and some of Isaiah, and some of Enoch;
101 But received not the gospel, neither the testimony of Jesus, neither the prophets, neither the everlasting covenant.
3) 102 Last of all, these all are they who will not be gathered with the saints, to be caught up unto the church of the Firstborn, and received into the cloud.
4) 103 These are they who are liars, and sorcerers, and adulterers, and whoremongers, and whosoever loves and makes a lie.

5) 104 These are they who suffer the wrath of God on earth.
6) 105 These are they who suffer the vengeance of eternal fire.
7) 106 These are they who are cast down to hell and suffer the wrath of Almighty God, until the fulness of times, when Christ shall have subdued all enemies under his feet, and shall have perfected his work; 107 When he shall deliver up the kingdom, and present it unto the Father, spotless, saying: I have overcome and have trodden the wine-press alone, even the wine-press of the fierceness of the wrath of Almighty God.

D&C 76:63-106 — Analysis 76J

4a/4b	Parallel concepts:	**4a-** An eight-element series of "these are they" listing the attributes of those who inherit the celestial world.
		4b- A seven-element series of "these are they" listing the attributes of those whose inherit the telestial world.
3a/3b	Parallel concepts:	**3a-** A statement of the glory of the terrestrial world.
		3b- A three-element chiasmus declaring the vision of the three degrees of glory.
2a/2b	Parallel concepts:	**2a-** A six-element series of "these are they" listing the attributes of those who inherit the terrestrial glory.
		2b- A five-element series of "these are they" listing the attributes of those who inherit the telestial glory.
1a/1b	Parallel concepts:	**1a-** And now this is the end of the vision which we saw of the terrestrial,
		1b- and again, we saw the glory of the telestial,

(For Analysis 76K, D&C 76:89-98, element 3b] of chiasmus 76J, see Chapter 6, page 99.)

D&C 88:34-39 — Chiasmus 136, 88D

5A] 34 *And again, verily I say unto you, that which is governed by law is also preserved by law and perfected and sanctified by the same.*

5B] 35 *That which breaketh a law, and abideth not by law, but seeketh to become a law unto itself, and willeth to abide in sin, cannot be sanctified by law, neither by mercy, justice, nor judgment. Therefore, they must remain filthy still.*

4A] 36 *All kingdoms*
4B] *have a law*
4C] *given;*
3] 37 *And there are many kingdoms;*
2] for *there is no space*
1] in the which *there is no kingdom;*
1] and *there is no kingdom*
2] in which *there is no space,*
3] *either a greater or a lesser kingdom.*
4A] 38 And unto *every kingdom*
4C] is *given*
4B] *a law;*
5A] and *unto every law there are certain bounds also and conditions.*
5B] 39 *All beings who abide not in those conditions are not justified.*

D&C 88:34-39 Analysis 88D

5Aa/5Ab	Parallel concepts:	**5Aa-** And again, verily I say unto you, that which is governed by law is also preserved by law and perfected and sanctified by the same. **5Ab-** unto every law there are certain bounds also and conditions.
5Ba/5Bb	Parallel concepts:	**5Ba-** That which breaketh a law, and abideth not by law, but seeketh to become a law unto itself, and willeth to abide in sin, cannot be sanctified by law, neither by mercy, justice, nor judgment. Therefore, they must remain filthy still. **5Bb-** All beings who abide not in those conditions are not justified.
4Aa/4Ab	Parallel concepts:	**4Aa-** All kingdoms **4Ab-** every kingdom
4Ba/4Bb	Identical words:	**4b-** a law
4Ca/4Cb	Identical word:	**4C-** given
3a/3b	Parallel concepts:	**3a-** And there are many kingdoms; **3b-** either a greater or lesser kingdom.
2a/2b	Identical words:	**2-** there is no space
1a/1b	Identical words:	**1-** there is no kingdom

D&C 93:7-23 **Chiasmus 150, 93B**

4] 7 And he bore record, saying: I saw his glory, that *he was in the beginning, before the world was;*

3] 8 *Therefore, in the beginning the Word was, for he was the Word, even the messenger of salvation—*

9 The light and the Redeemer of the world; the Spirit of truth, who came into the world, because the world was made by him, and in him was the life of men and the light of men.

10 The worlds were made by him; men were made by him; all things were made by him, and through him, and of him.

2A] 11 *And I, John, bear record that I beheld his glory,* as the glory of the Only Begotten of the Father, full of grace and truth, even the Spirit of truth, which came and dwelt in the flesh,

2B] *and dwelt among us.*

1A] 12 *And I, John, saw* that he received not of the fulness at first, but received grace for grace.

13 And he received not of the fulness at first, but continued from grace to grace, until he received a fulness;

1B] 14 *And thus he was called the Son of God,* because he received not of the fulness at the first.

1A] 15 *And I, John, bear record,* and lo, the heavens were opened, and the Holy Ghost descended upon him in the form of a dove, and sat upon him,

1B] *and there came a voice out of heaven saying: This is my beloved Son.*

2A] 16 *And I, John, bear record that he received a fulness of the glory of the Father.*

17 And he received all power, both in heaven and on earth, and the glory of the Father was with him,

2B] *for he dwelt in him.*

18 And it shall come to pass, that if you are faithful you shall receive the fulness of the record of John.

19 I give unto you these sayings that you may understand and know how to worship, and know what you worship, that you may come unto the Father in my name, and in due time receive of his fulness.

20 For if you keep my commandments you shall receive of his fulness, and be glorified in me as I am in the Father; therefore, I say unto you, you shall receive grace for grace.

3] 21 And now, verily I say unto you, *I was in the beginning with the Father, and am the Firstborn;*
22 And all those who are begotten through me are partakers of the glory of the same, and are the church of the Firstborn.
4] 23 *Ye were also in the beginning with the Father;* that which is Spirit, even the Spirit of truth;

D&C 93:7-23 — Analysis 93B

4a/4b	Parallel concepts:	**4a-** he was in the beginning, before the world was; **4b-** Ye were also in the beginning with the Father;
3a/3b	Parallel concepts:	**3a-** Therefore, in the beginning the Word was, for he was the Word, even the messenger of salvation— **3b-** I was in the beginning with the Father, and am the Firstborn;
2Aa/2Ab	Parallel concepts:	**2Aa-** And I, John, bear record that I beheld his glory, **2Ab-** And I, John, bear record that he received a fulness of the glory of the Father.
2Ba/2Bb	Parallel concepts:	**2Ba-**and dwelt among us. **2Bb-** for he dwelt in him.
1Aa/1Ab	Parallel concepts:	**1Aa-** And I, John, saw **1Ab-** And I, John, bear record
1Ba/1Bb	Parallel concepts:	**1Ba-** And thus he was called the Son of God, **1Bb-** and there came a voice out of heaven saying: This is my beloved Son.

D&C 93:44-52 — Chiasmus 157, 93I

4A] 44 Verily, I say unto *my servant Sidney Rigdon,* that in some things he hath not kept the commandments concerning his children; therefore, first set in order thy house.
4B] 45 Verily, I say unto *my servant Joseph Smith, Jun.,*
3] *or in other words, I will call you friends, for you are my friends,* and ye shall have an inheritance with me—

46 I called you servants for the world's sake, and ye are their servants for my sake—

2A] 47 *And now, verily I say unto Joseph Smith, Jun.—You have not kept the commandments, and must needs stand rebuked before the Lord;*

2B] 48 *Your family must needs repent and forsake some things, and give more earnest heed unto your sayings,*

2C] *or be removed out of their place.*

1] 49 What I say unto one I say unto all; pray always lest that wicked one have power in you, and remove you out of your place.

2A] 50 *My servant Newel K. Whitney also, a bishop of my church, hath need to be chastened,*

2B] *and set in order his family, and see that they are more diligent and concerned at home, and pray always,*

2C] *or they shall be removed out of their place.*

3] 51 *Now, I say unto you, my friends,*

4A] let *my servant Sidney Rigdon* go on his journey, and make haste, and also proclaim the acceptable year of the Lord, and the gospel of salvation, as I shall give him utterance; and by your prayer of faith with one consent I will uphold him.

4B] 52 And *let my servants Joseph Smith Jun., and Frederick G. Williams* make haste also, and it shall be given them even according to the prayer of faith; and inasmuch as you keep my sayings you shall not be confounded in this world, nor in the world to come.

D&C 93:44-52 — Analysis 93I

4Aa/4Ab	Identical words:	**4A-** my servant Sidney Rigdon,
4Ba/4Bb	Identical words:	**4B-** my servant(s) Joseph Smith Jun.,
3a/3b	Parallel concepts:	**3a-** or in other words, I will call you friends, **3b-** Now, I say unto you, my friends,
2Aa/2Ab	Parallel concepts:	**2Aa-** And now, verily I say unto Joseph Smith, Jun.—You have not kept the commandments, and must needs stand rebuked before the Lord; **2Ab-** My servant Newel K. Whitney also, a bishop of my church, hath need to be chastened,

2Ba/2Bb	Parallel concepts:	**2Ba-** Your family must needs repent and forsake some things, and give more earnest heed unto your sayings, **2Bb-** and set in order his family, and see that they are more diligent and concerned at home, and pray always,
2Ca2Cb	Identical words:	2C- or (they shall) be removed out of their place.
1	Central theme:	1- What I say unto one I say unto all; pray always lest that wicked one have power in you, and remove you out of your place.

D&C 94:3-12 — Chiasmus 158, 94A

2A] 3 *And let the first lot on the south be consecrated unto me*
2B] *for the building of a house for the presidency,*
2C] *for the work of the presidency, in obtaining revelations; and for the work of the ministry of the presidency, in all things pertaining to the church and kingdom.*
2D] 4 Verily I say unto you, that *it shall be built fifty-five by sixty-five feet in the width thereof and in the length thereof, in the inner court.*
5 *And there shall be a lower court and a higher court,* according to the pattern which shall be given unto you hereafter.
2E] 6 *And it shall be dedicated unto the Lord from the foundation thereof,* according to the order of the priesthood,
2F] *according to the pattern which shall be given unto you hereafter.*
7 And it shall be wholly dedicated unto the Lord for the work of the presidency.
1A] 8 And ye shall not suffer *any unclean thing*
  1B] *to come in unto it;*
1C] and *my glory shall be there,*
1D] *and my presence shall be there.*
  1B] 9 *But if there shall come into it*
1A] *any unclean thing,*
1C] *my glory shall not be there;*
1D] *and my presence shall not come into it.*
2A] 10 And again, verily I say unto you, *the second lot on the south shall be dedicated unto me*
2B] *for the building of a house unto me,*

2C] *for the work of the printing of the translation of my scriptures, and all things whatsoever I shall command you.*
2D] 11 *And it shall be fifty-five by sixty-five feet in the width thereof and the length thereof, in the inner court; and there shall be a lower and a higher court.*
2E] 12 *And this house shall be wholly dedicated unto the Lord from the foundation thereof,* for the work of the printing, in all things whatsoever I shall command you, to be holy, undefiled,
2F] *according to the pattern in all things as it shall be given unto you.*

D&C 94:3-12 **Analysis 94A**

2Aa/2Ab	Parallel concepts:	**2Aa-** And let the first lot on the south be consecrated unto me **2Ab-** the second lot on the south shall be dedicated unto me
2Ba/2Bb	Parallel concepts:	**2Ba-** for the building of a house for the presidency, **2Bb-** for the building of a house unto me,
2Ca/2Cb	Parallel concepts:	**2Ca-** for the work of the presidency, in obtaining revelations; and for the work of the ministry of the presidency, in all things pertaining to the church and kingdom. **2Cb-** for the work of the printing of the translation of my scriptures, and all things whatsoever I shall command you.
2Da/2Db	Identical words:	**2D-** And it shall be fifty-five by sixty-five feet in the width thereof and the length thereof, in the inner court; and there shall be a lower and a higher court.
2Ea/2Eb	Parallel concepts:	**2Ea-**And it shall be dedicated unto the Lord from the foundation thereof, **2Eb-** And this house shall be wholly dedicated unto the Lord from the foundation thereof,
2Fa/2Fb	Parallel concepts:	**2Fa-** according to the pattern which shall be given unto you hereafter. **2Fb-** according to the pattern in all things as it shall be given unto you.
1Aa/1Ab	Identical words:	**1A-** any unclean thing

1Ba/1Bb	Positive to negative:	**1Ba-** to come in unto it; **1Bb-** But if there shall come into it
1Ca/1Cb	Positive to negative:	**1Ca-** my glory shall be there, **1Cb-** my glory shall not be there;
1Da/1Db	Positive to negative:	**1Da-** and my presence shall be there. **1Db-** and my presence shall not come into it.

NOTE: Elements 1A to 1D form a three-element series, with the first two elements being chiastically arranged.

Chiasma Containing Triple Parallelisms

D&C 109:29-50 — Chiasmus 200, 109D

12] *if they will not repent, when the everlasting gospel shall be proclaimed in their ears;*

11A] 30 *And that all their works may be brought to naught, and be swept away by the hail,*

11B] and by the judgments which thou wilt send upon them in thine anger,

10] *that there may be an end to lyings and slanders against thy people.*

9] 31 *For thou knowest, O Lord, that thy servants have been innocent before thee in bearing record of thy name, for which they have suffered these things.*

8] 32 Therefore we plead before thee for a full and complete deliverance *from under this yoke;*

7] 33 *Break it off, O Lord;* break it off from the necks of thy servants, by thy power, that we may rise up in the midst of this generation and do thy work.

6] 34 *O Jehovah, have mercy upon this people,* and as all men sin forgive the transgressions of thy people, and let them be blotted out forever.
35 Let the anointing of thy ministers be sealed upon them with power from on high.
36 Let it be fulfilled upon them, as upon those on the day of Pentecost; let the gift of tongues be poured out upon thy people, even cloven tongues as of fire, and the interpretation thereof.
37 And let thy house be filled, as with a rushing mighty wind, with thy glory.

5A] 38 *Put upon thy servants the testimony of the covenant,*

5B] that when they go out and proclaim thy word *they may seal up the law,*

4] and prepare the hearts of thy saints for *all those judgments thou art about to send, in thy wrath, upon the inhabitants of the earth, because of their transgressions,*

3] *that thy people may not faint in the day of trouble.*

2A] 39 *And whatsoever city thy servants shall enter, and the people of that city receive their testimony,*

2B] *let thy peace and thy salvation be upon that city;*

2C] *that they may gather out of that city the righteous,*

1] that they may come forth to Zion, or to her stakes, the places of thine appointment, with songs of everlasting joy;
40 And until this be accomplished, let not thy judgments fall upon that city.

2A] 41 *And whatsoever city thy servants shall enter, and the people of that city receive not the testimony of thy servants,* and thy servants warn them to save themselves from this untoward generation,

2B] *let it be upon that city according to that which thou hast spoken by the mouths of thy prophets.*

2C] 42 *But deliver thou, O Jehovah, we beseech thee, thy servants from their hands,* and cleanse them from their blood.

3] 43 *O Lord, we delight not in the destruction of our fellow men; their souls are precious before thee;*
44 But thy word must be fulfilled. Help thy servants to say, with thy grace assisting them: Thy will be done, O Lord, and not ours.

4] 45 We know that *thou hast spoken by the mouth of thy prophets terrible things concerning the wicked, in the last days—that thou wilt pour out thy judgments, without measure;*

5A] 46 Therefore, O Lord, *deliver thy people from the calamity of the wicked;*

5B] *enable thy servants to seal up the law,* and bind up the testimony, that they may be prepared against the day of burning.

6] 47 *We ask thee, Holy Father, to remember those who have been driven by the inhabitants of Jackson county, Missouri, from the lands of their inheritance,*

7] and *break off, O Lord,*

8] *this yoke of affliction* that has been put upon them.

9] 48 *Thou knowest, O Lord, that they have been greatly oppressed and afflicted by wicked men; and our hearts flow out with sorrow because of their grievous burdens.*

10] 49 *O Lord, how long wilt thou suffer this people to bear this affliction,*

11A] *and the cries of their innocent ones to ascend up in thine ears, and their blood come up in testimony before thee,*

11B] *and not make a display of thy testimony in their behalf?*

12] 50 Have mercy, O Lord, upon the wicked mob, who have driven thy people, that they may cease to spoil, *that they may repent of their sins if repentance is to be found;*

D&C 109:29-50 **Analysis 109D**

12a/12b	Parallel concepts:	**12a-** if they will not repent, when the everlasting gospel shall be proclaimed in their ears; **12b-** that they may repent of their sins if repentance is to be found;
11Aa/11Ab	Persecutors vs persecuted:	11Aa- And that all their works may be brought to naught, and be swept away by the hail, **11Ab-** and the cries of their innocent ones to ascend up in thine ears, and their blood come up in testimony before thee,
11Ba/11Bb	Persecutors vs persecuted:	**11Ba-** and by the judgments which thou wilt send upon them in thine anger,

		11Bb- and not make a display of thy testimony in their behalf?
10a/10b	Parallel concepts:	**10a-** that there may be an end to lyings and slanders against thy people. **10b-** O Lord, how long wilt thou suffer this people to bear this affliction,
9a/9b	Parallel concepts:	**9a-** For thou knowest, O Lord, that thy servants have been innocent before thee in bearing record of thy name, for which they have suffered these things. **9b-** Thou knowest, O Lord, that they have been greatly oppressed and afflicted by wicked men; and our hearts flow out with sorrow because of their grievous burdens.
8a/8b	Parallel concepts:	**8a-** from under this yoke; **8b-** this yoke of affliction
7a/7b	Parallel concepts:	**7a-** Break it off, O Lord; **7b-** break off, O Lord,
6a/6b		**6a-** O Jehovah, have mercy upon this people, **6b-** We ask thee, Holy Father, to remember those who have been driven by the inhabitants of Jackson county, Missouri, from the lands of their inheritance,
5Aa/5Ab	Similar appeals to the Lord:	**5Aa-** Put upon thy servants the testimony of the covenant, **5Ab-** deliver thy people from the calamity of the wicked;
5Ba/5Bb	Parallel concepts:	**5Ba-** they may seal up the law, **5Bb-** enable thy servants to seal up the law,
4a/4b	Parallel concepts:	**4a-** all those judgments thou art about to send, in thy wrath, upon the inhabitants of the earth, because of their transgressions, **4b-** thou hast spoken by the mouth of thy prophets terrible things concerning the wicked, in the last days—that thou wilt pour out thy judgments, without measure;

3a/3b	Those of the kingdom vs those of the world:	**3a-** that thy people may not faint in the day of trouble **3b-** O Lord, we delight not in the destruction of our fellow men; their souls are precious before thee;
2Aa/2Ab	Positive to negative:	**2Aa-** And whatsoever city thy servants shall enter, and the people of that city receive their testimony, **2Ab-** And whatsoever city thy servants shall enter, and the people of that city receive not the testimony of thy servants,
2Ba/2Bb	Positive to negative:	**2Ba-** let thy peace and thy salvation be upon that city; **2Bb-** let it be upon that city according to that which thou hast spoken by the mouths of thy prophets.
2Ca/2Cb	Parallel concepts:	**2Ca-** that they may gather out of that city the righteous, **2Cb-** But deliver thou, O Jehovah, we beseech thee, thy servants from their hands,
1	Central theme:	**1-** that they may come forth to Zion, or to her stakes, the places of thine appointment, with songs of everlasting joy; And until this be accomplished, let not thy judgments fall upon that city.

Chiasma Containing Quadruple Parallelisms

D&C 11:1-30 — Chiasmus 21, 11A

16] 1 *A great and marvelous work is about to come forth among the children of men.*

15] 2 *Behold, I am God*; give heed to my word, which is quick and powerful, sharper than a two-edged sword, to the dividing asunder of both joints and marrow; therefore give heed unto my word.

14A] 3 Behold, the field is white already to harvest; *therefore, whoso desireth to reap*

14B] *let him thrust in his sickle* with his might, *and reap* while the day lasts,

13] *that he may treasure up for his soul everlasting salvation in the kingdom of God.*

12] 4 Yea, whosoever will thrust in his sickle and reap, *the same is called of God.*
5 Therefore, if you will ask of me you shall receive; if you will knock it shall be opened unto you.

11] 6 Now, as you have asked, behold, I say unto you, keep my commandments, and *seek to bring forth and establish the cause of Zion.*

10A] 7 *Seek not for riches but for wisdom;*

10B] and, *behold, the mysteries of God shall be unfolded unto you*, and then shall you be made rich. Behold, he that hath eternal life is rich.

9] 8 Verily, verily, I say unto you, even as you desire of me so it shall be done unto you; and, *if you desire, you shall be the means of doing much good in this generation.*

8] 9 *Say nothing but repentance unto this generation.*

7] *Keep my commandments*, and assist to bring forth my work,

6A] *according to my commandments,*

6B] *and you shall be blessed.*

5A] 10 Behold, thou hast a gift, or thou shalt have a gift *if thou wilt desire of me*

5B] *in faith*, with an honest heart,
believing in the power of Jesus
Christ, or in my power which
speaketh unto thee;
4] 11 For, behold, it is I that speak; *behold*, I am the light which shineth
in darkness, and *by my power I give these words unto thee.*
3] 12 And now, verily, verily, I say unto thee, *put your trust in that*
Spirit which leadeth to do good—yea, to do justly, to walk humbly,
2] *to judge righteously*; and this is my Spirit.
1] 13 Verily, verily, I say unto you, I will impart unto you of
my Spirit, which shall enlighten your mind, which shall fill
your soul with joy;
2] 14 And then shall ye know, or by this shall you know, all
things whatsoever you desire of me, which are *pertaining unto*
things of righteousness,
3] *in faith believing in me that you shall receive.*
4] 15 *Behold, I command you* that you need not suppose that you are
called to preach until you are called.
16 Wait a little longer, until you shall have my word, my rock, my
church, and my gospel, that you may know of a surety my doctrine.
5A] 17 And then, behold, *according*
to your desires,
5B] yea, *even according to your faith*
shall it be done unto you.
6A] 18 *Keep my commandments*; hold
your peace; appeal unto my Spirit;
6B] 19 Yea, cleave unto me with all
your heart, *that you may assist in*
bringing to light those things of
which has been spoken—yea, the
translation of my work; be patient
until you shall accomplish it.
7] 20 Behold, this is your work, to *keep*
my commandments, yea, with all your
might, mind and strength.
8] 21 Seek not to declare my word, but *first*
seek to obtain my word, and then shall your
tongue be loosed;

9] then, *if you desire, you shall have my Spirit and*
my word, yea, the power of God unto the con-
vincing of men.
10A] 22 But now hold your peace; *study my word which*
hath gone forth among the children of men, and
also study my word which shall come forth among
the children of men, or that which is now transla-
ting, yea, until you have obtained all which I shall
grant unto the children of men in this generation,
10B] *and then shall all things be added thereto.*
11] 23 Behold thou art Hyrum, my son; *seek the kingdom*
of God, and all things shall be added according to
that which is just.
12] 24 Build upon my rock, which is my gospel;
25 *Deny not the spirit of revelation, nor the spirit of*
prophecy, for wo unto him that denieth these things;
13] 26 Therefore, *treasure up in your heart until the time which*
is in my wisdom that you shall go forth.
14A] 27 Behold, *I speak unto all who have good desires,*
14B] *and have thrust in their sickle to reap.*
15] 28 *Behold, I am Jesus Christ, the Son of God.* I am the life and the
light of the world.
29 I am the same who came unto mine own and mine own
received me not;
16] 30 *But verily, verily, I say unto you, that as many as receive me, to them*
will I give power to become the sons of God, even to them that believe
on my name. Amen.

D&C 11:1-30 — Analysis 11A

16a/16b	General to specific:	**16a-** A great and marvelous work is about to come forth among the children of men. **16b-** But verily, verily, I say unto you, that as many as receive me, to them will I give power to become the sons of God, even to them that believe on my name.
15a/15b	Parallel concepts:	**15a-** Behold, I am God; **15b-** Behold, I am Jesus Christ, the Son of God.

14Aa/14Ab	Parallel concepts:	**14Aa-** Therefore, whoso desireth to reap **14Ab-** I speak unto all who have good desires,
14Ba/14Bb	Future to past:	**14Ba-** let him thrust in his sickle . . . and reap **14Bb-** and have thrust in their sickle to reap.
13a/13b	Eternal to temporal:	**13a-** that he may treasure up for his soul everlasting salvation in the kingdom of God. **13b-** treasure up in your heart until the time which is in my wisdom that you shall go forth.
12a/12b	Positive to negative:	**12a-** the same is called of God. **12b-** Deny not the spirit of revelation, nor the spirit of prophecy,
11a/11b	Temporal to eternal:	**11a-** seek to bring forth and establish the cause of Zion. **11b-** seek the kingdom of God,
10Aa/10Ab	General to specific:	**10Aa-** Seek not for riches but for wisdom; **10Ab-** study my word which hath gone forth among the children of men, and also study my word which shall come forth among the children of men, and also study my word which shall come forth among the children of men, or that which is now translating, yea, until you have obtained all which I shall grant unto the children of men in this generation,
10Ba/10Bb	Parallel concepts:	**10Ba-** behold, the mysteries of God shall be unfolded unto you, **10Bb-** and then shall all things be added thereto.
9a/9b	General to specific:	**9a-** if you desire, you shall be the means of doing much good in this generation. **9b-** if you desire, you shall have my Spirit and my word, yea, the power of God unto the convincing of men.

8a/8b	Specific to general:	**8a-** Say nothing but repentance unto this generation. **8b-** first seek to obtain my word, and then shall your tongue be loosed;
7a/7b	Identical words:	**7-** Keep my commandments,
6Aa/6Ab	Parallel concepts:	**6Aa-** according to my commandments, **6Ab-** Keep my commandments;
6Ba/6Bb	General to specific:	**6Ba-** you shall be blessed. that you may assist in bringing to light those things of which has been spoken—yea, the translation of my work; **6Bb-** that you may assist in bringing to light those things of which has been spoken—yea, the translation of my work; **5Ab-** according to your desires,
5Ba/5Bb	Parallel concepts:	**5Aa-** in faith **5Ab-** even according to your faith
4a/4b	Parallel actions:	**4a-** behold . . . by my power I give these words unto thee **4b-** Behold, I command you
3a/3b	Parallel concepts:	**3a-** put your trust in that Spirit which leadeth to do good— **3b-** in faith believing in me that you shall receive.
2a/2b	Parallel concepts:	**2a-** to judge righteously; **2b-** pertaining unto things of righteousness,
1	Central theme:	**1-** verily, verily, I say unto you, I will impart unto you of my Spirit, which shall enlighten your mind, which shall fill your soul with joy;

Interdigitated Parallelisms and Chiasma

D&C 29:32 **Chiasmus 48, 29D**

2] 32 First *spiritual,*
1] secondly *temporal,*
which is the beginning of my work;
1] and again, first *temporal,*
2] and secondly *spiritual,*
which is the last of my work—

D&C 29:32 **Analysis 29D**

2a/2b Identical word: **2-** spiritual,
1a/1b Identical word: **1-** temporal,
NOTE: Interdigitated parallelism and chiasmus, parallelism is underlined.

Parallel comparison—
1a/1b Identical word: **1-** first
2a/2b Identical word: **2-** secondly
3a/3b First to last: **3a-** which is the beginning of my work
3b- which is the last of my work

D&C 74:1 **Chiasmus 104, 74A**

2] For the unbelieving *husband*
1] is sanctified by the *wife*
1] and the unbelieving *wife*
2] is sanctified by the *husband*

D&C 74:1 **Analysis 74A**

2a/2b Identical word: **2-** husband
1a/1b Identical word: **1-** wife
NOTE: Interdigitated parallelism and chiasmus, parallelism is underlined.

Parallel comparison—
1a/1b Identical word: **1-** unbelieving
2a/2b Identical words: **2-** is sanctified

D&C 77:2 **Chiasmus 119, 18G**

2] that which is *spiritual*
1] being in the likeness of that which is *temporal*
1] and that which is *temporal*
2] in the likeness of that which is *spiritual*

D&C 77:2 **Analysis 18G**

2a/2b Identical word: **2**— spiritual
1a/1b Identical word: **1**— temporal
Parallel comparison—
1a/1b Identical words: **1**— that which is
2a/2b Identical words: **2**— in the likeness of that which is

NOTE: Interdigitated parallelism and chiasmus, parallelism is underlined.

D&C 112:8 **Chiasmus 205, 112B**

8 And by thy word
2] *many high ones*
1] *shall be brought low,*
and by thy word
1] *many low ones*
2] *shall be exalted*

D&C 112:8 **Analysis 112B**

2a/2b Parallel concepts: **2a-** many high ones
2b- shall be exalted
1a/1b Parallel concepts: **1a-** shall be brought low,
1b- many low ones

NOTE: Interdigitated parallelism and chiasmus, parallelism is underlined.

Parallel comparison—
1a/1b Identical words: **1-** and by thy word

BIBLIOGRAPHY

Abbott, E. A., *Johannine Grammar*. London: A. & C. Black, 1906.

Albright, W. F. and Mann, C. S., *Matthew.*, Garden City: Doubleday, 1971.

Albright, W. F., *Yahweh and the Gods of Canaan; A Historical Analysis of Two Contrasting Faiths*. London: Athlone Press, Univ. of London, 1968.

Alden, Robert L., "Chiastic Psalms: A study in the Mechanics of Semitic Poetry in Psalms 1—50." *Journal of the Evangelical Theological Society*, 17, pp. 11-28, 1974.

Alden, Robert L., "Chiastic Psalms (II): A Study in the Mechanics of Semitic Poetry in Psalms 51-100." *Journal of the Evangelical Theological Society*, 19, pp. 199-210, 1978.

Alden, Robert L., "Chiastic Psalms (III): A Study in the Mechanics of Semitic Poetry in Psalms 101-150." *Journal of the Evangelical Theological Society*, 21, pp. 199-200, 1978.

Anbar, Moshe, "Changement des noms des Tribus Nomades Dans la Relation d'un Meme e Evenement." *Biblica*, 49, pp. 221-32, 1968.

Anderson, Francis I., *Job*. London: Inter-Varsity Press, 1976.

Anderson, Francis I., *The Sentence in Biblical Hebrew*. The Hague: Mouton & Co. 1974.

Anderson, Richard Lloyd, "Paul and the Athenian Intellectuals." *Ensign*, 6, pp. 50-55, Feb. 1976.

Auffret, Pierre, "Note Sur la Structure Litteraire de Psaume 3." *Zeitschrift fuer die Alttestamentliche Wissenschalft*, 91, pp. 93-106, 1979.

Auffret, Pierre, "Essai Sur la Structure Litteraire de Psaume 11." *Zeitschrift fuer die Alttestamentliche Wissenschalft*, 93, pp. 401-17, 1981.

Auffret, Pierre, "Essai Sur la Structure Litteraire de Psaume XV." *Vetus Testamentum*, 31, 4, pp. 358-99, Oct. 1981.

Auffret, Pierre, "Essai Sur la Structure Litteraire de Psaume 90." *Biblica*, 61, pp. 262-76, 1980.

Auffret, Pierre, "Essai Sur la Structure Litteraire de Psaume 137." *Zeitschrift fuer die Alttestamentliche Wissenschalft*, 92, pp. 346-77, 1980.

Auffret, Pierre, "Essai Sur la Structure Litteraire de Psaume 8." *Vetus Testamentum*, 34, 3, pp. 257-69, July 1984.

Auffret, Pierre, "The Literary Structure of Exodus 6:2-8." *Journal for the Study of the Old Testament*, 27, pp. 46-54, 1983.

Auffret, Pierre, "Note Sur la Structure Litteraire de Psaume 136." *Vetus Testamentum*, 27, 1, pp. 1-12, Jan. 1977.

Bailey, Kenneth B., "Parallelism in the New Testament; Needed: A New Bishop Lowth." *The Bible Translator*, 26, pp. 333-38, July 1975.

Bailey, Kenneth B., *Poet and Peasant: A Literary Cultural Approach to the Parables in Luke*. Grand Rapids: Wm. B. Eerdmans Publishing Company, 1976.

Bailey, Kenneth B., "Recovering the Poetic Structure of 1 Corinthians 1:17-2:2." *Novum Testamentum*, 17, pp. 265-96, 1975.

Bailey, Kenneth B., "The song of Mary: Vision of the New Exodus (Luke 1:46-55)." *Near Eastern School of Theology Theological Review*, 2, pp. 29-35, 1979.

Bailey, Kenneth B., *Through Peasant Eyes: More Lucan Parables, Their Culture and Style.*, Grand Rapids: Wm. B. Eerdmans Publ. Co., 1980.

Bailey, Kenneth B., *A Study of Some Lucan Parables in Light of Oriental Life and Poetic Style*. St. Louis: Doctoral Thesis, Concordia Theological Seminary, 1972.

Baldwin, Joyce G., *Haggai, Zachariah, Malachi*. London: Tyndale House, 1972.

Bar-Efrat, S., "Some Observations on the Analysis of Structure in Biblical Narrative." *Vetus Testamentum*, 30, 2, pp. 154-73, Apr. 1980.

Barensten, Jack, "Restoration and its Blessings: A Theological Analysis of Psalms 51 and 32." *Grace Theological Journal*, 5, 2, pp. 247-69, Fall 1984.

Barmouin, M., "Recherches Numeriques Sur la Genealogie de Genesis 5." *Revue Biblique*, 77, 10, pp. 347-65, July 1970.

Barre, Michael L., "Paul as Eschatologic Person: A New Look at 2 Cor. 11:29." *Catholic Biblical Quarterly*, 37, pp. 500-26, Oct. 1975.

Barrett, C. K., *A Commentary of the First Epistle to the Corinthians, Harper's New Testament Commentaries*. New York: Harper and Row, 1968.

Bartina, S., "La Vida Como Historia, en el Prologo al Cuarto Evangelio." *Biblica*, 49, pp. 91-96, 1968.

Bassett, Samuel E., "Hysteron Proteron Homerikos." *Harvard Studies in Classical Philology*, 31, pp. 39-57, 1920.

Bazak, Jacob, *Structures and Contents in the Psalms*, Jerusalem: Dvir, 1984.

Bazak, Jacob, "Structural Geometric Patterns in Biblical Poetry." *Poetics Today*, 6, 3, pp. 475-502, 1985.

Bazak, Jacob, "The Geometric-Figurative Structure of Psalm 136." *Vetus Testamentum*, 35, 2, pp. 129-38, 1985.

Bee, Ronald E. "Statistical Methods in the Study of the Masoretic Text of the Old Testament." *Journal of the Royal Statistical Society*, Series A., 134, 135, pp. 611-22, 1971.

Begrich, Jochim, *Gesamkmelte Studien zum Alten Testament*. Munchen: C. Kaiser, 1964.

Bellerini, T., *Introduzione alla Biblia*. 2, Turin: n.p., 1971.

Bencze, Dom Anselm, "An Analysis of Romans 13:8-10." *New Testament Studies*, 20, pp. 90-92, Oct. 1983.

Bengel, J. A., *Gnomon Novi Testamenti*. Tuebingen: William and Norgate, 1742, [R], 1862.

Benoit, Pierre, "Review of Jacques Dupont's 'Les Beatitudes: Le Probleme Litteraire, Le Message Doctrinal." *Revue Biblique*, 62, pp. 420-24, 1955.

Beregovskaia, F. M., "K Feorii Figur: Semantiko-Funktsinnal'naia Kharakteristika Khiazma." *Izvestiya Akademii Nauk. S.S.S.R.*, 43(3), pp. 227-37, May-June 1984.

Beregovskaya, E. M., "K Teorii Figur: Semantiko-Funktsional Naya Kharakteristika Khiazma (To the Theory of Figures Semantic and Functional Characteristics of Chiasmus)." *Izvestiya Akademii Nauk. S.S.S.R., Seriya Literatury i Yazyka*; 43, 3, pp. 227-37, May-June 1984.

Bertram, Stephen, "Symmetrical Design in the Book of Ruth." *Journal of Biblical Literature*, 84, pp. 165-168, June 1965.

Bettenzoli, Guiseppe, "GLI Anziani di Israele." *Biblica*, 64, 1, pp. 47-73, 1983.

Betz, Hans Dieter, *Galatians, Hermeneia*. Philadelphia: Fortress Press, 1979.

Biays, Paul, "Parallelism in Romans." in *Fort Hays Studies*, 5, Hays: Kansas State College, Mar. 1967.

Blass, Friedrich, *Grammatik des Neutestamentlichen Griechisch,* Edited by Albert Debrunner, 10th Edition. Gottingen: Vandenhoech & Ruprecht, 1959.

Blass, Friedrich, and Debrunner, Albert, *Grammatik des Neutestamentlichen Griechisch,* Edited by Friedrich Rehkopf, 14th Edition. Gottingen: Vandenhoeck & Ruprecht, 1976.

Blass, Friedrich, and Debrunner, Albert, *A Greek Grammar of the New Testament and Other Early Christian Literature*. Translated and revised by Robert Funk, Chicago: University of Chicago Press, 1961.

Blenkinsopp, J., "Structure and Style in Judges 13-16." *Journal of Biblical Literature*, 82, pp. 65-76, Mar. 1963.

Bliese, Loren F., *Psalm 34, An Acrostic, Chiastic Poem.* Stuttgart: United Bible Society Transactions Workshop, May 1984.

Bliese, Loren F., *Metrical Sequences and Climas in the Poetry of Joel.* Stuttgart, United Bible Society Transactions Workshop, May 1984.

Bliese, Loren F., "The Negative Particle in the Metric Lines of Joel." *Afretcon Workshop*, June 1985.

Bliese, Loren F., *Relationships Between Hebrew Narrative and Poetry*. Stuttgart: United Bible Society Transasctions Workshop, May 1984.

Bligh, John, "The Structure of Hebrews." *Heythrop Journal*, 5, pp. 170-77, 1964.

Bligh, John, *Galatians in Greek: A Structural Analysis of Paul's Epistle to the Galatians*. University of Detroit Press, 1966.

Bligh, John, *Galatians—A Discussion of St. Paul's Epistle*. London: St. Paul Publishers, 1969.

Blomberg, Craig L., "Midrash, Chiasmus, and the Outline of Luke's Central Section," *Gospel Perspectives*, 3, pp. 217-61, 1983.

Boadt, Lawrence, "The A:B:B:A Chiasm of Identical Roots in Ezekiel." *Vetus Testamentum*, 25, pp. 693-99, 1975.

Boccaccio, Petrus, and Berardi, Guido, *Bereshit—Gn 1-11*. Rome: Fano, 1960.

Bogaers, Maurice, "Chiastiche Strukturen in St. Trudperter Hohen Lied." *Rodopi*, p. 226, 1988.

Boismard, M. E., *Le Prologue de Saint Jean*. Paris: Cerf, 1953.

Boling, R. G., *Judges*. Garden City: Doubleday, 1975.

Boogaart, T. A., "Stone for Stone: Retribution in the Story of Abimelech and Shechem." *Journal for the Study of the Old Testament*, 32, pp. 45-56, 1985.

Borgen, Peder, "Observations on the Targumic Character of the Prologue of John." *New Testament Studies*, 16, pp. 288-95, Apr. 1979.

Borgen, Peder, "Logos was the True Light." *Novum Testamentum*, 14, pp. 115-30, Apr. 1982.

Borig, Rainer, *Der Wahre Weinstock: Untersuchungen zu Johannes 15:1-10*. Munich: Koesel, 1967.

Bourke, J., "Le Jour de Yahve dans Joel." *Revue Biblique*, 66, pp. 5-31, 1959.

Boys, Thomas, *Tactica Sacra*. London: T. Hamilton, 1824.

Boys, Thomas, *Key to the Book of Psalms*. London: L. B. Seeley, 1825.

Bratcher, Robert G., Klijne, J. J. and Smalley, W. W., *Understanding and Translating the Bible: Papers in Honor of Eugene A. Nida*. New York: American Bible Society, 1974.

Braus, Ira, "Brahm's Liebe und Fruhling II, op. 3, no. 3: A New Path to the Artwork of the Future?" *19th Century Music*, 10, pp. 135-56, Fall 1986.

Bream, H. N., Heim, R. D., and Moore, C. A., *A Light Unto My Path: Old Testament Studies in Honor of Jacob M. Myers, zum 70. Geburtstag*. Philadelphia: Temple University, 1974.

Breck, John, Biblical Chiasmus: "Exploring Structure for Meaning." *Biblical Theology Bulletin*, 17, 2, pp. 70-75, Apr. 1987.

Bronznick, Norman M., "'Metathetic Parallelism' An Unrecognized Subtype of Synonymous Parallelism." *Hebrew Annual Review*, 3, pp. 25-39, 1979.

Brown, Raymond E., *The Gospel According to John 1, 2.* Garden City: Doubleday, 1966/1970.

Brownlee, W. N., *Meaning of the Qumran Scrolls for the Bible.* New York: Oxford University Press, 1964.

Bruegemann, Walter, "On Coping with Curse: A Study of 2 Samuel 15:5-14." *Catholic Biblical Quarterly*, 36, pp. 175-92, Apr. 1974.

Brunot, Amedee, *Le Genie Litteraire de Saint Paul, Lectio Divina 15.* Paris: Les Editions du Cerf, 1955.

Buchanan, George W., *To the Hebrews.* Garden City: Doubleday, 1972.

Bullinger, E.W., *Figures of Speech Used in the Bible.* London: Eyre and Spottiswoode, 1898.

Buttrick, G. A., ed., *Interpreter's Dictionary of the Bible.* Nashville: Abingdon, 1962.

Cadbury, Henry J., "Review of Lund's 'Chiasmus in the New Testament'." *Journal of Religion*, 23, pp. 62-3, Jan. 1943.

Cambell, Edward F., *Ruth.* Garden City: Doubleday, 1975.

Casanowicz, I. M., "Parallellism in Hebrew Poetry." *Jewish Encyclopedia*, 9, pp. 520-22.

Ceresko, Anthony R., "A Poetic Analysis of Psalm 105, With Attention to its Use of Irony." *Biblica*, 64, pp. 20-46, 1983.

Ceresko, Anthony R., "The Function of Chiasmus in Hebrew Poetry." *Catholic Biblical Quarterly*, 40, 1, pp. 1-10, 1978.

Ceresko, Anthony R., "The Chiastic Word Pattern in Hebrew." *Catholic Biblical Quarterly*, 38, pp. 303-11, 1976.

Ceresko, Anthony, R., "The A:B: :B:A Word Pattern in Hebrew and Northwest Semitic with Special Reference to the Book of Job." *Ugarit-Forschungen*, 7, pp. 73-88, 1975.

Chang, Peter Shiu-Chi, *Repetitions and Variations in the Gospel of John.* Doctoral Dissertation, Universite des Sciences Humaines de Strasbourg, 1975.

Charles, R. H., ed., *The Apocrypha and Pseudepigrapha of the Old Testament.* 2, Oxford: The Clarendon Press, 1912-13.

Charlesworth, James H. and Dykers, Pat, *Pseudepigrapha and Modern Research.* Missoula: Scholars Press, 1976.

Christensen, Duane L., "Reading the Bible as an Icon." *TSF Bulletin*. pp. 4-6, Jan.-Feb. 1985.

Christenson, Allen J., "The Use of Chiasmus by the Ancient Maya-Quiche." *Latin American Indian Literatures Journal: A Review of American Indian Texts and Studies* v4(20), pp. 125-50, Fall 1988.

Christensen, Duane L., "Two Stanzas of a Hymn in Deuteronomy 33." *Biblica*, 65, pp. 382-89, 1984.

Christensen, Duane, L., "Andrzej Panufnik and the Structure of the Book of Jonah: Icons, Music and Literary Art." *Journal of the Evangelical Theological Society*, 28, 2, pp. 133-40, June 1985.

Christensen, Duane L., "Zephaniah 2:4-15: A Theological Basis for Josiah's Program of Political Expansion." *Catholic Biblical Quarterly*, 46, 4, pp. 669-82, Oct. 1984.

Christensen, Duane L., "Hulday and the Men of Anathoth: Women in Leadership in the Deuteronomic History." *Society of Biblical Literature Seminar Papers*, pp. 400-04, 1984.

Christensen, Duane L., "Josephus and the Twenty-Two-Book Canon of Sacred Scripture." *Journal of the Evangelical Theological Society*, 29, 1, pp. 37-46, Mar. 1986.

Christensen, Duane L., "Form and Structure in Deuteronomy 1-11." *Bibliotheca Ephemeridum Theologicarum Lovanien*, 68, pp. 135-44, 1985.

Christensen, Duane L., "Anticipatory Paranomasia in Jonah 3:7-8 and Genesis 37:2." *Revue Biblique*, 2, pp. 261-63, Apr. 1983.

Christensen, Allen J., "The Use of Chiasmus by the Ancient Maya-Quiche." *Latin American Literature Journal*, 4, 2, pp. 135-50, Fall 1988.

Christensen, Duane L., "The song of Jonah: A Metrical Analysis." *Journal of Biblical Literature*, 104, 2, pp. 217-31, 1985.

Christensen, Duane L., "Summary of Prosodic Analysis of the book of Nahum." *American Baptist Seminary of the West*, Nov. 1986.

Clark, D. J., "Criteria for Identifying Chiasm." *Linguistica Biblica*, 35, pp. 63-72, Sept. 1975.

Clifford, Richard J., "Psalm 89: A Lament Over the Davidic Ruler's Continued Failure." *Harvard Theological Review*, 73, 1-2, pp. 35-48, Jan.-Apr. 1980.

Coats, George W., "Redactional Unity in Genesis 37-50." *Journal of Biblical Literature*, 83, pp. 15-21, Mar. 1974.

Cohn, Robert L., "Literary Technique in the Jeroboam Narrative." *Zeitschrift fuer die Alttestamentliche Wissenschaft*, 97, 1, pp. 23-35, 1985.

Cohn, Robert L., "Literary Technique in the Jeroboam Narrative." *Zeitschrift Fuer Die Alttestamentliche Wissenschaft*, 97, 1, pp. 23-35, 1985.

Cohn, Robert L., "Form and Perspective in 2 Kings 5." *Vetus Testamentum*, 33, 2, pp. 171-184, Apr. 1983.

Cole Ronald Dennis, "The Idolatry Polemics in the Book of Jeremiah: A Study in Prophetic Rhetoric." *Dissertation Abstracts International*, 45, 12-A, p. 3668, 1984.

Collins, J. J., "Chiasmus, the 'aba' Pattern and the Text of Paul." *Studiorum Paulinorum Congr. Internat. Catholicus*, 2, Rome: Paepstliches Bibelinsitut, pp. 575-83, 1963.

Collins, Adela Y., *The Combat Myth in the Book of Revelation*. Missoula: Scholars Press, 1976.

Comber, Joseph A., "The Composition and Literary Characteristics of Matthew 11:20-24." *The Catholic Biblical Quarterly*, 39, 4, pp. 497-504, Oct. 1977.

Condamin, Albert, *Le Livre de Jeremie, 3rd Edition*. Paris: Libraire Lecoffre, 1936.

Condamin, Albert, *Poemes de la Bible avec une Introduction sur la Strophe Hebraique, 2nd Edition*. Paris: G. Beauchesne et ses Fils, 1933.

Coogan, Michael D., "A Structural and Literary Analysis of the Song of Deborah." *The Catholic Biblical Quarterly*, 40, 2, pp. 143-66, Apr. 1978.

Coote, Robert, "The Meaning of the Name 'Israel'." *Harvard Theological Review*, 65, pp. 137-42, Jan. 1972.

Cross, Frank Moore, Jr., *Canaanite Myth and Hebrew Epic*. Harvard University, 1973.

Corngold, Stanley, "Metaphor and Chiasmus in Kafka." *Newsletter of the Kafka Society of America*, 5, 2, pp. 23-31, Dec. 1981.

Corngold, Stanley, "Restoring the Image of Death: On Death and the Figure of Chiasm in Kafka." *Journal of the Kafka Society of America*, 9(1-2), pp. 49-68, June-Dec. 1985.

Cracroft, Paul, "A Clear Poetic Voice." *Ensign*, pp. 28-31, Jan. 1984.

Craven, Toni Anne, "Artistry and Faith in the Book of Judith." *Dissertation Abstracts International*, 41, 10-A, pp. 4423, 1980.

Critchley, Simon, "The Chiasmus: Levinas, Derrida and the Ethical Demand for Deconstruction." *Textual Practice*, 3, 1, pp. 91-106, Spring 1989.

Culpepper, R. Alan, "The Pivot of John's Prologue." *New Testament Studies*, 27, pp. 1-31, Oct. 1980.

Dahood, Mitchell J., "Chiasmus." *Interpreter's Dictionary of the Bible*, Nashville: Abingdon, p. 145, 1976.

Dahood, Mitchell J., "Ugaritic-Hebrew Syntax and Style." *Ugarit-Forschungen*, 1, pp. 15-36, 1968.

Dahood, Mitchell J., "Vocative Lamedh in Psalm 74:14." *Biblica*, 59, 2, pp. 252-63, 1978.

Dahood, Mitchell J., "Vocative Lamedh in the Psalter." *Vetus Testamentum*, 16, pp. 299-311, July 1966.

Dahood, Mitchell J., *Psalms 1, 2, 3.* Garden City: Doubleday, 1965-66/1968/1970.

Dahood, Mitchell J., *The Ras Shamra Parallels: Text from Ugarit and the Hebrew Bible, 1-2.* Rome: Pontifical Biblical Institute, 1972, 1975.

Dahood, Mitchell J., "Hebrew-Ugaritic Lexicography IX." *Biblica*, 52, pp. 337-56, 1971.

Dahood, Mitchell J., "Proverbs 8:22-31." *The Catholic Biblical Quarterly*, 30, pp. 512-21, Oct. 1981.

Dahood, Mitchell J., "Chiastic Breakup in Isaiah 58:7." *Biblica*, 57, 1, pp. 105, 1976.

Dahood, Mitchell J., "Hebrew-Ugaritic Lexicography I-VI." *Biblica*, 1963-1968.

Dalton, William J., *Christ's Proclamation to the Spirits.* Rome: Paepstliches Bibelinstitut, 1965.

de Vaux, Roland, "Les Hurrites de L'historie et les Horites de la Bible." *Revue Biblique*, 74, pp. 481-503, Oct. 1967.

De Waard, J., "The Chiastic Structure of Amos 5:1-17." *Vetus Testamentum*, 27, 2, pp. 170-77, Apr. 1977.

Deakyne, Kathi Ellen, *Meiotic Patterns and Chiasma Frequency in Malacothrix (Asteraceae)*. University of Louisville, Masters Abstracts, 19, 2, p. 154, 1980.

Deeks, David, "The Structure of the Fourth Gospel." *New Testament Studies*, 15, pp. 107-28, Oct. 1968.

Deimel, A., *'Enuma Elis' und Hexaemeron.* Rome: Paepstliches Bibelinstitut, 1934.

Delong, Richard A., "How Was the Book of Mormon Translated?" *Foundation for Ancient Research and Mormon Studies*, pp. 1-3, 20 Sept. 1982.

Deroche, Michael, "Structure, Rhetoric, and Meaning in Hosea 4:4-10." *Vetus Testamentum*, 33, pp. 185-98, Apr. 1983.

Des Places, E., "Actes" 17:27, *Biblica*, 48, pp. 1-6, 1967.

Dewey, Joanna, "The Literary Structure of the Controversy Stories in Mark 2:1-3:6." *Journal of Biblical Literature*, 92, pp. 394-401, Sept. 1973.

Di Marco, Angelico, "Der Chiasmus in der Bibel 1: Ein Beitrag zur Strukturellen Stilistik." *Linguistica Biblica*, 36, pp. 21-97, Dec. 1975.

Di Marco, Angelico, "Der Chiasmus in der Bibel 2: Ein Beitrag zur Strukturellen Stilistik." *Linguistica Biblica*, 37, pp. 49-68, May 1976.

Di Marco, Angelico, "Der Chiasmus in der Bibel 3: Ein Beitrag zur Strukturellen Stilistik." *Linguistica Biblica*, 39, pp. 37-85, Dec. 1976.

Di Marco, Angelico, "Der Chiasmus in der Bibel 4: Ein Beitrag zur Strukturellen Stilistik." *Linguistica Biblica*, 44, pp. 3-70, Jan. 1979.

Dillard, Raymond B., "The Literary Structure of the Chronicler's Solomon Narrative." *Journal for the Study of the Old Testament*, 30, pp. 85-93, 1984.

Dinkler, E., ed., *Zeit und Geschichte: Dankesgabe an Rudolf Bultmann zum 80. Gerburtstag*. Tuebingen: Mohr, 1964.

Dixon, Poaul Bergstom, "The Forms and Functions of Ambiguity in 'Dom Casmurro,' 'Pedro Paramo,' 'Grande Sertao: Veredas,' and 'Cien años de Soledad.'" *Dissertation Abstracts International*, 42, 6-A, p. 2696, 1981.

Dominy, Bert B. ed., "Current Issues in New Testament Study." *Southwestern Journal of Theology*, 22, 2, pp. 60-71, Spring 1980.

Dommershausen, Werner, *Die Estherrolle: Stil und Ziel einer Alttestamentlichen Schrift*. Stuttgart: Katholisches Bibelwerk, 1968.

Doran, R., *Temple Propaganda: The Purpose and Character of 2 Maccabees*. Washington, D.C.: The Catholic Biblical Association of America, 1981.

Doukhan, Jacques, "The Seventy Weeks of Daniel 9: An Exegetical Study." *Andrews University Semitic Studies*, 17, pp. 1-22, Spring 1979.

Dow, James R., "Chiasmus Structural Symmetry, and Nonverbal Communication: Toward an Understanding of the Old Order Amish Gemee." *Zeitschrift fuer Dialektologie und Linguistik*, supplement 64, pp. 125-36, 1989.

Drijvers, Pius, *The Psalms: Their Structure and Meaning*. New York: Herder & Herder, 1965.

Driver, G. R., "Review of M. Dahood's 'Proverbs and Northwest Semitic Philology,'" *Journal of Semitic Studies*, 10, pp. 112-18, 1965.

Dupont, Jacques, "La Parabole du Figuier Qui Bourgeonne." *Revue Biblique*, 75, pp. 526-48, Oct. 1968.

Dupont, Jacques, *Les Beatitudes: Le Probleme Litteraire, Le Message Doctrinal*. Bruges: Editions de L'abbaye de Saint Andre, 1954.

Dupont, Jacques, "Le Probleme de la Structure Litteraire de l'Epitre aux Romains." *Revue Biblique*, 62, pp. 36-84, 1955.

Dupont, Liliane; Lash, Christopher; and Levesque, Georges, "Recherche sur la structure de Jean 20." *Biblica*, 54, pp. 482-98, 1973.

Ehrman, Bart D. and Plunkett, Mark A., "The Angel and The Agony: The Textual Problem of Luke 22:43-44." *The Catholic Biblical Quarterly*, 45, pp. 401-16, July 1983.

Eissfeldt, Otto, *Einleitung in das Alte Testament, 3rd Edition.* Tuebingen: J. C. B. Mohr, 1964.

Ellis, Peter F., "Patterns and Structures of Mark's Gospel." In *Biblical Studies in Continental Thought*, Edited by Miriam Ward, Burlington, Vermont. Trinity College Biblical Institute, 1975.

Eslinger, Lyle, "More Drafting Techniques in Deuteronomic Laws." *Vetus Testamentum*, 34, pp. 221-26, Apr. 1984.

Eslinger, Lyle M., "Hosea 10:5A and Genesis 32:29: A Study in Inner Biblical Exegesis." *Journal for the Study of the Old Testament*, 18, pp. 91-99, Oct. 1980.

Exum, J. Cheryl, "A Literary and Structural Analysis of the Song of Songs." *Zeitschrift fuer die Alttestamentliche Wissenschaft*, 85, pp. 47-79, 1973.

Exum, J. Cheryl, and Talbert, Charles H., "The Structure of Paul's Speech to the Ephesian Elders (Acts 20)18-35)." *The Catholic Biblical Quarterly*, 29, pp. 233-36, 1967.

Faris, Wendy B., "The Return of the Past: Chiasmus in the Texts of Carlos Fuentes." *World Literature Today*, 57, pp. 578-84, Autumn 1983.

Farrer, A., *St. Matthew and St. Mark.* London: A. & C. Black, 1954.

Fenton, John C., "Inclusio and Chiasmus in Matthew." *Studia Evangelica*, 1, pp. 174-79, Ed. by K. Aland et al, 2 volumes. Berlin: Akademie-Verlag, 1959-64.

Fenton, John C., *Matthew, Pelical Gospel Commentaries.* Baltimore: Penguin Books, 1963.

Fenton, John C., "The Order of the Miracles Performed by Peter and Paul in Acts." *Expository Times*, 77, pp. 831-83, 1965/1966.

Feuillet, A., "La Citation d'Habacue 24 et les Huit Premiere Chapitres de L'Epitre aux Romans." *New Testament Studies*, 6, pp. 52-80, Oct. 1959.

Finnegan, Patrick Owen, "Les Figures de Satre." *Dissertation Abstracts International*, 51(4), p. 1249A, Oct. 1990.

Fiorenza, Elisabeth, "The Eschatology and Composition of the Apocalypse." *The Catholic Biblical Quarterly*, 30, pp. 537-69, Oct. 1968.

Fiorenza, Elisabeth, "The Composition and Structure of the Revelation of John." *The Catholic Biblical Quarterly*, 39, pp. 364-66, 1977.

Fisher, Loren R., ed., *The Ras Shamra Parallels: The Texts from Ugarit and the Hebrew Bible, 1, 2.* Rome: Pontifical Biblical Institute, 1972/1975/19--.

Flender, H., *St. Luke, Theologian of Redemptive History,* Translated by Reginald H. and Ilse Fuller. Philadelphia: Fortress Press, 1967.

Forbes, John, *Symmetrical Structure of Scripture.* Edinburgh: T. & T. Clark, 1854.

Forbes, John, *Analytical Commentary on the Epistle to the Romans.* Edinburgh: T. & T. Clark, 1868.

Ford, Josephine M., *Revelation.* Garden City: Doubleday, 1975.

Fowden, G., "Bishops and Temples in the Eastern Roman Empire AD. 320-435." *Journal of Theological Studies*, 29,1, pp. 53-78, Apr. 1978.

France, Richard T., Wenham, David, eds. *Gospel Perspectives: Studies in Midrash and Historiography.* Sheffield, England: Jsot Press, University of Sheffield, 3, p 299, 1983.

Fredericks, Daniel C., "Chiasm and Parallel Structure in Qoheleth 5:9-6:9." *Journal of Biblical Literature*, 108,1, pp. 17-35, 1989.

Freedman, David Noel, "The Structure of Job 3." *Biblica*, 49, pp. 503-09, 1968.

Fukuchi, Michael Seiji, "A Study of Old English Riddles." *Dissertation Abstracts International*, 41, 4-A, p. 1609, 1980.

Gaechter, Paul, *Matthaeus Evangelium.* Innsbruck, 1964.

Gaechter, Paul, "Semitic Literary Forms in the Apocalypse and Their Import." *Theological Studies*, 8, pp. 547-73, 1947.

Gaechter, Paul, *Die Literarische Kunst im Mathaus-Evangelium.* Stuttgart: Verlag Katholisches Bibelwerk, 1965.

Gaeta, G., *Il Dialogo con Nicodemo.* Brescia: Paideia, 1974.

Gaisser, Julia Haig, "Structural Analysis of the Digressions in the Iliad and the Odyssey." *Harvard Studies in Classical Philology*, 73, pp. 1-44, 1969.

Galop, Jane, "Freud's Invisible Chiasmus: or You Can't Judge a Book by its Cover." *Visible Language: The Quarterly Concerned with All That Is Involved In Our Being Literate*, 14(93), pp. 273-82, 1988.

Garner, Donald William, "Forms of Communication in the Book of Ezekiel." *Dissertation Abstracts International*, 41, 11-A, p. 4743, 1980.

Garr, W. Randall, "The Qinah: A study of Poetic Meter, Syntax and Style." *Zeitschrift fuer die Alttestamentliche Wissenschaf*, 95, 1, pp. 54-75, 1983.

Garrett, Duane A., "The Structure of Amos as a Testimony to its Integrity." *Journal of Evangelical Theological Studies*, 27, pp. 275-76, Sept. 1984.

Geller, Stephen A., "The Dynamics of Parallel Verse: A Poetic Analysis of Deut. 32:6-12." *Harvard Theological Review*, 75, 1, pp. 35-36, Jan. 1982.

Giavini, Jean, "La Structure Litteraire d'Eph. II.11-22." *New Testament Studies*, 16, pp. 209-11, 1970.

Gibboryahu, H.; Hukhramen, Y.; Lahab, M.; and Luria, B. Z., editors., *Sefer Zer-Kabod (M. Zer-Kabod Festschrift)*. Jerusalem: Kiryat Sefer, 1967.

Giblin, Charles Homer, "Two Complementary Literary Structures in John 1:1-18." *Journal of Biblical Literature*, 104, pp. 87-183, Mar. 1986.

Giblin, Charles H., "Revelation 11:1-13: Its Form, Function, and Contextual Integration." *New Testament Studies*, 30, 3, pp. 433-59, July 1984.

Girard, Marc, "The Literary Structure of Psalm 95." *Theology Digest*, 30, 1, pp. 55-58, Spring 1982.

Girard, Marc, "L'Unite de Composition de Jean 6, au Regard de L'Analyse Structurelle, Eglise." *Theology*, 13, pp. 17-110, Jan. 1982.

Glasson, "Chiasmus in St. Matt. 7:6." *Expository Times*, 68, pp. 302, July 1957.

Goedicke, Hans, ed., *Near Eastern Studies in Honor of W. F. Albright.* Baltimore: Johns Hopkins Press, 1971.

Good, E. M., *Irony in the Old Testament.* Philadelphia: Westminster University Press, 1964-65.

Gordon, Cyrus H., *Ugaritic Literature: A Comprehensive Translation of the Poetic and Prose Texts.* Rome: Paepstliches Bibelinstitut, 1949.

Gordon, Cyrus H., "Higher Critics and Forbidden Fruit." *Christianity Today*, 4, pp. 131-34, Nov. 1959.

Gordon, H. Paul, "The Critical Double: Figurative Meaning in Protagoras, James, and Kafka (Greece, Czechoslovakia, United States)." *Dissertation Abstracts International*, 46, 3-A, p. 696, 1984.

Gose, Elliott B., Jr., "Destruction and Creation in a Portrait of the Artist as a Young Man." *James Joyce Quarterly*, 22, 3, pp. 259-70, Spring 1985.

Gottwald, Norman K., "Samuel, Book of." *Encyclopaedia Judaica*, 14, p. 795.

Goulder, M. D., *Type and History in Acts.* London: SPCK, 1964.

Goulder, M. D., "Midrash and Lectino in Matthew." *Society for the Promotion of Christian Knowledge*, 1974.

Goulder, M. D., "The Chiastic Structure of the Lucan Journey." *Studia Evangelica*, 2, pp. 1995-2202, Edited by F. L. Cross, 2 vols. Berlin: Akademie-Verlag, 1959-64.

Gow, Murray D., "The Significance of Literary Structure for the Translation of the Book of Ruth." *The Bible Translator*, 35, pp. 309-20, July 1984.

Grassi, Joseph, "The Role of Jesus's Mother in John's Gospel." *The Catholic Biblical Quarterly*, 48, pp. 67-80, Jan. 1986.

Gray, George Buchanan, *The Forms of Hebrew Poetry.* London: Hodder and Stoughton, 1915.

Green, Barbara Gail, "A Study of Field and Seed Symbolism in the Biblical Story of Ruth." *Dissertation Abstracts International*, 41, 4-A, pp. 1647, 1980.

Grobel, William K., "Chiastic Retribution-Formula in Romans 2." *Zeitschrift und Geschichte: R. Bultmann; ed. by E. Dinkler*, 255-61, 1964.

Gros-Louis, K. R. R., Acherman, J. S. and Warshaw, T. S., eds., *Literary Interpretations of Biblical Narratives.* Nashville: Abingdon, 1974.

Grosholz, Emily, "Angels, Language and the Imagination: A Reconsideration of Rilke's Poetry." *The Hudson Review*, 35, 3, pp. 419-38, Autumn 1982.

Habel, Norman C., *Literary Criticism of the Old Testament.* Philadelphia: Fortress Press, 1971.

Halpern, Baruch; Friedman, Richar Elliott, "Composition and Paronomasia in the Book of Jonah." *Hebrew Annual Review*, 4, pp. 79-92, 1980.

Halpern, Baruch, "The Ritual Background of Zechariah's Temple Song." *The Catholic Biblical Quarterly*, 40, 2, pp. 157-90, Apr. 1978.

Hartman, Lars, *Prophecy Interpreted: The Formation of Some Jewish Apocalyptic Texts and of the Eschatological Discourse Mark 13.* Gleerup: Lund, 1966.

Hatton and Clark, "From the Harp to the Sitar." *Bible Translator*, 26, pp. 132-38, Jan. 1975.

Havemann, Jacob Coenraad Trichardt, *The Meaning and Function of the Chiasm as a Figure of Style in the Letter to the Romans.* University of Pretoria, South Africa, Masters Abstracts, 20, 3, p. 291, 1981.

Havers, Wilhelm, *Handbuch der Erklaerenden Syntax.* Heidelberg: Carl Winters Universitaetsbuchhandlung, 1931.

Heck, Joel D., "The Missing Sanctuary of Deut. 33:12." *Journal of Biblical Literature*, 103, pp. 523-29, Dec. 1984.

Heidel, Alexander, *The Gilgamesh Epic and Old Testament Parallels, 2nd Edition.* University of Chicago, 1949.

Helfgott, B. W., *The Doctrine of Election in Tannaitic Literature.* Columbia University, 1954.

Henry, Matthew and Scott, Thomas, "General Remarks on the Poetical Books." in *Commentary on the Holy Bible,* Grand Rapids: Baker Book House, 1973.

Hibbard, F. G., *The Psalms Chronologically Arranged With Historical Introduction, etc. 2 parts in 1 volume.* New York: Carton & Porter, 1856.

Hiebert, Theodore, "Isaiah 1:25-27." *Society of Biblical Literature*, 1986.

Hillers, D. R., *Lamentations.* Garden City: Doubleday, 1972.

Holliday, William L., "Chiasmus, the Key to Hosea XII 3-6." *Vetus Testamentum*, 16, 1, pp. 53-64, Jan., 1966.

Holliday, William L., "The Covenant with the Patriarchs Overturned: Jeremiah's Intention in Terror on Every Side." *Journal of Biblical Literature*, 91, pp. 305-20, Sept. 1972.

Holliday, William L., "The Recovery of Poetic Passages of Jeremiah." *Journal of Biblical Literature*, 85, pp. 401-35, Dec. 1966.

Holmgren, F., "Chiastic Structure in Isaiah 50:1-11." *Vetus Testamentum*, 19, pp. 196-201, Apr. 1969.

Hongisto, Leif, "Literary Structure and Theology in the Book of Ruth." *Andrews University Semitic Studies*, 23, pp. 19-28, Spring 1985.

Hooker, Morna, "John the Baptist and the Johannine Prologue." *New Testament Studies*, 16, pp. 354-58, 1969/1970.

Horne, T. H., *An Introduction to the Critical Study and Knowledge of the Holy Scriptures.* Philadelphia: Desilver Thomas & Company, 1836.

Horne, T. H., *A Compendious Introduction to the Study of the Bible: Being an Analysis of "An Introduction to the Critical Study of the Holy Scriptures."* Revised Edition, New York: J. Arthur, 1833/1835/1850.

Hornung, Estella B., "Chiasmus, Creedal Structure, and Christology in Hebrews 12:1-2." *Biblical Research*, 23, pp. 37-48, 1978.

Howard, George, "Stylistic Inversion and the Synoptic Tradition." *Journal of Biblical Literature*, 97, 3, pp. 375-89, Sept. 1978.

Hull, W. E., *John.* in The Broadman Bible Commentary, edited by Clifton J.Allen, 12 volumes. Nashville: Broadman Press, 1969-72.

Hurvitz, A., "Diachronic Chiasm in Biblical Hebrew (Hebrew)." *Bible & Jewish History Dedicated to the Memory of J. Liver*, pp. 248-55, 1971.

Hyland, C. F., and Freedman, David Noel, "Psalm 29: A Structural Analysis." *Harvard Theological Review*, 66, pp. 237-56, Apr. 1983.

Irwin, William H., "Syntax and Style in Isaiah 26." *The Catholic Biblical Quarterly*, 41, 2, pp. 240-61, Apr. 1979.

Jackson, Jared J., and Dessler, Martin, eds., *Rhetorical Criticism: Essays in Honor of James Muilenburg.* Pittsburg: Pickwick, 1974.

Jacob, B., *Das Erste Buch der Tora: Genesis.* Berlin: Schocken, 1934.

Jebb, John, *Sacred Literature.* London: T. Cadell and W. Davies, 1820.

Jeremias, J., "Chiasmus in den Paulusbriefen." *Zeitschrift fur die Neutestamentliche Wissenschaft*, 49, pp. 145-56, 1958.

Jungel, Eberhard, "Das Gesetz Swischen Adam un Christus (Eine Theologische Studie zu Romer 5, 12-21)." *Zeitschrift fur die Theologie und Kirche*, 60, pp. 42-74, 1963.

Kasemann, Ernst, *An die Romer, Handbuch sum Neuen Testament, 8a, Mohr.* Tubingen, 1973 .

Kidder, Derek, *Psalms 1-71*, Downers Grove: Intervarsity Press, 1983.

Kidder, S. Joseph, "'This Generation' in Matthew 24:34." *Andrews University Semitic Studies*, 21, pp. 203-09, Autumn 1983.

Kilroy, James, "The Chiastic Structure of 'In Memoriam'." *Philological Quarterly*, 56, 3, pp. 358-73, Summer 1977.

Knox, Alexander and Jebb, John, *Thirty Years of Correspondence Between John Jebb and Alexander Knox*, C. Forster, Editor. Philadelphia: Esquire, pp. 258-63, 1835.

Knutson, F. Brent, *Literary Parallels Between the Texts of Le Palais Royal d'Ugarit IV and the Hebrew Bible.* Doctoral Dissertation, Claremont Graduate School, 1970.

Knutson, F. Brent, "The Ras Shamra Parallels: The Text from Ugarit and the Hebrew Bible." *Pontifical Biblical Institute, Rome*, 1-3, 6, 1972, 1975.

Koch, K., *Was ist Formgeschichte?*, Neukirchen, 1961.

Koenig, E., "Poetry-Biblical." *Jewish Encyclopedia*, 10, pp. 93-98.

Kogut, Simkha, "On Chiasm and its Roll in Exegesis (Hebrew)." *Shnaton*, 2, pp. 196-204, 1977.

Kosmala, Hans, "Form and Structure in Ancient Hebrew Poetry." *Vetus Testamentum*, 14, pp. 435-45, Oct. 1964.

Kosmala, Hans, "Form and Structure in Ancient Hebrew Poetry (cont.)." *Vetus Testamentum*, 16, pp. 152-80, 1966.

Krinetzke, L., *Das Hohe Lied.* Duesselforf: Patmos-Verlag, 1964.

Kselman, John, S., "Psalm 72: Some Observations on Structure." *Bulletin of American Schools of Oriental Research*, 220, pp. 77-81, Dec. 1975.

Kselman, John S., "Semantic-Sonant Chiasmus in Biblical Poetry." *Biblica*, 58, pp. 219-33, 1977.

Kselman, John S., "Note on Isaiah 2:2." *Vetus Testamentum*, 25, pp. 225-27, Apr. 1975.

Kugle, James E., *The Idea of Biblical Poetry: Parallelism and its History.* New Haven: Yale University Press, 1981.

Kuntz, J. Kenneth, "Perceiving Biblical Hebrew Poetry Through Rhetorical Criticism." *University of Iowa Bulletin*, Feb. 1987.

Laato, Antli, "The Composition of Isaiah 49-55." *Journal of Biblical Literature*, volume 109, pp. 202-28, Summer 1990.

Laconi, M. E., et al., in *Il Messaggio dell Salvezzay, 3-4.* Turin: Leumann, 1967-69.

Lafaro, Joseph R. "From God to Chiasm in Merleau-Ponty." *Dissertation Abstracts International*, 36, 5-A, p. 2926, 1974.

Lamarche, Paul, *Zacharie IX-XIV: Structure Litteraire et Messianisme.* Paris: J. Gabalda, 1961.

Lambrecht, J., "Structure and Line of Thought in 2 Corinthians 2:14-4:6." *Biblica*, 64, pp. 344-80, 1983.

Lambrecht, I., *Die Redaktion der Markus-Apokalypse.* Rome: 1967.

Landy, Francis, "The Song of Songs in the Garden of Eden." *Journal of Biblical Literature*, 98, 4, pp. 513-28, 1979.

Langlamet, F., "Les Recits de L'institution de la Royaute (I Sam. VII-XII)." *Revue Biblique*, 77, pp. 161-200, 1970.

Laymon, Charles M., ed. *The Interpreter's One-Volume Commentary on the Bible.* Nashville: Abingdon, 1971.

Leigh, David J., "Augustine's Confessions as a Circular Journey." *Thought*, volume 68, pp. 73-88, March 1985.

Lenglet, A., "La Structure Litteraire de Daniel 2-7." *Biblica*, 53, pp. 169-90, 1972.

Leon-Dufour, Pere X., "Trois Chiasmus Johanniques." *New Testament Studies*, 7, pp. 249-54, Apr. 1961.

Lepeau, John Philip, "Psalm 68: An exegetical and Theological Study." *Dissertation Abstracts International*, 42, 7-A, p. 3195, 1981.

Lete, G. Del Olmo, "David's Farewell Oracle (2 Samuel 23:1-7: A Literary Analysis." *Vetus Testamentum*, 345, 4, pp. 414-37, Oct. 1984.

Levie, J., "Review of Chiasmus in the New Testament, by Nils Wilhelm Lund." *Nouvelle Revue Theologique*, 69, p. 541, 1947.

Licht, Jacob, "Time and Eschatology in Apocalyptic Literature in Qumran." *Journal of Jewish Studies*, 16, pp. 177-82, 1965.

Lichtenstein, Murray H., "Chiasm and Symmetry in Proverbs 31." *The Catholic Biblical Quarterly*, 44, 2, pp. 202-11, Apr. 1982.

Liddell, Henry G., and Scott, Robert, *A Greek-English Lexicon,* Revised by Henry Stuart James and Roderick McKenzie, 2 volumes. Oxford: At the Clarendon Press, 1991.

Lieberman, S. J., ed., *Sumerological Studies in Honor of Thorkild Jacobsen on his Seventieth Birthday June 7, 1974, in Orientale Institute of Assyriological Studies, 20.* Chicago: University of Chicago Press, pp. 205-316, 1976.

Liebrich, Leon J., "The Compilation of the Book of Isaiah." *Jewish Quarterly Review*, 46, pp. 259-77, Jan. 1956.

Liebrich, Leon J., "The Compilation of the Book of Isaiah." *Jewish Quarterly Review*, 47, pp. 114-38, Oct. 1956.

Liebrich, Leon J., "Psalms 34 and 145 in the Light of Their Key Words." *Hebrew Union College Annual*, 27, pp. 181-92, 1956.

Lipsinki, E., "Macarismes et Psaumes de Congratulation." *Revue Biblique*, 75, pp. 321-67, 1968.

Lipsinki, E., *Essais sur la Revelation et la Bible.* Paris: Editions du Cerf, 1970.

Lodge, John G., "James and Paul at Cross-Purposes, James 2:22." *Biblica*, 62, 2, pp. 195-213, 1981.

Lohfink, N., "Darstellungskunst und Theologie." *Biblica*, 41, pp. 403-35, Oct. 1961.

Lohfink, N., *Lectures in Deuteronomy*. Rome: Pontifical Biblical Institute, 1968.

Lohfink, N., *Das Hauptgebot: Eine Untersuchung Literarischer Einleitungsregeln zu Dtn 5-11.* Rome: Pontifical Biblical Institute, 1963.

Lohfink, N., *Hoere Israeli.* Duesseldorf: Patmos-Verlag, 1965.

Lohmeyer, Ernst, *Das Evangilium des Matthaeus,* 3rd Edition. Goettingen: Vandenhoech & Ruprecht, 1962.

Lohr, Charles, "Oral Techniques in Gospel of Matthew." *The Catholic Biblical Quarterly*, 23, pp. 403-35, Oct. 1961.

Lowrie, Joyce O., "Pretexts and Reflections: A Reflection upon Pre-Texts in Les Liaisons Dangereuses." *Modern Language Studies* 18(1), pp. 150-64, Winter 1988.

Lund, Nils, *Studies in the Book of Revelation.* Chicago: Covenant Press, 1955.

Lund, Nils, "The Significance of Chiasmus for Interpretation." *Crozer Quarterly*, 20, pp. 105-23, Apr. 1943.

Lund, Nils, "The Presence of Chiasmus in the New Testament." *Journal of Religion*, 10, 1, pp. 74-93, Jan. 1930.

Lund, Nils, "The Presence of Chiasmus in the Old Testament." *American Journal of Semitic Languages and Literature*, 46, pp. 104-26, Jan. 1930.

Lund, Nils, *Chiasmus in the New Testament.* Chapel Hill: University of North Carolina Press, 1942.

Lund, Nils, "The Influence of Chiasmus Upon the Structure of the Gospels." *Anglican Theological Review*, 13, 1, Jan. 1931.

Lund, Nils, "Chiasmus in the Psalms." *American Journal of Semitic Languages and Literature*, 49, 4, pp. 281-312, July 1933.

Lundbom, Jack R., *Jeremiah: A Study in Ancient Hebrew Rhetoric.* Missoula: Scholars Press, 1975.

Lundbom, Jack R., "Elijah's Chariot Ride." *Journal of Jewish Studies*, 24, pp. 39-50, Spring 1973.

Lundgren, Alice, "In the Learning of the Jews." *Zarahemla Record*, pp. 14-15, Winter/Spring 1985.

Magonet, Jonathan, "Some Concentric Structures in Psalms." *Heythrop Journal*, 23, 4, pp. 365-76, Oct. 1982.

Magonet, Johathan, "The Rhetoric of God: Exodus 6:2-8." *Journal for the Study of the Old Testament*, 27, pp. 56-67, 1983.

Malateste, Edward, *The Epistles of St. John.* Rome: Pontifical Gregorian, 1973.

Malateste, Edward, "The Literary Structure of John 17." *Biblica*, 52, pp. 190-214, 1971.

Man, Ronald E., "The Value of Chiasm for New Testament Interpretation." *Bibliotheca Sacra*, 141, 562, pp. 146-57, Apr. June, 1984.

Man, Ronald E., *Chiasm in the New Testament.* Dallas Theology Masters Thesis, Dallas Theological Seminary, 1982.

Mannati, Marina, and de Solms, E., "Les Psaumes, 1." *Desclee de Brouwer*, 1966-67.

Manns, Frederic, "Philippians 2:6-11: A Judeo-Christian Hymn." *Theological Digest*, 26, 1, pp. 4-12, Spring 1978.

Manson, W., "Review of Chiasmus in the New Testament, by Nils Wilhelm Lund." *Journal of Theological Studies*, 45, pp. 81-84, 1944.

Mays, Amos: *A Commentary.* Philadelphia: Westminster Press, 1969.

McCarthy, Dennis J., "Plagues and Sea of Reeds: Exodus 5-17." *Journal of Biblical Literature*, 85, pp. 137-58, June 1966.

McCarthy, Dennis J., "Moses' Dealings with Pharoah: Exodus 7:8-10:27." *The Catholic Biblical Quarterly*, 27, pp. 336-47, Oct. 1965.

McGinley, Laurence J., "Review of Chiasmus in the New Testament, by Nils Wilhelm Lund." *Theological Studies*, 13, pp. 452-54, 1942.

McEvenue, Sean E., *The Narrative Style of the Priestly Writer.* Rome: Paepstliches Bibelinstitut, 1971.

McKenzie, J. L., *Second Isaiah.* Garden City: Doubleday, 1968.

McKenzie, Steve, "'You Have Prevailed': The Function of Jacob's Encounter at Peniel in the Jacob Cycle." *Restoration Quarterly*, 23, 4, pp. 225-31, 1980.

Meek, T. James, "The Structure of Hebrew Poetry." *Journal of Religion*, 9, pp. 523-50, 1929.

Mermall, Thomas, "The Chiasmus: Unamuno's Master Trope." *PKLA*, 105, pp. 245-55, Mar. 1990.

Metzger, Bruce M., *An Introduction to the Apocrypha.* Oxford: Oxford University Press, 1969.

Meynet, Roland, "Comment Etablir un Chiasme. A Propos des 'Pelerins d'Emmaus." *Nouvelle Revue Teoligique*, 100, pp. 233-49, 1978.

Miesner, Donald R., "The Circumferential Speeches of Luke-Acts: Patterns and Purpose." *SBL Seminary Papers*, 14, pp. 223-37, 1978.

Miesner, Donald A. "The Missionary Jouneys Narrative: Patterns and Implications," in *Perspectives on Luke-Acts,* editor, C. Talbert. pp. 199-214, 1978.

Miesner, Donald Robert, "Chiasm and the Composition and Message of Paul's Missionary Sermons." *Dissertation Abstracts international*, 36, 5-A, p. 2926, 1974.

Moeller, H., *Zeitschrift fuer die Neutestamentliche Wissenschaft*, 9, 1908.

Mollat, D., and Braum, F. M., *L'Evangile et les Epitres de Saint Jean, La Sainte Bible, 50.* Paris: Les Editions du Cerf, 1953.

Morgenthaler, R., *Die Lukanische Geschichteschreibung als Zeugnis, 1.* Zurich: Zwingli-Verlag, 1948.

Montagnini, F., *Libro di Isaia 1-39.* Breschia: Paideia, 1966.

Morisette, R., "Un Midrash sur al Mort: 1 Cor 15:54-57." *Revue Biblique*, 79, pp. 161-88, Apr. 1972.

Mosca, Paul G., Psalm 26: "Poetic Structure and the Form-Critical Task." *The Catholic Biblical Quarterly*, 47, 2, pp. 212-37, Apr. 1985.

Moule, C. F. D., *An Idiom Book of New Testament Greek.* Cambridge: University Press, 1953.

Moulton, R. G., *The Literary Study of the Bible.* Boston: D. C. Heath, 1899.

Moulton, J. H., Howard, W. F. and Turner, N., *A Grammar of New Testament Greek, 4th Edition, 3.* Edinburgh: T. & T. Clark, 1963.

Mounin, Georges, "Hebraic Rhetoric and Faithful Translation." *Bible Translator*, 30, pp. 336-40, 1979.

Muilenburg, James, "Form Criticism and Beyond." *Journal of Biblical Literature*, 88, pp. 1-18, Mar. 1969.

Muilenburg, James, "A Study in Hebrew Rhetoric: Repetition and Style." *Vetus Testamentum*, Supplement 1, pp. 97-111, 1953.

Muilenburg, James, "The Literary Character of Isaiah 34." *Journal of Biblical Literature*, 59, pp. 339-65, 1940.

Muilenburg, James, "Poetry-Biblical." *Encyclopaedia Judaica*, 13, pp. 671-680.

Mulka, Arthur L., "Fidaes quae per Caritatem Operatur," *The Catholic Biblical Quarterly*, 28, pp. 174-88, 1966.

Murphy-O'Connor, Jerome, "Structure of Matthew XIV-XVII." *Revue Biblique*, 82, pp. 350-84, July 1975.

Nagelsbach, Karl Friedrich von and Muller, Iwan, *Lateinische Stilistik*, 9th Edition. Nurnberg: Konrad Geiger, 1905.

Naidoff, Bruce D., "The Two-fold Structure of Isaiah 45:9-13." *Vetus Testamentum*, 31, 2, pp. 180-185, Apr. 1981.

Nanny, Max, "Chiasmus in Literature: Ornament or Function?, Word & Image", *Journal of Verbal/Visual Enquiry*, 4(1), p. 51-59, Jan.-Mar. 1988.

Naveh, J., "Old Hebrew Inscriptions in a Burial Cave." *Israel Exploration Journal*, 13, 074-92, 1963.

Nelson, Edwin Sterling, "Paul's First Missionary Journey As Paradigm: A Literary-Critical Assessment of Acts 13-14." *Dissertation Abstracts International*, 43, 4-A, p. 1203, 1282.

Newman, Barclay M., "Some Observations Regarding the Argument, Structure and Literary Characteristics of the Gospel of John." *The Bible Translator*, 26, pp. 234-39, Apr. 1975.

Nida, Eugene, "Rhetoric and the Translator: With Special Reference to John 1," *The Bible Translator*, pp. 324-28, July 1982.

Nielsen, Edward, *Oral Tradition: A Modern Problem in Old Testament Introduction.* London: SCM Press, 1954.

O'Toole, Robert F., "Philip and the Ethiopian Eunuch (Acts 8:25-40)." *Journal for the Study of the New Testament,* 17, pp. 25-34, Fall 1983.

O'Conner, M., *Hebrew Verse Structure.* Winona Lake: Eisenbrauns, 1980.

Oliva, Manuel, "Interpretacion Teologica del Culto en la Pericopa del Sinai de la Historia Sacerdotal." *Biblica*, 49, pp. 345-54, 1968.

Parunak, Henry Van Dyke, "Oral Typesetting: Some Uses of Biblical Structure," *Biblica*, 62, pp. 153-68, 1981.

Parunak, Henry Van Dyke, "Transitional Techniques in the Bible." *Journal of Biblical Literature*, 102, p. 525-48, Dec. 1983.

Penna, A., *Isaia*, Rome: Marietti, 1957.

Peterson, David O., "Chiasmus, The Hebrews and the Pearl of Great Price." *New Era*, 2, pp. 40-43, Aug. 1972.

Plummer, A., *The Gospel According to St. Luke, International Critical Commentary.* Edinburgh, T. & T. Clark, 1896: 7th ed., New York: Chas. Scribner's Sons, 1906.

Porten, B., "The Structure and Theme of the Solomon Narrative: 1 Kings 3-11." *Hebrew Union College Annual*, 38, pp. 93-128, 1967.

Porten, B., and Rapport, U., "Poetic Structure in Genesis 9:7." *Vetus Testamentum*, 21, pp. 363-69, July 1971.

Prete, in *Il Messaggio dell Salvezza*, 4. Turin: Leumann, 1967-69.

Prewitt, Terry J., "Story Structure and Social Structure in Genesis: Circles and Cycles," in *Semiotics*, J. N. Deely, Editor. New York: Plenum Press, pp. 529-43, 1983.

Radday, Yehuda T., "Chiasmus." *Beth Mikra*, pp. 48-72, 1964.

Radday, Yehuda T., "Chiasm in Joshua, Judges and Others." *Linguistica Biblica*, 27-28, pp. 6-13, Sept. 1973.

Radday, Yehuda T., "Chiasm in Samuel." *Linguistica Biblica*, 9-10, 3, pp. 21-31, 1973.

Radday, Yehuda T., "Chiasm in Tora." *Linguistica Biblica*, 19, p. 12-23, Sept. 1972.

Radday, Yehuda T., "Chiasm in Kings." *Linguistica Biblica*, 31, pp. 52-67, May 1974.

Radday, Yehuda T., "Studies in the Poetic Sections of Samuel." *Israel Bible Society*, 19, pp. 355-66, 1967.

Radday, Yehuda T., "Le Chiasme dans le Recit Biblique." *Les Nouveaux Cahiers*, 38, pp. 44-55, 1974.

Radday, Yehuda T., and Welch, John W., "Chiasmus in the Scroll of Ruth." *Beth Mikra*, 77, pp. 180-87, 1979.

Redford, Donald B., *A Study of the Biblical Story of Joseph.* Leiden: E. J. Brill.

Reese, James J., "Literary Style of John 13:31-14:31; 16:5-6, 16-33." *The Catholic Biblical Quarterly*, 34, pp. 321-31, July 1972.

Reese, James J., "Plan and Structure in the Book of Wisdom." *The Catholic Biblical Quarterly*, 27, pp. 39-399, 1965.

Reumann, J., "Philippians 3:20-21: A Hymnic Fragment?" *New Testament Studies*, 30, 4, pp. 593-609, Oct. 1984.

Revell, E. J., "Pausal Forms and the Structure of Biblical Poetry." *Vetus Testamentum*, 31, pp. 186-99, Apr. 1981.

Reynolds, Noel B., "Nephi's Outline." *BYU Studies*, 20, pp. 131-49, Winter 1980.

Rice, George E., "The Chiastic Structure of the Central Section of the Epistle to the Hebrews." *Andrews University Semitic Studies*, 19, pp. 243-46, Autumn 1981.

Richter, W., *Exegese als Literaturwissenschaft.* Goettingen: Vandenhoeck & Ruprecht, 1971.

Rickenbacher, O., *Weisheitsperikopen bei Ben Sira.* Goettingen: Vandenheoch & Ruprecht, 1973.

Ridderbos, N. H., *Die Psalemn, Stilistische Verfahren und Aufbau mit Besonderer Beruecksichtigung von Ps. 1-41.* Berlin: 1972.

Ridderbos, N. H., *Studies in Scripture and its Authority.* Grand Rapids: Wm. B. Eerdman Publishing Company, 1978.

Riding, Charles B., "Psalm 95:1-7c as a Large Chiasm." *Zeitschrift fuer die Alttestamentliche Wissenschaft*, 88, 3, pp. 418, 1976.

Ridout, Charles B., *Prose Compositional Techniques in the Succession Narrative.* Berkeley: Doctoral Dissertation, Graduate Theology Union, 1971.

Rigaux, Beda, *The Testimony of St. Mathew,* Translated by P.J. Oligny. Chicago: Franciscan Herald, 1968.

Robertson, A. T., *A Grammar of the Greek New Testament in the Light of Historical Research.* Nashville: Broadman Press, 1934.

Robinson, Bernard P., "Israel and Amalek: The Context of Exodus 17:8-16." *Journal for the Study of the Old Testament*, 32, pp. 15-22,1985.

Robinson, D. W. B., "The Literary Structure of Hebrews 1:1-4." *Australian Journal of Biblical Archaelogy*, 2, pp. 178-86, 1972.

Sampley, J. P., *'And the Two Shall Become One Flesh': A Study of Traditions in Ephesians 5:21-33.* Cambridge: Univerity Press, 1971.

Sanders, James A., ed., *Essays in Honor of Nelson Glueck: Near Eastern Archaeology in the Twentieth Century.* Garden City: Doubleday, 1970.

Sanders, James A., *The Dead Sea Psalms Scroll.* Cornell University, 1967.

Sarna, Nahm, *Understanding Genesis: The Heritage of Biblical Israel,* New York: Schocken Books, 1970.

Schenk, Gunter, "What is the History of Logic." *Deut. Z. Phil*, 28, pp. 1443-1452, 1980.

Schenk, Wolfgang, "Testlinguistische Aspekte der Strukturanalyse, Dargestellt am Beispiel von 1 Kor 15:1-11." *New Testament Studies*, 23, pp. 469-77, July 1977.

Schieber, Hans, "Konzentrik im Matthausschluss: Ein form- und Gattungskritischer Versuch zu Matthaus 28," *Zeitschrift fuer Religionswissenschaft und Theologie,* 19, pp. 286-307, 1960.

Schmiel, Robert, "Moschus' Europa." *Classical Philology*, 76, 4, pp. 261-72, Oct. 1981.

Schnackenburg, Rudolf, "Strukturanalyse von Johannes 17." *Biblische Zeitschrift*, 17, pp. 67-78, 196-292, 1973.

Schnider, F., and Stenger, W., "Beobachtungen zur Struktur der Emmausperikope (Lukas 24:13-35)." *Bibl. Zeitschrift*, 16, pp. 94-114, 1972.

Schoors, "The Ras Shamra Parallels: The Texts from Ugarit and the Hebrew Bible, 1-2," Rome. *Pontifical Biblical Institute*, 1972,1975.

Schreiner, S., "Erwaegengen zum Text von Hab. 2:4-5." *Zeitschrift fuer die Alttestamentliche Wissenschaft*, 86, pp. 538-42, 1974.

Schurfranz, Barbara D., "Strophic Structure versus Alternative Divisions in the Prise d'Orange." *Romance Philology*, 33, 2, pp. 247-64, Nov. 1979.

Schwartz, D. R., "Viewing the Holy Utensils." *New Testament Studies*, 32, 1, pp. 153-59, Jan. 1986.

Scott, M. Philip, "Chiastic Structure: A Key to the Interpretation of Mark's Gospel." *Biblical Theological Bulletin*, 15, 1, pp. 17-26, Jan. 1985.

Segbroeck, F. Van, "Jesus Rejete par sa Patri," *Biblica*, 49, pp. 167-97, 1968.

Sharrock, Graeme E., "Psalm 74: A Literary-Structural Analysis." *Andrews University Seminary Studies*, 21, pp. 211-23, Autumn 1983.

Shea, William H., "Revelation 5 and 19 as Literary Reciprocals." *Andrews University Semitic Studies*, 22, pp. 249-57, Summer 1984.

Shea, William H., "Chiasmus and the Structure of David's Lament." *Journal of Biblical Literature*, 105, 1, pp. 13-25, 1986.

Shea, William H., "Chiasm in Theme and by Form in Revelation 18." *Andrews University Semitic Studies*, 20, pp. 249-56, Autumn 1982.

Shea, William H., "David's Lament." *Bulletin for American Schools of Oriental Research*, 221, pp. 141-44, Feb. 1976.

Shea, William H., "The Chiastic Structure of the Song of Songs." *Zeitschrift fuer die Alttestamentliche Wissenschaft*, 92, pp. 378-96, 1980.

Smalley, William A., "Recursion Patterns and the Sectioning of Amos." *The Bible Translator*, 30, 1, pp. 118-27, Jan. 1979.

Smalley, William A., "Discourse Analysis and Bible Translation." *The Bible Translator*, 31, 1, pp. 119-25, Jan. 1980.

Smalley, William A., "Toward an Etic Taxonom of Language in Discourse." *Rueschlikon: UBS Staff Workshop*, May 1975.

Smith, Gary V., "Amos 5:13: The Deadly Silence of the Prosperous." *Journal of Biblical Literature*, 107, pp. 289-91 June 1988.

Smith, Robert, "Another View of the New English Bible." *Dialogue: A Journal of Mormon Thought*, 6, pp. 101-03, Spring, 1971.

Sparks, H. F. D., "The Semitisms of St. Luke's Gospel." *Journal of Theological Studies*, 44, pp. 129-38, 1943.

Staley, Jeff, "The Structure of John's Prologue: Its Implications for the Gospel's Narrative Structure." *The Catholic Biblical Quarterly*, 48, pp. 241-63, April 1986.

Steempvoort, P. A. van, "Eine Stilistische Losung einer alten Schwierigkeit in 1 Thessaloniker 5,23." *New Testament Studies*, 7, pp. 262-65, 1961.

Steele, R. B., "Anaphora and Chiasmus in Livy." *Transactions and Proceedings of the American Philosophical Association*, 32, 1901.

Steele, R. B., *Chiasmus in Sallust, Ceaser, Tacitus and Justinus.* Northfield, Min.: Press of Independent Publishing Company, 1981.

Stock, Augustine, "Chiastic Awareness and Education in Antiquity." *Biblical Theology Bulletin*, 14,1, pp. 23-27, Jan. 1984.

Strand, Kenneth A., "Chiastic Structure and Some Motifs in the Book of Revelation." *Andrews University Semitic Studies*, 16, pp. 401-08, Autumn 1978.

Strand, Kenneth A., "Some Modalities of Symbolic Usage in Revelation 18." *Andrews University Seminary Studies*, 24, pp. 37-46, Spring 1986.

Suter, David W., *Tradition and Composition in the Parables of Enoch.* Doctoral Thesis, University of Chicago Divinity School, 1977.

Talbert, Charles H., "Artistry and Theology: An Analysis of the Architecture of John 1:19-5:47." *The Catholic Biblical Quarterly*, 32, pp. 341-66, July 1970.

Talbert, Charles H. and Exum, C., "The Structure of Paul's Speech to the Ephesian Elders (Acts 20:18-35)." *The Catholic Biblical Quarterly*, 29, pp. 233-36, Apr. 1967.

Talbert, Charles H., *Literary Patterns: Theological Themes and the Genre of Luke-Acts.* Missoula: Scholars Press, 1974.

Testa, P. E., *Genesi 1-11.* Turni: 1969.

Testa, P. E., in *Il Messaggio della Salvezza, 3.* Turin: Leumann, 1967-69.

Thackeray, H. St. John, *The Septuagint and Jewish Worship.* London: H. Milford, 1923.

Thiering, Barbara, "The Poetic Forms of the Hodayot." *Journal of Semitic Studies*, 8, pp. 189-209, Fall 1963.

Thomas, Kenneth J., "The Old Testament Citations in Hebrews." *New Testament Studies*, 11, pp. 303-25, July 1965.

Thompson, William G., *Matthew's Advice to a Divided Community, Mt. 17, 22-18, 35.* Rome: Paepstliches Bibelinstitut, 1970.

Tournay, R., "Notes sur les Psaumes." *Revue Biblique*, 79, pp. 39-58, Jan. 1972.

Tourney, R., "Un Cylindre Babylonien Decouvert en Transjordanie." *Revue Biblique*, 74, pp. 248-54, Apr. 1867.

Tov, E., Pap. "Giessen 13, 19, 22, 26: A Revision of LXX (Planches X-XI)." *Revue Biblique*, 17, pp. 31-54, 1971.

Traill, David A., "Catullus 63: Rings Around the Sun." *Classical Philology*, 76, 3, pp. 211-14, July 1981.

Treat, Raymond C., "Chiasmus Help Prove." *Restoration Voice*, pp. 12-13, Jan.Feb.1983.

Treat, Raymond C., "Another Ancient Pattern: Chiastic Structure in the Book of Mormon." *The Zarahemla Record*, pp. 8-12, Summer/Autumn 1982.

Tsumura, David T., "The Literary Structure of Psalm 46:2-8." in *Annual of the Japanese Biblical Institute*, 6, ed. M. Sekine, pp. 29-55, 1980.

Van Grol, H. W. M., "Paired Tricola in the Psalms, Isaiah and Jeremiah." *Journal for the Study of the Old Testament*, 26, pp. 55-73, 1983.

Van Leeywen, Raymond C., "What Comes Out of God's Mouth: Theological Wordplay in Deuteronomy 8." *The Catholic Biblical Quarterly*, 47, pp. 55-57, Jan. 1985.

Vander Kam, James C., "The Poetry of I. Q. Ap. Gen, XX, 2-8A." *R. Qu.*, 10, 1, pp. 119-25, Jan. 1980.

Vanhoye, Albert, "La Composition de Jean 5.19-30." in *Melanges Bibliques,* Duculot, Gambloux, France, 1970.

Vanhoye, Albert, "Structure de Benedictus." *New Testament Studies*, 12, pp. 382-88, July 1966.

Vanhoye, Albert, "A Structured Translation of the Epistle to the Hebrews." *Pontifical Biblical Institute*, Rome, 1970.

Vogels, W., "A Structural Analysis of Psalm 1." *Biblica*, 60, pp. 410-16, 1979.

Vanhoye, Albert, *La Structure Litteraire de L'Epitre aux Hebreux.* Brussels: Brues, 1963.

Varebeke, Albert Jassens de, "La Structure des Scenes du Recit de la Passion en Joh. 18-19." *Ephemerides Theol. Lavanienses*, 38, pp. 504-22,1962.

Vogels, W., "Egypte Mon Peuple: L'Universalisme d'Is. 19:16-25." *Biblica*, 57, 4, pp. 494-514, 1976.

Von Rad, Gerhard, *Genesis: A Commentary,* Revised Edition. Philadelphia: Westminster, 1973.

Voslo, W., "Balance Structures in the Old Testament: A Brief Survey." *Theologica Evangelica*, 12, p. 48, 1979.

Walker, H. H., and Lund, N. W., "The Literary Structure of the Book of Habakkuk." *Journal of Biblical Literature*, 53, 4, pp. 355-70, 1934.

Wallis, Wilber B., "The Problem of an Intermediate Kingdom in 1 Corinthians 15:20-28." *Journal of the Evangelical Theological Society*, 18, pp. 229-42, 1975.

Watson, Wilfred G. E., "Classical Hebrew Poetry," *Journal for the Study of the Old Testament*, Sheffield, England. 1984.

Watson, Wilfred G. E., "Gender-Matched Synonymous Parallelism in the Old Testament." *Journal of Biblical Literature*, 99, 3, pp. 321-41, 1980.

Watson, Wilfred G. E., "Further Examples of Semantic-Sonant Chiasmus." *The Catholic Biblical Quarterly*, 46, 1, pp. 31-33, Jan. 1984.

Webster, Edwin C., "Strophic Patterns in Job 29-42." *Journal for the Study of the Old Testament*, 30, pp. 95-109, 1984.

Webster, Edwin C., "Pattern in the Song of Songs." *Journal for the Study of the Old Testament*, 22, pp. 73-93, 1982.

Weise, M., "Jesaja 57:5." *Zeitschrift fuer die Alttestamentliche Wissenschaft*, 72, pp. 25-32, 1960.

Weiser, Artur, *The Psalms: A Commentary.* Philadelphia: The Westminster Press, 1962.

Weiss, Johannes, *Earliest Christianity,* 2 Volumes. New York: Harper & Bros., 1937.

Weiss, Raphael, "De Chiasmo in Scriptura." *Beth Mikra*, 13, pp. 46-57, 1962.

Weiss, Raphael, "Chiasm in the Bible, (Hebrew)." *Studies of the Text and Language of the Bible*, pp. 259-73, 1981.

Weiss, Meir, "Wege der Neuen Dichtungs Wissenschaft in Ihrer Anwendung Auf die Psalmenforschung." *Biblica*, 42, pp. 255-302, 1962.

Welch, John W., ed., *Chiasmus in Antiquity: Structures, Analyses, Exegesis.* Hildesheim: Gerstenberg, p. 353, 1981.

Welch, John W., "A Book You Can Respect." *Ensign*, 7, pp. 45-48, Sept. 1977.

Welch, John W., "Criteria for Identifying the Presence of Chiasmus," Provo, Utah: *Foundation for Ancient Research and Mormon Studies.*

Welch, John W., "Paul's Hymn to Love (Agape): 1 Cor. 13," Provo, Utah: *Foundation for Ancient Research and Mormon Studies.*

Welch, John W., "Chiasmus in the Book of Mormon." *BYU Studies*, 10, 1, pp. 69-84, Autumn 1969.

Welch, John W., "Chiasmus in the Book of Mormon or The Book of Mormon Does It Again." *New Era*, 2, pp. 6-11, Feb. 1972.

Welch, John W., "Chiasmus in Ugaritic." *Ugaritic-Forschungen*, 6, pp. 421-36, 1974.

Welch, John W., *Chiasmus im Buch Mormon.* Munich: South German Mission, 1970.

Welch, John W., *A Study Relating Chiasmus in the Book of Mormon to Chiasmus in the Old Testament, Ugaritic Epics, Homer, and Selected Greek and Latin Authors*. Provo: Masters Thesis, Brigham Young University, 1970.

Wenham, Gordon J., "The Coherence of the Flood Narrative." *Vetus Testamentum*, 28, 3, pp. 336-48, 1978.

Wenham, David, "The Structure of Matthew 13." *New Testament Studies*, 25, 4, pp. 516-22, July 1979.

Wenham, David, "A Note on Matthew 24:10-12." *Tyndale Bulletin*, 31, pp. 155-62, 1980.

Westcott, B. F., and Hort, F. J. A., *The New Testament in the Original Greek*. New York: Harper & Bros., 1890.

Wicke, Donald W., "The Literary Structure of Exodus 1:2-2:10." *Journal for the Study of the Old Testament*, 24, pp. 99-107, 1982.

Williams, James G., "The Power of Form: A Study of Biblical Proverbs." *Semeia*, 17, pp. 35-58, 1980.

Willis, John T., "Psalm 1—An Entity." *Zeitschrift fuer die Alttestamentliche Wissenschaft*, 91, pp. 381-400, 1979.

Willis, John T., "The Juxtaposition of Synonymous and Chiastic Parallelism in Tricola in Old Testament Hebrew Psalm Poetry." *Vetus Testamentum*, 29, 4, pp. 465-80, Oct. 1979.

Willis, John T., *Zeitschrift fuer die Alttestamentliche Wissenschaft*, 81, pp. 191-214.

Willis, John T., "The Song of Hannah and Psalm 113." *The Catholic Biblical Quarterly*, 35, pp. 139-54, Apr. 1973.

Willis, John T., "The Structure of Micah 3-5 and the Function of Micah 5:9-14 in the Book," *Zeitschrift fuer die Alttestamentliche Wissenschaft*, 81, 1969.

Wolfe, Kenneth R., "The Chiastic Structure of Luke-Acts and some Implications for Worship." *Southwestern Journal of Theology*, 22, pp. 60-67, 1980.

Wright, Addison G., "The Structure of the Book of Wisdom." *Biblica*, 48, pp. 165-84, 1967.

Yee, Gale A., "An Analysis of Proverbs 8:22-31 According to Style and Structure." *Zeitschrift fuer die Alttestamentliche Wissenschaft*, 94, pp. 58-65, 1982.

Zehnle, Richard, "Peter's Pentacost Discourse, Tradition and Lukan Reinterpretation in Peter's Speeches of Acts 2 and 3." *Society of Biblical Literature Monograph Series*, 15, Abingdon, Nashville, 1971.

Zerwick, M., *Untersuchungen zum Markusstil*. Rome: Pontificio Instituto Biblico, 1937.

INDEX

Wednesday Sept. 18, 96

After Jamie left me on Feb. 24, 96 I cried and cried all day long,* I cried myself unto utter despair. I cried until I cried dried tears until my soul did almost drown in sorrow. I remember lying in bed and realizing that I was too weak to pray. For three days my heart cried out in silence, as I was too weak to form any words for a praye On my fourth day, I finally prayed one word, "LORD!"..., as this was all I had strength for. On the second day I prayed, "LORD, Be WITH ME..." On the third day I prayed, "LORD, BE WITH ME - I Need YOU NEAR..." On the fourth day, I added, "... TO COMFORT AND LOVE MY WEAKENED SPIRIT..." On the fifth day I added, "... I SHANT NOT CRY WHILE YOU'RE NEAR BY..." The sixt I added, "... AND SO I SIGH,

LORD, BE WITH ME." So this whole prayer took me 10 days to complete. I knew when I was too weak to pray, that my spirit was calling out to GOD to bless me and help me to pray. I do believe that my prayer was prompted by the Comforter - The Holy Spirit of Promise.

This prayer took place on May 6, 1993. I bought this book on Sept. 16, 96 without any previous knowledge of Chiasmus literary form. "I'll have to search my journals. I had not started a journal until May of '94, but possibly I may have added it in afterwords.

* every day, all day for 3 months.

LORD, Be With Me
I Need You Near
To Comfort And Love
My Weakened Spirit.

I Shan't Not Cry
While You're Near By
And So, I Sigh
LORD, Be WITH Me.

This chiasmus structure is quite simple and yet it still wasn't natural to me. I had to diagram it out several times before I wrote it out.

---

3 LORD, Be With Me
2 I Need You Near
1 < To Comfort And Love
My Weakened Spirit
2 < *I Shan't Not Cry
While You're Near By
3 < *And So, I Sigh
LORD, Be With Me.

---

* I believe these lines should be off to the side of the basic structure as shown on page 19 for the first chiasmus.

DESERET BOOK CO.

SAN DIEGO, CA #61 619-535-1404

Please Keep This Receipt For Refund

61 1 34324 58935 Sale

3113059
CA CUT COPY SCRAPBK EARLY Y 7.95
954138
CLASS ITEMS/TEACHING AIDS 4.40
1750401
OP CASS TIME FOR REFLECTION 3.97
2478113
OP CHAINBREAKERS 0.97
2595806
LANGUAGE OF THE LORD - CHIA 19.98
50.0% Discount -9.99
2351091
BK REM 2 RING 8X14 BLACK 10.95
954129 2@1.95
CLASS ITEMS/OFFICE SUPPLIES 3.90
Subtotal 42.13
Discount code 11
7.75% Total Tax 3.27
Tax code SD

Total 45.40 *
Check 45.40

Account: 002092810
20:13 09/16/96

Thank You And Let Us Serve You Again

For Mail Orders, or Catalogs Call
1-800-453-4532